Beyond the Welfare State?

The New Political Economy
of Welfare

Third Edition

Christopher Pierson

polity

This third edition first published in 2006 by Polity Press

First edition published 1991; second edition 1998; reprinted 2007

Polity Press
65 Bridge Street
Cambridge CB2 1UR, UK

Polity Press
350 Main Street
Malden, MA 02148, USA

ISBN-13: 978-07456-3521-7 (pb)

A catalogue record for this book is available from the British Library.

Typeset in 10/12 pt Times New Roman
by SNP Best-set Typesetter Ltd, Hong Kong
Printed and bound in Great Britain by MPG Books Ltd, Bodmin, Cornwall.

For further information on Polity, visit our website: www.polity.co.uk

Contents

Acknowledgements

Much has happened to the welfare state since the second edition of this book was published in 1998. This third edition has been comprehensively revised to take account of these changes. I continue to be indebted to those who helped to make the original writing of this book possible: Virginia Bovell, Peter Flora, Anthony Giddens, David Held, John Keane, Desmond King, Meridee Pierson; participants at the British Sociological Association annual conference, the American Sociological Association annual conference, and at seminars in the departments of Politics and Sociology at the universities of Edinburgh and Stirling. Research for the first edition was supported by the Carnegie Trust for the Universities of Scotland and the University of Stirling. In preparing the second edition, I was fortunate enough to spend a period as a Visiting Research Fellow at the Australian National University in Canberra and my work there and in New Zealand was supported by the British Academy and the Carnegie Trust for the Universities of Scotland as well as the ANU itself. I have learned a great deal from staff and students at the Public Policy Program in Canberra and at the University of Nottingham. I am especially grateful to Professor Francis Castles for sharing his expertise about the Australian system of social protection (and much else), and to Nick Ellison.

Thanks are due to all the editorial staff at Polity Press.

Christopher Pierson

The author and publisher would also like to thank the following for permission to reproduce material in the book:

Blackwell Publishing Ltd for table 5.1 from N. Ploug, 'The welfare state in liquidation?', *International Social Security Review*, 2 (1995).

MIT Press for figure 2.1 from C. Offe, *Contradictions of the Welfare State* (1984).

Organization for Economic Cooperation and Development, Paris, for figure 4.4 from *Social Expenditure 1960–1990*, © OECD 1985; and for figure 4.3 and table 4.5 from *The Future of Social Protection*, © OECD 1988.

Oxford University Press for table 6.1 from table 5.4 (p. 85), chapter 5, 'Comparative welfare regimes re-examined' in G. Esping-Andersen, *Social Foundations of Postindustrial Economies* (Oxford University Press, 1999).

Solo Syndication Ltd/Associated Newspapers for the cartoon by David Low from the *Evening Standard*, 1950.

Transaction Publishers for figure 4.2 from A. Flora and A. J. Heidenheimer, *The Development of Welfare States in Europe and America* (1981), copyright © 1981 by Transaction Publishers.

Every effort has been made to trace copyright holders, but if any have been inadvertently overlooked, the publishers will be pleased to make suitable arrangements at the first opportunity.

Introduction

Transforming welfare is now at the top of almost every politician's domestic agenda. The welfare state, which was once a defining cause for social democrats and, by turns, a source of despair and indifference for those on the right, is now the object of almost universal demands for urgent and profound change. The stakes have been raised, as welfare reform has been transformed into the key strategy for 'reviving the economy' and 'mending the social fabric', but faith in traditional solutions is in seemingly terminal decline. We are told that, in anything like its traditional form, the welfare state cannot survive. But, as yet, the workable alternatives are quite unclear. Indeed, we now are confronted with a perplexing diversity of possible futures all of which somebody promises will resolve our current difficulties. What explains this change in the terms of the welfare state debate and where is it headed? How do we pick our way through the abundance of competing explanations? Most importantly, are we really moving, as some suppose, to circumstances that are 'beyond the welfare state'? These are the questions addressed in this book. We shall find that the answers are more complex (and the process of reform more difficult) than many contemporary commentators suggest. We shall find, too, that to understand the newer trajectories of reform we need to know rather more about how we got to be where we are and, indeed, to understand rather more clearly just how and for whom existing welfare states work.

Welfare States: The Changing Object of Debate

For a lengthy period after the Second World War, the dominant academic view was that the emergence of the welfare states could be seen either as the completion of the centuries' long movement towards full and equal citizenship, or else as the price exacted by the organized labour movement for a cessation of open hostilities with capital. For some, the institutionalization of the welfare state represented a decisive victory for the political arm of the labour movement, a vindication of the 'positive-sum' reformism of social democracy. For others, it was the technologically rather than politically determined 'side-effect' of industrial and economic progress, the final act in the process of 'civilizing' the brute forces of industrialization. Again, while for some it consummated the transformation of capitalism into a distinctively new form of social and political organization, (which might or might not be called socialism), for others it represented the further and benevolent development of capitalism. For the latter, the welfare state constituted a form in which the excesses of nineteenth-century laissez-faire capitalism had been curbed and a more rational, equitable, sociable (and thus secure) basis for the private ownership of the economy put in its place. As we shall see, such views were never universally shared, still less unequivocally welcomed. Some on the left insisted that the rise of the welfare state sapped the transformative energies of the working class while subsidizing the reproduction costs of capital. At the same time, critics to the right maintained that the welfare state undermined the fundamental premises of the liberal society that had been created by the great revolutionary movements of the seventeenth and eighteenth centuries. But despite these dissenting opinions, enough of a common view prevailed in the postwar years of Western economic growth and welfare state expansion for us to speak of a widespread (though often unarticulated) professional consensus on the broad lines of welfare state development.

Just as certainly, we may speak of the last twenty-five years having seen an extremely widespread challenge to this orthodoxy. This dissent has been heard from most points of the political compass. In the heyday of 'postwar consensus', outright hostility to the welfare state settlement was widely characterized as a maverick disposition of the political extremes of both left and right. But this was to alter under the pressure of the economic reverses and social upheavals of the late 1960s and early 1970s, and the political changes these brought in their wake. In this period, the belief that the welfare state was 'in crisis', indeed, that many of the social, economic and political ills of the modern era were directly attributable to the continuing growth of the welfare state, established itself, with astonishing rapidity, as something like a new orthodoxy. Elements of both the New Left and the New Right found common ground in identifying the incompatibility of a working market economy with the state provision of welfare. At the same time, criticism of the particular consequences of the welfare state for women and for ethnic minorities, long a suppressed undercurrent in social policy, gained a new prominence with the general resurgence in feminist and anti-racist writing and thinking from the early 1970s onwards. Still more recently, the impact of the green movement, with its character- istic concern for the harmful consequences of unsustainable economic growth and bureaucratized public services, has represented a further chal- lenge to the benign assumptions of the defenders of the social democratic welfare state.

Paralleling this increased political interest and controversy has been a change in the academic study of the welfare state. However wrongly, the welfare state was for long seen as the worthy, if rather dull, province of a group of concerned specialists, mostly in the fields of social policy and social administration, working on a particular and practical agenda of (diminishing) poverty and (expanding) welfare provision. By contrast, in the last twenty years, the welfare state has increasingly been colonized by students of political theory and the 'new political economy', who have drastically broadened the domain of welfare state studies, seeking, under this rubric, to construct broad explanations of the general nature of the social, economic and political arrangements of advanced capitalism. In the most recent period, with the demise of the Soviet Union and the seem- ingly uncheckable advance of a fully globalized capitalism, the 'problem' of the welfare state has (once again) been presented as amenable to a tech- nical fix – only this time the 'fixers' are more likely to be economic spe- cialists from the World Bank than the 'traditional' welfare professionals of the postwar period.

From both these political and academic sources has come, in recent years, increasing support for the claim that the advanced capitalist soci- eties are undergoing a process of transformation which is carrying them towards social and political arrangements which are, in some sense, *beyond the welfare state*. Most prominent among these claims are the following:

Proposition 1
In the long term, the welfare state is incompatible with a healthy market- based economy. Only the exceptionally favourable circumstances for eco- nomic growth of the postwar period allowed simultaneously for an expansion of the economy *and* the welfare state. Under changed interna- tional economic conditions this means, for the political right, that eco- nomic growth can only be restored by severely lessening the drain of the welfare state on the productive economy. For the left, it has implied that the welfare aspirations embodied in the idea of a welfare state can only be met by instituting new forms of economic organization and ownership.

Proposition 2
The development of the welfare state was an integral part of the evolu- tion of modern capitalist societies. However, the period of its remarkable

growth was also historically unique. The welfare state has now 'grown to its limits'. Wholesale dismantling is neither necessary nor likely, but any further (costly) growth will begin to undermine the basis of its popular support.

Proposition 3

Changes in the international political economy, above all the processes of *globalization*, have undermined the circumstances for the promotion of national welfare states. The powers of national governments, national labour movements and nationally based capital – between whom agreements about national welfare states were typically constructed – have been undermined by the greater internationalization and deregulation of the modern world economy. The Keynesian Welfare State is incompatible with this new international political economy.

Proposition 4

The postwar welfare state represented a 'historic compromise' between the powers/interests of capital and organized labour. That 'compromise' has now broken down (on some accounts because of the comprehensive defeat of the labour interest). While at one time welfare state policies served both capital and labour, they are now becoming increasingly unattractive to both and will be able to mobilize decreasing support within both camps. At the same time, these interests have been reorganized in ways which make any future return to corporatism improbable.

Proposition 5

The development of welfare state provision (especially in public health and public education) has itself generated social changes which undermine the continuing necessity for state welfare provision and attenuate the basis of continuing support for public provision. In particular, the development of the welfare state has transformed the *class* structure of advanced capitalism in such a way as to undermine the *class* basis for its own continuation. Most significantly, these changes undermine that alliance between middle and working classes (or, alternatively, that commonality of working-class experience) on which the welfare state was built. This furnishes for an ever growing section of the population an incentive to *defect* from (the support of) public welfare provision.

Proposition 6

The welfare state represented an appropriate institutional means for delivering certain welfare services at a given level of social and economic development. Continued economic growth has rendered these forms of welfare provision increasingly inappropriate. Most notably, the expansion of consumer choice/affluence within Western industrialized economies engenders increasing dissatisfaction with state-administered welfare and a greater defection of consumers to market-provided welfare services.

Proposition 7
While the welfare state political project should be understood as historically progressive, further progress cannot be effected through the continued promotion of conventional welfare state policies. This is because the welfare state is tied to a productivist/economic growth strategy which is not (any longer) consonant with the meeting of real human needs and the securing of genuine social welfare.

It is with these claims about development 'beyond the welfare state' that this book is principally concerned. It is not however a study in futurology. Future 'tendencies' in the welfare states must depend on their historical evolution and those powers and structures that they currently embody. This is reflected in the structure of the book. The first three chapters deal with the major theoretical approaches to the welfare state out of which prognoses for its future development arise. More specifically, they are concerned with the relationship between the welfare state, social democracy and the structure of advanced capitalism. To assist the reader through this minefield of competing explanations, I include at the end of each section a brief thesis summarizing the main claims that have been outlined. Chapter 4 reviews major trends in the international development of welfare states down to the early 1970s.

For most commentators, the conditions for moving 'beyond the welfare state' have only ripened or become manifest over the past thirty years. This is the period that has been dominated by the spectre of a 'crisis in the welfare state'. Correspondingly, chapters 5 and 6 give detailed consideration to varying explanations of this crisis and measures these against the actual experience of developed welfare states since the early 1970s. Chapter 7 returns to questions about future developments 'beyond the welfare state', considering specifically claims about the impact of globalization, demographic change and 'new social risks'. While we shall see that the casual elision of social democracy and the welfare state is historically and theoretically misplaced, especial attention is directed throughout the book to the changing relationship between the welfare state and social democracy.

PART I

Capitalism, Social Democracy and the Welfare State

1
Industrialism, Modernization and Social Democracy

The purpose of these first three chapters is to establish how the (contested and changing) relationship between capitalism, social democracy and the welfare state has been understood. It would perhaps be as well to begin by clarifying how these terms will be employed within this study. *Capitalism* refers to an economic (and social) system based on the production and exchange of privately owned commodities. *Advanced capitalism* refers to this economic (and social) system as it has evolved within the most developed societies of North America, Western Europe, Japan and Australasia. Both systems are seen to be more or less dependent on markets, but neither is premised on pure 'free' markets in either labour or commodities. *Social democracy* refers to those political movements, ideologies and practices which are founded on the reformist promotion of the interests of organized labour within a developed capitalist economy. It tends to afford definitive status to the development of representative democratic institutions within capitalist societies as the means of gradually reforming these societies in the direction of greater fairness and equality, largely through the promotion of welfare state strategies.

Use of the expression *welfare* has always been inexact. At its simplest, *welfare* may describe 'well-being' or 'the material and social preconditions for well-being' (*Shorter Oxford English Dictionary*; Weale, 1983, p. 23). As such, it may be distinguished from three common subclassifications: (1) *social welfare*, which broadly refers to the collective (and sometimes sociable) provision or receipt of welfare; (2) *economic welfare*, which usually describes those forms of welfare secured through the market or the formal economy; and (3) *state welfare*, which refers to social welfare provision through the agency of the state. A good deal of confusion has arisen from the tendency of commentators to argue as if one of these subclassifications was exhaustive of *all* forms of welfare or as if they were interchangeable (as, for example, in the supposition that state welfare is the same as social welfare). These definitional issues have been extensively discussed elsewhere (see Titmuss, 1963; Madison, 1980, pp. 46–68; Weale, 1983, pp. 1–21; Jones, 1985, pp. 13–14; Rose, 1981; on classical definitions of economic welfare, see Pigou, 1912 and 1929). Here, comment can be confined to two points. First, in this study the primary focus of attention is on *state*-provided forms of welfare and their interconnection with the structure of the formal economy. Secondly, and given this emphasis, it should be stressed that the ways in which welfare is delivered *outside* the state or the formal economy, through the church, through voluntary organizations and, above all, through the family, is just as important.

In a narrow sense, the *welfare state* may refer to state measures for meeting key welfare needs (often confined to health, education, housing, income maintenance and personal social services). This provision may take the form of either *services* (provided by, or funded by the state) or income *transfers*. Increasingly broadly, the welfare state is also taken to define (1) a particular form of state; (2) a distinctive form of polity; or (3) a specific type of society. In this study, the *welfare state under capitalism* is generally understood in this third sense as defining a society in which the state intervenes within the processes of economic reproduction and distribution to reallocate life chances between individuals and/or classes.

Capitalism against the Welfare State: Classical Political Economy

In this book, attention is focused on the nature of the relationship between capitalism, the welfare state and social democracy. In considering the competing ways in which this relationship has been understood, perhaps the most primitive line of division is between those who perceive the welfare state to be *incompatible* with the principles and practices of (any form of) capitalism and those who understand the welfare state as a possible or even as a *necessary* component of any developed capitalist economy. Both forms of explanation can be seen to focus on (differing) aspects of capitalism as a market-based form of economic organization. For both, social democracy may be either an indispensable third term or else largely irrelevant.

The conviction that state responsibility for social welfare is incompatible with the efficient working of a capitalist economy can be persuasively retraced to capitalism's greatest advocate – Adam Smith. In common with many later commentators, Smith understood welfare, or the means to welfare, rather narrowly, as being secured primarily through the production and exchange of goods and services within the formal economy. Since, he argued, the general welfare of society is but the sum of the welfare of the individuals within it, social welfare would be best secured by maximizing the sum of individual welfares. Such maximization could best be achieved by allowing individuals, within an overall legal framework of tort and contract, to pursue their own economic interests without external restraint. The form for such economic maximization was a freely competitive market economy in which production was directed solely by the laws of supply and demand and in which each sought to maximize his or her welfare within the marketplace by selling dear and buying cheap such marketable resources or 'commodities' (including labour) as lay within his or her command. The great beauty of the market economy – its 'cunning of reason' – was that though every man entered into market transactions solely to serve his own selfish (and generally short-term) ends, in so doing he was 'led by an invisible hand to promote an end which was not part of his intention', that is the maximization of general social welfare or the common good (A. Smith, 1976b). If not quite the product of either God or Nature, markets nonetheless maximized the liberty of the individual and effectively directed man's (natural) self-interest and greed towards the optimization of general social welfare.

Smith, like the more thoughtful of his latter-day followers, was not an uncritical admirer of the market. He noted, for example, the pernicious effect that the minute division of labour might have on the labouring poor. Nor did he discount the importance of a state exercising centralized political authority. However, the proper exercise of such state power was limited to (1) the defence of the realm against external assault; (2) the guarantee of the rule of law; and (3) the maintenance of 'certain public works and certain public institutions' which the market could not competently provide. Even were the latter to include some sort of state responsibility for the relief of destitution, it is clear that the state could not have a *duty* to provide (nor its citizens a corresponding *right* to claim) generalized social welfare.

Just why such a welfare-securing state was incompatible with a capitalist market economy is made clear in the work of other classical political economists – notably by Nassau Senior and Thomas Malthus (Senior, 1865; Malthus, 1890; see also Bowley, 1967, pp. 282–334; Rimlinger, 1974, pp. 38–47). Within a capitalist economy, the 'free' owners of labour power – as Marx ironically noted, 'free' in the twin sense of being legally at liberty to sell their labour power to an employer and being 'free' of any other means of supporting themselves – *must* be obliged to sell this labour power *at the prevailing market price* in order to support themselves and their families (Marx, 1973a, pp. 270–1). Without this compulsion to work – the requirement to undergo the disutility of labour in order to enjoy the utility of welfare – an efficient (and welfare-maximizing) market economy could no longer function. If welfare were to be granted, still more were it to be guaranteed, independent of the willingness (and/or capacity) to work, there would remain no incentive for the worker to sell his or her labour power. Workers could then dissipate themselves (as Malthus feared) in idle living (and breeding) at the expense of the productive members of society and the economy would in turn be undermined to the eventual ruination of the whole society. Thus it was the very uncertainty of the wage-earner's continued welfare that was the mainspring of capitalist economic growth.

Capitalism against the Welfare State: Marx

Marx was perhaps the most sophisticated (and admiring) critic of this clas-sical political economy. In turning to his account of the relationship between capitalism and welfare, we find broad agreement about the struc-ture and dynamics of the capitalist economy and about its incompati-bility with state-secured welfare. As the status of his definitive study of *Capital* as 'a critique of political economy' suggests, Marx's intention was to take the work of the classical political economists and to press what he saw as their authentic premises to radically new conclusions (Marx, 1973a). The radical divergence between Marx and classical political economy lies not in his view of the relationship between capitalism and the welfare-securing state, but in his account of the (ever more acute) inability of capitalist economic organization to secure 'genuine' individual and social welfare.

At the heart of Marx's critique of capitalism were three basic claims drawn from classical political economy: first, that capitalism is an eco-nomic system based on the production and exchange of privately owned commodities within an unconstrained market; secondly, that the value of any commodity is an expression of the amount of human labour power expended on its production. On these premises, Marx develops an account of capitalism as a necessarily exploitative and class-based system, one in which unpaid labour is extracted from the sellers of labour power by the owners of capital under the form of a 'free and equal exchange' in the marketplace. Such market exchanges do not however optimize individual (and thus social) welfare. Rather, the radically unequal exchange (the extraction of surplus value) that is masked by a formally 'free and equal' market in commodities means that capitalist economic organization only secures the welfare of the capitalists (as individuals and as a numerically declining class) while prescribing *dis*welfare for the great majority of the exploited working class.

The third element that Marx derives from classical political economy is the claim that capitalism is a dynamic system in which the competitive search for profit and responses to the long-term tendency for the rate of profit to fall lead to the intensification of exploitation and the heightening of class conflict. It is also a system chronically prone to periodic crises (of overproduction). While such crises do not straightforwardly occasion the economic collapse of capitalism, they do determine a cyclical intensification of the contradictions that are to lead to its eventual demise. As a part of this process, capitalism in its historically 'declining' phase comes to be ever less efficient and less equitable in delivering individual and collective social welfare.

This radical inequality of welfare outcomes is endemic to capitalism and, for Marx, not open to remedy or amelioration by an interventionist state. As we shall see later, views on the welfare state in twentieth-century Marxism are complex and sometimes contradictory. However, the most essential points of Marx's own understanding of the state, and of its capacity to secure general social welfare, may be summarized as follows:

1   While some insist that Marx's central works of political economy constitute not an economic but a *materialist* critique of capitalism, the core of Marx's historical materialism depicts the political in general, and the state in particular, as derived from essentially economic relationships.
2   That economic relationship which the state and politics expresses is one of systematic class-based exploitation. In every age, the state mobilizes *exclusively* the interests of the ruling class. This is true of the capitalist state, as it will be of the proletarian state under a transitional socialist order. Only under communism, with the final elimination of class oppression, will the state 'wither away'.
3   The state cannot serve two masters (or classes) nor can the transformation from one type of state to another be peaceful and/or gradual (other than under very exceptional circumstances). The bitter historical experience of the workers' movement has been that the existing state has to be 'smashed' and replaced with new and distinctively proletarian state institutions. (Marx, 1973b, p. 125, p. 71; C. Pierson, 1986, pp. 7–30)
4   This relationship is not changed by the winning of popular parliamentary democracy. Certainly, Marx held democracy to be a progressive principle, but he rejected the claim that the winning of parliamentary democracy so transformed the existing order that it became possible to effect transition through the institutions of the existing state. (Marx, 1973b, pp. 238, 190)

In summary, the state under capitalism might intervene in the reproduction of social relations, but it could not (1) intervene in such a way as to undermine the logic of the capitalist market economy; or (2) act against the long-term interests of the capitalist class. Whatever institutional form the state under capitalism might take (and even under the governance of social democratic forces), it remained in essence a *capitalist* state. For Marx, securing the *real* welfare of the broad working population and articulating their *real* needs were simply incompatible with the structure of a capitalist economy.

It is possible then to find in the work of classical political economy and its fiercest opponent a broadly shared view of the incompatibility between capitalist economic organization and the state provision of welfare. The distribution of utilities under capitalism is taken to reflect not 'needs', however these are understood, but market capacity. It was not so much this analysis of the nature of the capitalist economy that divided socialists from capitalism's defenders. Rather it was the socialists' argument that responsiveness to markets rather than 'needs' made capitalism unacceptable and required that it be replaced by a form of social organization of production (whether communal, cooperative or state directed) in which the distribution of welfare reflected 'real need' rather than 'market capacity'. Down to the early twentieth century and the prospect of the welfare state as an alternative socialist strategy, this was a view embraced not just by revolutionary Marxists but also by most other (and more circumspect) species of socialism. The defenders of liberal capitalism responded to this criticism by insisting that, while not perfect, markets were the most effective way of promoting general and improving levels of welfare. If the anonymous and impersonal 'coercion' of the market were to be removed and society's material needs still to be met, this would require *more* oppressive and directive forms of coercion by the state (Kristol, 1978).

Capitalism and the Welfare State: Symbiosis and Support

There were those writing in the eighteenth and nineteenth centuries who believed that capitalist economic organization was compatible with securing collective provision for the welfare of the working class (Owen, 1927; T. Paine, 1958, pp. 246ff). However, down to the last third of the nineteenth century there was widespread agreement among both capitalism's defenders and its detractors that state welfare was incompatible with the dynamics of a capitalist economy. The twentieth century saw opinion much more evenly divided. Indeed, in certain phases, there was a broadly based consensus, again shared on both left and right, that the state provision of welfare is fully compatible with, or even indispensable to, a developed capitalist economy. This mutual compatibility of capitalism and state welfare is not always welcomed and some see the welfare state as a way of reinforcing the inequitable welfare outcomes dictated by the market economy. But, whether for good or ill, in the period after the Second World

War, the logic of *symbiosis* between the welfare state and capitalism came to define the prevailing orthodoxy.

The context for this changed approach to the relationship between capitalism and the welfare state was the emergence or maturing of a series of deep-seated economic, social and political changes in the structure of the developing capitalist societies towards the end of the nineteenth century. For those who perceive a symbiotic relationship between capitalism and public welfare, the emergence of the welfare state can be understood in terms of those societal changes which arose out of the great historical transformation from essentially agrarian, localized and traditional to definitively industrialized, (inter)national and modern societies that occurred between the eighteenth and twentieth centuries. More specifically, these transformations could be traced to the interaction between industrial revolution (expanding from its origins in eighteenth-century Britain) and political revolution (most spectacular in America and France in the eighteenth century, but just as importantly in the widespread extension of democracy in the late nineteenth and early twentieth centuries).

Summarily, the most important of these societal developments were:

(1) **The impact of industrialization** The coming of large-scale industrial production led to:

- a long-term decline in agricultural employment and the rural population;
- extensive urbanization – the growth of large cities and of typically urban 'ways of life';
- the creation of a landless (manual) urban working class, concentrated in particular economic sectors and based in distinctive urban neighbourhoods.

Its *further* development led to:

- the requirement for a (partially) skilled, literate and reliable workforce;
- the recognition of 'unemployment' as a condition in which workers were *involuntarily* unable to find paid work;
- the growth of white-collar employment and the middle classes;
- the creation of societies of historically unprecedented wealth (however inequitably this wealth might be distributed), and of sustained and long-term economic growth.

(2) **Population growth and the changing social composition of the population** Everywhere industrialization was accompanied by a rapid growth of population. It was also associated with other demographic changes:

- changing patterns of family and community life;

- a growing division between working and non-working populations and between 'home' and 'work';
- decreasing infant mortality and increased life expectancy (at least in the long run);
- the emergence of publicly sanctioned non-participation in the labour force (through retirement in old age, sickness, disability, childrearing, involvement in full-time education).

(3) **The growth of nation-states**   The locus of industrialization consisted increasingly of nations and states. In some cases, state formation and nation-building were directly associated with the management and coordination of industrial development (as, for example, in Germany and Italy). The growth of industrialized nation states was itself widely associated with:

- internal pacification;
- the centralization of governmental powers;
- the development of a 'professional' civil service;
- growing state competence through new techniques of surveillance and advanced communications.

For most (though certainly not for all) significant commentators, one further element should be added to these basic characteristics of industrialization:

(4) **The growth of political democracy/the rise of political citizenship**   Industrialization often coincided with growth in a number of elements of political citizenship:

- the expansion of legal citizenship;
- the extension of the franchise;
- the development of social democratic parties;
- the increased salience of 'the social question'/the political 'problem' of the working class.

For the great majority of more recent commentators, these constitute the necessary, but not sufficient, bases for an explanation of the development of the welfare state. There is some disagreement about which of these constitute the more important causes. For example, some commentators dismiss the independent impact of *political* forces in shaping the welfare state, while others regard political mobilization as indispensable. There is also violent disagreement about those other variables whose interaction with industrial development can persuasively account for the emergence of the welfare state. But it is widely maintained that without these basic processes of industrialization (the growth of industrial production, economic growth, urbanization, demographic change, state development) it would be impossible to imagine the modern welfare state.

Industrialism and the Welfare State

For some, the principal mobilizing force behind the growth of the welfare state was a *moral* one, based on public or elite reactions against the excessive hardships inflicted by early industrialization. In such accounts, particular stress is laid on the growth of humanitarian and charitable sentiment among the governing and middle classes, the growth of knowledge of social and medical conditions affecting the industrial population, and a growing awareness of the nature and importance of public health provision. Thus Penelope Hall, in a standard British text of the 1950s (and beyond), insists that the basis of the welfare state rests in 'the obligation a person feels to help another in distress, which derives from the recognition that they are in some sense members one of another' (Hall, 1952, p. 4). In a more historical mode, Derek Fraser writes of 'the public conscience . . . shocked into action', and Malcolm Bruce of the welfare state as 'the result of a fit of conscience' (D. Fraser, 1973, p. 23; Bruce, 1968, p. 294).

However much this 'moral' approach may continue to reflect popular justifications of the welfare state, its intellectual authority has been rapidly eroded over the past fifty years, particularly as the welfare state has become increasingly the object of study for those interested in the dynamics of comparative political science. Perhaps more lastingly influential have been those who depict the coming of the welfare state as a product of '*the logic of industrialism*'. From the perspective of (Anglo-Saxon) functionalist sociology in the postwar period, the rise of the interventionist state and the curbing of the 'excesses' of liberal capitalism could be seen as a response to the new 'needs' generated by the development of industrial societies. On such an explanation, the origins of the welfare state were seen to lie in secular changes associated with the broad processes of industrialization and, particularly, the breakdown of traditional forms of social provision and family life. These changes included economic growth and the associated growth in population (especially of an aged population), the developed division of labour, the creation of a landless working class, the rise of cyclical unemployment, changing patterns of family and community life, and industry's increasing need of a reliable, healthy and literate workforce.

The most authoritative advocate of this industrialism thesis has been Harold Wilensky, whose early work concluded that 'over the long pull, economic level is the root cause of welfare-state development'. The effects of the level of economic development are expressed 'chiefly through demographic changes . . . and the momentum of the programs themselves once established'. The effects of 'political elite perceptions, mass pressures, and welfare bureaucracies' may hasten its coming, but the welfare state is essentially a product of the 'needs' of an industrialized society. While

Wilensky allows some weight at the margins to the influence of 'democratic corporatism', in essence, political ideology and political systems are largely irrelevant in explaining a technologically determined development which occurs more or less independently of the will of either political elites or mass publics (Wilensky, 1975, p. 47; 1976, pp. 21–3).

This thesis on the welfare state, which achieved its greatest prominence in the 1950s and 1960s, belonged within a much broader explanation of the evolution of industrial societies. This broader account enjoined that conventional political divisions between capitalist and socialist (or communist) societies were increasingly irrelevant. What characterized societies in the developed world (capitalist or communist) was that they were *industrial* societies, the nature of whose social and economic arrangements was given by the technological logic of industrial production and economic growth. Thus, Wilensky argued,

> economic growth and its demographic and bureaucratic outcomes are the root cause of the general emergence of the welfare state . . . such heavy brittle categories as 'socialist' versus 'capitalist' economies, 'collectivistic' versus 'individualistic' ideologies, or even 'democratic' versus 'totalitarian' political systems . . . are almost useless in explaining the origins and general development of the welfare state. (1975, p. xiii)

Accordingly, such theorists maintained both that the welfare state was an indispensable part of this structure of the industrial societies, and that 'the primacy of economic level and its demographic and bureaucratic correlates is support for a convergence thesis: economic growth makes countries with contrasting cultural and political traditions more alike in their [welfare state] strategy' (Wilensky, 1975, p. 27).

Thesis 1

The welfare state is a product of the *needs* generated by the development of industrial societies

---

Commentary: The Industrialism Thesis

As the orthodoxy of the 1950s and 1960s, the industrialism thesis – with its central claim that the welfare state was a product of both the new *needs* and the new *resources* generated by the process of industrialization – has received considerable attention. A series of empirical surveys (most influentially those of Cutright and Wilensky) suggested 'the primacy of economic level and its demographic and bureaucratic correlates' in determining welfare state development. In a survey of seventy-six nation-states outside Africa, Cutright found that 'the degree of social security coverage is most powerfully correlated with its level of economic development' (Cutright, 1965, p. 537). Wilensky's later survey among a range of twenty-two developed and underdeveloped nation-states maintained that economic level, when combined with the dependent effects of the proportion of aged in the population and the age of the social security system, explained in excess of 85 per cent of the international variance in social security effort. Accordingly, 'there is not much variance left to explain' by other causes (Wilensky, 1975, pp. 22–5, 48–9).

However, this view has been frequently challenged. In a survey of seventeen developed Western capitalist democracies, Stephens argues that Wilensky's 'finding that public spending is heavily influenced by the demographic and bureaucratic outcomes of economic growth does not hold' (1979, p. 101). Similarly, James O'Connor (1988) finds very limited evidence of convergence in the OECD countries, and then only on a very particular definition of 'welfare effort' and for a very limited period. In a survey of the long-term experience of four Western European states, Hage, Hanneman and Gargan find that 'previous research has overestimated the importance of GNP in welfare state development'. While 'social need is an important determinant of the growth in welfare expenditures . . . the availability of resources has no relationship to the growth in welfare expenditures' (Hage et al., 1989, pp. 104–8). Indeed, in certain contexts, Hage et al. and David Cameron find that the growth of welfare expenditure is in fact *counter*cyclical, that is it is negatively related to economic growth. (On France and Britain, respectively, see Hage et al., 1989, p. 107; Cameron, 1978, p. 1245.)

More recently, Manfred Schmidt has adapted the 'industrialist' thesis developed by Dethev Zollner to assess social policy development in a range of thirty-nine 'rich and poor countries'. Zollner's original thesis was that the share of social spending as a percentage of GDP (as a surrogate of welfare state development) could be correlated with 'the non-agricultural dependent labour force–population ratio' (as an index of industrialization). Amending the thesis so as also to include previous levels of affluence and of social expenditure, Schmidt finds that, in its amended form, Zollner's industrialism thesis will explain about 75 per cent of total variation in social spending effort among his sample of thirty-nine nations. The fit between the amended Zollner thesis and the empirical data is thus 'remarkably good'. However, for a small subsample of nine nations (both 'underspenders' and 'overspenders'), the fit was 'remarkably bad'. In the case of these 'social policy surplus' and 'deficit' nations, Schmidt insists that an explicitly *political* explanation is required (Schmidt, 1989).

Schmidt's assessment may in fact direct us towards a more general conclusion about the utility of the industrialism thesis. Undoubtedly, the experience of industrialization and economic growth has had a profound impact on the development of welfare states. Even among those who challenge the relationship of economic development to welfare state growth, there is widespread recognition of changing social need as a spur to social policy innovation. However, following Uusitalo, it is clear that the significance of economic development in explaining *variation* in social policy between nations depends very substantially on the size and diversity of the sample under review. It may also depend on the precise ways in which crucial variables, such as 'welfare effort', are specified (J. S. O'Connor and Brym, 1988). In samples which draw on a wide range of very differently developed nations (as when, for example, contrasting the first and third worlds), economic development emerges as a very powerful indicator of welfare state growth. However, among similarly developed nations (for example, in studies confined to OECD countries), much less can be explained by variation in levels of economic development (Uusitalo, 1984). More recently, Castles (1998, 50–3, 301–6) argues that economic development is crucial to the capacity of states to develop extensive welfare regimes but, beyond a certain threshold, industrial development no longer explains the diversity in welfare state experiences (and expenditures). Correspondingly, we can argue that the industrialism thesis (stripped of its teleological functionalist element) demonstrates that economic and industrial development has been a necessary background condition for the development of welfare states. However, given this premise, especially within the developed capitalist states, the *particular form* that the welfare state takes may be crucial, and it is here that the space remains for other forms of explanation.

This is an insight which was developed with particular effect by Göran Therborn. Concentrating on the logic of market economies rather than the logic of industrialism, Therborn insists that the dominance of capitalist markets, far from eliminating the necessity of state institutions, generates new and pressing demands for (welfare) state intervention. He draws attention to what he calls 'the modern *universality* of welfare states', as the form which *all* developed and industrial societies (and not only capitalist ones) must necessarily take. For Therborn, such universality necessarily arises from a uniform feature of all such societies, namely '*the failure of markets in securing human reproduction*'. Echoing the classical analysis of Karl Polanyi on the coming of a market society, he insists that 'markets require states'. He identifies a 'double historical process, in which the modern welfare state emerged, a process of market expansion and a countermovement of protection against the market' (Therborn, 1987, p. 240). As feminist writers have done most to establish, the market has never provided competently for the reproduction of human labour power. For this it has always had to rely on either private provision (through the family) or public provision (through the state's education and health services).

Welfare states then are the necessary corollary of the rise of the market economy.

This account of the welfare state as provider of those conditions of human reproduction not secured by the market is developed through a further distinction between *public* goods and *private* goods.[1] Therborn argues that state provision for simple human reproduction and some provision for expanded reproduction constitutes a public good in virtually all developed countries. Some other public goods – beyond the simple reproduction of the species – are widely acknowledged (for example, in the area of natalist or health policies). Others have become more or less deeply institutionalized as 'national norms' or 'social citizenship rights'. However, the state provision of private (rivally consumed) goods is seen to constitute a much more fiercely contested area of welfare state policy. The provision of private goods is, by definition, redistributive, whether progressively or regressively. It is here, over the redistribution of resources through taxation, pensions, social security transfers and so on, that the fiercest disputes occur.

In essence, Therborn's view is that a minimum of state provision of welfare (broadly that which can be understood as constituting public goods) is a necessity dictated by the structure of societies dependent on markets and is not vulnerable to political retrenchment. Only the form and extent of the welfare state, rather than its very existence, is a political issue in market-dependent societies, and this form will be largely determined by the balance of social forces in conflict. This may be illustrated through Therborn's own 'ideal types' of the welfare state as these might reflect the conflicting interests of owners and workers (see table 1.1).

A strong, interventionist welfare state is seen to be closer to the working-class model and better able to resist pressure for retrenchment. By contrast, a market-oriented, weak welfare state is closer to the bourgeois model. As we shall see later (pp. 125n, 171–7 below), this is something of an oversimplification. Employers large and small have often taken an active interest in the nature (and funding) of (especially workers') welfare provision. But differing types of employers in differing sectors of the economy have often taken a quite different view of what the appropriate form (and size) of such a welfare state should be (see, for example, Swenson, 2002; Mares, 2003). Generally, the conflict engaged in has been over the *form* or *extent* of the welfare state, not over the welfare state set against some other state form.

In this way, Therborn characterizes the welfare state as 'irreversible' or as a 'functional necessity'. It is an indispensable means of overcoming the

---

[1] *Public goods* are 'non-rivally consumed' goods or goods from which it is impractical to exclude non-paying consumers. *Private goods* are those which, even if provided by the state, are rivally consumed.

Table 1.1   Two types of welfare state

'Proletarian' welfare state	*'Bourgeois' welfare state*
1 Welfare state arrangements to assert workers' right to a livelihood	Welfare state arrangements adjusted to needs of capital accumulation, incentives to work, and so on
2 Right to work, right to safety at work, leisure and so on	Primarily geared to provision of skilled, able, loyal and fit workforce
3 Statutory public social insurance and public income maintenance; worker controlled (state controlled a second-best option)	Limited (discretionary) system of social provision, administered by employers (state controlled a second-best option)
4 A wide coverage and uniform/ universal provision on a class (rather than 'social citizenship') basis	No uniform/universal provision; provision on a 'needs' basis
5 Redistributive financing of welfare state	Welfare state financed on (actuarially sound) insurance principles

Source: Therborn, 1986, pp. 155–6.

limitations of market provision under *any* social formation. However, its actual form may represent the interests of either capital or organized labour. The balance of interests represented will be determined by the effective strengths of these (and other) opposing political forces. Therborn's account thus shares with the original industrialism thesis the claim that the welfare state is a product of the *needs* generated by the development of market-based societies. But he also maintains that the actual level of welfare state provision will be an expression of the strength of social democratic forces, thus anticipating the 'power resources model' (pp. 30–3 below).

The industrialism thesis, in either its original or this amended form, remains of considerable importance. It is clear that massive changes in the social and industrial character of capitalist societies in the nineteenth century did transform the context for state action, and the view that the dominance of capitalist markets, far from eliminating the necessity of state intervention, generates new and pressing demands for state involvement carries considerable conviction. Nonetheless, such accounts are very significantly weakened by the misplaced assumption that the identification of changing 'needs' in itself *explains* the development of new institutions to meet such needs. In the case of Therborn's work, it is not clear that the identification of potential public goods makes their (indefinitely continued) provision unproblematic. Public choice theory makes it clear that there is no guarantee that a public good will be produced even if it is in the interests of every member of society to have such a good provided (Offe, 1987, p. 516; Olson, 1965). Furthermore, many of Therborn's proposed public goods, resting on 'national norms' or 'social citizenship rights' look extremely vulnerable to political retrenchment or 'redefinition'. Too often, the 'logic of industrialism' has been seen as a sufficient *explanation* of the rise of welfare state institutions, without identifying the political and historical actors/forces which were to make such changes happen.

Modernization and the Welfare State

The modernization approach may be represented, simply if rather approximately, as a *politicized* version of the industrialism thesis. It too is concerned with what distinguishes modern from traditional societies and sees the welfare state as a part of that complex which defines modern society. It too is shaped by a progressive-evolutionary logic, a historical transition towards more complex and developed societies which is seen to be carrying all traditional societies towards some variant of the modern form. But it can be distinguished from the industrialism thesis by the (differing) ways in which it complements the logic of industrialism with the dynamics of democratization. Thus modern societies are to be defined as much by the processes of institutional change that they have undergone under the rubric of political democratization as by the technological changes that have followed on industrialization.

The modern world (including the welfare state) is seen to be the product of two revolutionary changes – not just the 'industrial revolution' but also the political revolution that transformed national publics from subjects to citizens. The latter process – most explicit in the revolutionary experience of France and America – saw its more prosaic but equally important fulfilment in the widespread universalization of the franchise around the turn of the twentieth century. In the words of Flora and Heidenheimer, the welfare state is 'a general phenomenon of modernization . . . a product of the increasing differentiation and the growing size of societies on the one hand and of processes of social and political mobilization on the other' (1981a, p. 8). Thus 'the historical constellation in which the European welfare state emerged' was one of 'growing mass democracies and expanding capitalist economies within a system of sovereign nation states' (1981b, pp. 23, 22).

Theorists of modernization have not fought shy of identifying capitalism (as opposed to industrialism) as an important and independent component in the shaping of (at least Western) modern societies. They also confer considerable importance on political mobilization and especially the mobilization of the emergent working class as an important component in the rise of the welfare state, particularly in the period before 1945.[2] However, at least in the modernization writing of the 1950s and 1960s, such political mobilization was depicted less as the implementation of the class aspirations of the organized working class than as the natural correlate of full citizenship (Lipset, 1969; Flora and Heidenheimer, 1981a). Certainly, the expansion of the franchise around the turn of the twentieth century did bring the working class more fully into political life. But perhaps more importantly for the modernization theorists, it tended in the longer term to de-emphasize class politics through (1) the social concessions made to the working class public (partly through social welfare), and (2) the shared status which everyone now enjoyed as full citizens of the nation-state. Thus, the securing of the early welfare state was seen both to constitute a success for working-class politics but also to lessen the requirement for further class-based political action. Indeed, it was suggested that in a reformed polity, the equality of political citizenship might predominate over the economic inequalities that arose within the capitalist marketplace. Thus Reinhard Bendix wrote: 'it may appear . . . that the growth of citizenship and the nation-state is a more significant dimension of modernization than the distributive inequalities underlying the formation of social classes', while 'the growth of the welfare state . . . provides a pattern of accommodation between competing social groups' (1970, p. 313).

On this account, the coming of the welfare state is one aspect of a more widespread process of modernization. It is associated historically with the extension of political citizenship and especially the rapid expansion of suffrage (and the consequent development of mass political parties) of the turn of the twentieth century. It is seen as a response to working-class political pressure (or, at least, the anticipation of such pressure), but also through its very institutionalization of social reform as a means of defusing the demand for further class-based and/or more revolutionary political action.

Perhaps the clearest statement of this position is to be found in the work of T. H. Marshall. Addressing the specifically British experience, Marshall characterizes the process of modernization over the past three hundred years as one of the general expansion of citizenship. It is a history of the

---

[2] Typically, Flora and Heidenheimer insist that 'up to 1914, and to a large extent through the inter-war period, the social forces most relevant to welfare state development were those of the working class' (1981b, p. 28).

Table 1.2 Types of rights

	Civil rights	Political rights	Social rights
Characteristic period	18th century	19th century	20th century
Defining principle	Individual freedom	Political freedom	Social welfare
Typical measures	Habeas corpus, freedom of speech, thought and faith; freedom to enter into legal contracts	Right to vote, parliamentary reform, payment for MPs	Free education, pensions, health care, (the welfare state)

———————————▶ Cumulative ———————————▶

Source: Marshall, 1963, pp. 70–4.

expansion of the rights of the citizen and a growth in the numbers of those entitled to citizen status.

Marshall identifies three species of rights, civil, political and social – each with its own 'typical' historical epoch – which have been cumulatively secured over the last three hundred years (see table 1.2). The macro-history of the period since 1688 in Britain is seen as one of progress from the securing of a body of civil rights – the rights of the freely contracting individual, sometimes identified with the structure of a capitalist market economy – which, in turn, made possible the expansion of political rights – principally, the expansion of voting rights, which meant in its turn the enfranchisement of the working class and the rise of mass social democratic parties. The winning of civil rights (in the eighteenth century) and of political rights (in the nineteenth century) made possible the securing in the twentieth century of an epoch of social rights. Such rights, which Marshall describes as embracing 'the whole range from the right to a modicum of economic welfare and security to the right to share to the full in the social heritage and to live the life of a civilized being according to the standards prevailing in the society', are frequently identified with a broadly based definition of the welfare state. On such an account, the coming of the welfare state is indeed a historical process, but one which is part of a broader progressive history of expanding citizenship. The coming of the welfare state in the early twentieth century is thus the product of the exercise of the expanded political citizenship of the late nineteenth century, broadly under social democratic auspices (Marshall, 1963).[3]

Thesis 2

The welfare state is a product of successful political mobilization to attain full citizenship, in the context of industrialization

---

Traditional or 'Classical' Social Democracy and the Welfare State

Very similar assumptions underlie much traditional social democratic thinking on the development of the welfare state. Here again there is an emphasis on the process of modernization (associated with the rise of an industrial civilization), and once more an acknowledgement of the importance of the capitalist organization of the economy. Also repeated is the belief that political changes effected under the rubric of extended citizenship (and under the pressure of working-class political mobilization) may, in fact, have *undermined* the conditions for further class-based political mobilization.

The distinctiveness of the traditional social democratic position may be established around three key points. First, while classical social democrats recognize that the birth of capitalism had severe and oppressive consequences for the formative working class, they insist that its further development has not, as Marxist critics have insisted, seen an inexorable worsening of the relative position of the working class. The situation of the urban-industrial working class (often through their own mobilization and agitation first in trade unions and then in social democratic political parties) has improved not worsened. Thus capitalism has proved capable of reform. The excesses of liberal capitalism have been checked by an increasingly interventionist 'social state' which has counteracted the inequitable outcomes of liberal capitalism through legislative interference.

Secondly, the class structure of capitalism, again in defiance of Marxist expectations, has not been increasingly polarized but has, in practice, grown to be ever more diffuse and differentiated. Significantly, the development of capitalism has been accompanied by the secular growth of the middle class. In the twentieth century, the growing division between the

---

[3] In fact, Marshall's was not a straightforwardly evolutionary view. He repeatedly stressed the potential clash between citizenship equality and class/economic inequality (Marshall, 1963). For a critical commentary, see Barbalet, 1988.

legal ownership of capital and its effective control (the 'managerial revolution') is seen to have weakened the power of capital as a class. At the same time, the expansion of the interventionist state not only ameliorates the position of the working class, but, in creating an expanding public employment sector, increasingly unseats the logic of the market and further complicates and differentiates class structure.

Thirdly, since a (reformed) capitalism is capable of growth without crises, and furnishes an increasingly complex class structure, the social democrats argue that further social progress (towards conceptually rather indistinct 'socialist' ends) is best effected, indeed is only possible, through the continued promotion of (capitalist) economic growth.[4]

All of these strategic claims and conclusions rely on a fourth and decisive element in the classical social democrats' position. This is their belief in the definitive importance of the winning of mass parliamentary democracy and the changing balance of social forces this occasions between the attenuated economic power (of the owners of industry) and the enhanced political power (of elected governments). The expansion of the franchise within the core societies of developed capitalism in the late nineteenth and early twentieth centuries – which generally corresponded with the rise of social democratic parties – is afforded an unchallenged primacy in social democratic accounts as the key to subsequent social development. Such social development is best explained not by concentrating on patterns of capitalist development alone, but rather by considering the impact of the expansion of democratic institutions and political rights against a background of economic growth. Of decisive importance is the winning of democracy, which brings a new social and political order under which it is *political* authority which exercises effective control over the *economic* seats of power.[5] Buttressed by the increased power of organized labour and the diffusion of the capitalist interest through the 'managerial revolution', the state emerges as the principal directing authority within the advanced capitalist societies. Increasingly, outmoded and irrational direction by the market, responsible to no one, gives way to the planning and administrative logic of an accountable political authority.

Further, the securing of democratic institutions allows for the *gradual* transformation of both state and society. Before the coming of mass

---

[4] According to the leading turn-of-the-century revisionist, Eduard Bernstein, 'the prospects of socialism depend not on the decrease but on the increase of social wealth' (1909, p. 142).
[5] According to Sidney Webb, 'collectivism is the obverse of democracy'; if the working man is given the vote, 'he will not forever be satisfied with exercising that vote over such matters as the appointment of the Ambassador to Paris, or even the position of the franchise . . . he will more and more seek to convert his political democracy into what one may roughly term an industrial democracy, so that he may obtain some kind of control as a voter over the conditions under which he lives' (cited in J. Hay, 1975, p. 14).

democracy, the exclusion of the mass of the people from within 'the pale of the constitution' justified, indeed necessitated, the call for the revolutionary overthrow of capitalism. However, the winning of parliamentary democracy transformed this relationship, allowing (indeed requiring) that the now-legal mass political and industrial organizations of the working class should effect the gradual transformation of capitalism into socialism by first securing democratic control of the state and then using such state power to effect social and economic transformation. For some classical social democrats, the 'social state' or welfare state – the state which intervenes in the processes of economic production and exchange to redistribute life chances between individuals and classes – became the principal mechanism for prosecuting such a transformative political strategy.

Social Democracy and the Coming of the 'Keynesian Welfare State'

However, this perspective still left practising social democrats with the theoretical 'problem' of the long-term socialization of the economy. As we have seen, early social democrats were distinguished from their more radical socialist opponents not by rejection of the final *aim* of socialization of the economy (which formally, at least, they endorsed) but by their differing (gradualist or evolutionary) *method* for achieving such an end. Neoclassical economics insisted that capitalism required the free play of untrammelled market forces. It seemed that for its socialist (including social democratic) opponents, socialism must by contrast be premised on some form of centralized and directive planning and investment. However, the social, political and economic costs of transition to such a socialized/planned economy were great, perhaps insurmountable, for social democrats pledged to the introduction of socialism through the medium of liberal parliamentary democracy.[6] The 'solution' to this social democratic dilemma was to be found in the development of Keynesian economic policy in association with the promotion of an expanded welfare state – the so-called *Keynesian Welfare State*. It is in this way that the welfare state comes to assume its familiar centrality in traditional social democratic thinking.

For social democracy, the vital importance of Keynesianism resided in its status as 'a system of political control over economic life' (Skidelsky, 1979, p. 55). Its great strategic beauty lay in its promise of effective political control of economic life without the dreadful social, economic and

---

[6] On the costs and difficulties of revolutionary transition, see Emmanuel, 1979; Offe, 1985; Przeworski, 1985; Przeworski and Sprague, 1986.

political costs that social democrats feared 'expropriation of the expropriators' would bring. Though Keynes was not a socialist, he was an opponent of the belief that capitalism was a self-regulating economic system. Above all, it was the neoclassical belief in a self-regulating market mechanism securing full employment that Keynes sought to subvert, indeed to invert. Say's Law – that under capitalism supply created its own sufficient demand – held true, Keynes claimed, only under the peculiar conditions of full employment. It did not however itself *guarantee* this equilibrium at full employment. Such a balance could only be secured *outside* the market, by the state's manipulation of 'those variables which can be deliberately controlled or managed by central authority' (Keynes, 1973). The key variables which governments could manipulate were the propensity to consume and the incentive to invest. It was the duty of governments to intervene in the market to generate an enhanced level of 'effective demand', promoting the propensity both to consume and to invest, so as to ensure sufficient economic activity to utilize all available labour and thus to secure equilibrium at full employment. To achieve this, a whole range of indirect measures – including taxation policy, public works, monetary policy and the manipulation of interest rates – were available to the interventionist government.

Keynes's advocacy of a 'managed capitalism' offered a neat solution to the social democratic dilemma of how to furnish reforms for its extended constituency and maintain its long-term commitment to socialism without challenging the hegemony of private capital. It was Keynesian economics that provided the rationale for social democracy's abandonment of the traditional socialist aspiration for socialization of the economy. Keynes himself had famously insisted:

> It is not the ownership of the instruments of production which it is important for the state to assume. If the state is able to determine the aggregate amount of resources devoted to augmenting the instruments and the basic rate of reward to those who own them, it will have accomplished all that is necessary. (1973, p. 378)

In this way, it was possible for social democrats to represent formal ownership of the economy (and the traditional strategy of socialization/ nationalization) as (largely) irrelevant. Economic *control* could be exercised through the manipulation of major economic variables in the hands of the government. The owners of capital could be *induced* to act in ways which would promote the interests of social democracy's wide constituency. At the same time, social democratic governments could shape the propensity to consume, through taxation and monetary policy, as well as through adjusting the level of public spending. They could also rectify the disutilities of the continuing play of market forces through the income transfers and social services that came to be identified with the welfare state. Happily, the raising of workers' wages and income transfers to the poor, a 'vice' in classical economics, suddenly became, given the tendency of lower income groups to consume the greater part of their incomes, a Keynesian 'virtue'. Social democracy was thus able simultaneously to secure the 'national interest' and to service its own constituency.

For traditional social democrats, then, the development of the welfare state institutionalized the successes of social democratic politics. The Keynesian revolution made possible the transition from the (zero-sum) politics of production to what, under conditions of economic growth, were the (positive-sum) politics of (re)distribution. As Berthil Ohlin described it in the 1930s, 'the tendency is in the direction of a "nationalization of consumption" as opposed to the nationalization of the "means of production" of Marxian socialism' (1938, p. 5). It was a twofold strategy built on active government intervention through (1) the macro-management of the economy to ensure economic growth under conditions of full employment, and (2) a range of social policies dealing with 'the redistribution of the fruits of economic growth, the management of its human effects, and the compensation of those who suffered from them' (Donnison, 1979, pp. 146–50).

> **Thesis 3**
>
> The welfare state is a product of industrial and political mobilization. It embodies the successes of the social democratic political project for the gradual transformation of capitalism

The Power Resources Model

The power resources model offers a distinctive variant of the social democratic approach. At its heart is a perceived division within the advanced capitalist societies between the exercise of economic and of political power, often presented as a contrast between markets and politics. It is insisted that 'the types of power resources that can be mobilized and used in politics and on markets differ *in class-related ways*' (Korpi, 1989, p. 312; emphasis added). Thus, in the *economic* sphere, the decisive power resource is control over capital assets, the mechanism for its exercise is the (wage labour) contract and its principal beneficiary the capitalist class. However, in the *political* sphere, power flows from the strength of numbers, mobilized through the democratic process and tends to favour 'numerically large collectivities', especially the organized working class.

Institutionalized power struggles under advanced capitalism are then best understood as a struggle between the logic of the market and the logic of politics and 'this tension between markets and politics is likely to be reflected in the development of social citizenship and the welfare state' (Korpi, 1989, p. 312). The more successful the forces of the organized working class, the more entrenched and institutionalized will the welfare state become and the more marginalized will be the principle of allocation through the market (Korpi, 1989; Esping-Andersen, 1985; Shalev, 1983; Esping-Andersen and Korpi, 1984, 1987).

In response to his critics, Korpi has insisted that the power resources model is not to be understood as a 'one-factor theory claiming to explain welfare state development more or less exclusively in terms of working class or left strength' (1989, p. 312n). A more complex position – including, for example, the role of confessional parties, party coalitions and pre-emptive conservative reforms – may be developed through the application of a 'games theoretical perspective' to a range of protagonists in the struggle over the welfare state (Korpi, 1989, p. 313). However, to date the principal application of the power resources model has been to underwrite a distinctive left social democratic account of the welfare state as an entrenchment of the power of organized labour and as an avenue of gradual transition towards socialism.

The two core claims of this left social democratic position are succinctly summarized by John Stephens: first, 'the welfare state is a product of labour organization and political rule by labour parties', and secondly, it 'thus represents a first step towards socialism' (1979, p. 72). While recognizing that the welfare state is not universally an expression of the strength of the organized working class, these left social democrats insist that, under the right circumstances, the inauguration and promotion of welfare state policies and institutions has been and can be an effective strategy for the gradual transition from capitalism to socialism. However, their position differs decisively from traditional social democracy in its belief that the coming of democracy, social democratic parties and the welfare state do not transform the social and political nature of the advanced capitalist societies. The logic of Marx's analysis of the contradictions of capitalism and the centrality of class struggle still holds, but parliamentary democracy and the interventionist state are seen to provide new channels for the prosecution of the class politics of socialism.[7]

Generally, the inception of welfare state policies is seen to follow on the universalization of the franchise, itself seen as a victory for the organized working class. Initially, social policy may represent an attempt to pre-empt

---

[7] In fact, Marxism has always embraced such a radical social democratic wing (with a strategy for socialism built on incrementalism and parliamentary democracy), perhaps best represented by Karl Kautsky and the Austro-Marxists (Kautsky, 1909, 1910, 1983; C. Pierson, 1986, pp. 58–83; Bottomore and Goode, 1978).

political reform or else to disorganize or demobilize the organized working class. But it is insisted that under wise and far-sighted social democratic governance, welfare state policies can be used both to counteract the dominance of capital that market relationships entail and to reinforce the effective solidarity of organized labour. The left social democrats afford much greater independent importance to political power than do many others in the Marxist tradition, and social democratic governments elected under universal franchise are seen to constitute an effective counter to the power exercised by capital within the privately owned economy. Where social democratic governments become more or less permanently entrenched in office (and this is an essential precondition) an effective balance or at least stalemate may be established between the political powers of social democracy and the economic powers of capital. Under these circumstances, some sort of working compromise between capital and labour is likely to emerge, characteristically under the rubric of the welfare state.

But the left social democrats insist that, however longstanding, such a compromise is in essence temporary. Indeed, if the social democrats govern wisely and make the right strategic choices, it is argued that the (Marxian) logic of continuing capitalist development will increasingly tilt the balance of power in favour of organized labour and against private capital. Thus it is suggested that continuing capitalist development will tend to produce an expanding and homogeneous broad working class. Social democratic governments that mobilize this constituency and promote its internal solidarity (through, for example, nationally agreed and uniform salary increases, the support of 'full employment' and the provision of generous unemployment and sickness benefits) can undermine the effectiveness of traditional market disciplines and further entrench their own political power. At a certain point in the strengthening of the powers of organized labour, conditions of balance/stalemate with capital no longer apply. At this point, it is possible for the social democratic movement to advance beyond the 'political' welfare state, with its indirect (Keynesian) influence on the management of the economy and to engage directly the traditional socialist issue of socialization of the economy.

This process was seen to have attained its highest expression in Sweden. Writing at the end of the 1970s, John Stephens argued that in Sweden, where 'the welfare state has been developed by a strongly organized and highly centralized trade union movement . . . in co-operation with a social democratic government that remained in office for 44 years . . . the welfare state is characterized by high levels of expenditure and progressive financing and thus represents a transformation of capitalism towards socialism' (1979, p. 129).

In more recent years, and in a colder climate for social democratic forces, the advocacy of a power resources model has been more circumspect and more nuanced. So, for example, Huber and Stephens insist that power resources – or the balance of class power – is still 'the primary determinant of variations through time and across countries in welfare state effort' (2001, p. 3). But they see this as mediated by historical legacies ('path dependency'), constitutional/state structures (particularly the number of veto points in a state's lawmaking processes) and the (positive) impact of women's increasing participation in both economy and politics. Similarly, Korpi and Palme (2003) insist that, even in an era of welfare state retrenchment, the levels and extent of welfare cutbacks correlate strongly with the partisanship of class-based parties. The cutbacks made by social democratic parties have been smaller and slower to arrive (at least in the period down to 1995 which they consider).

Summarily, this is an approach which suggests that the most 'successful' social democratic welfare states will be associated with:

- the extension of the franchise;
- the rise of social democratic parties;
- a strong (and centralized) trade union movement;
- weak parties of the right;
- sustained social democratic governmental incumbency;
- sustained economic growth;
- strong class identity and correspondingly weak cleavages of religion, language and ethnicity.

Thesis 4

The welfare state is the product of a struggle between the political powers of social democracy and the economic powers of capital. A generous and expansive welfare state is an expression of the strength of working-class forces (in both parties and trade unions)

Commentary: Modernization, Social Democracy and Working-Class Power

Some of the weaknesses identified in the industrialism thesis are at least addressed in the literature of modernization and traditional social democracy and in the 'power resources' model of welfare state development. In fact, there has sometimes been a tendency to elide explanations in terms of modernization with those premised on industrialization. However, Hage et al. insist upon the need 'to separate the independent effects of modernization from those of industrialization' and argue that 'the modernization process has much more impact than the industrialization process on the expansion in social welfare expenditures'. Specifically, they isolate urbanization and the increasing density of communication (measured by quantities of mail and electronic/telegraphic communications) rather than industrialization or economic growth as decisive indicators of welfare state growth (Hage et al., 1989, pp. 100–10). Similarly, Peter Flora and Jens Alber prefer the 'vague and ambiguous' but 'multi-dimensional' concept of modernization to either industrialization or democratization as the key to explaining the development of European welfare states (1981, pp. 37–8).

However, the major issue that has divided advocates of modernization and social democratic theses on the welfare state from the claims of industrialism is the independent importance that they attribute to *political* forces in shaping the development of the welfare state. Often, this advocacy of the political causes of welfare state development is simply an inversion of the claims of industrialism. Thus, for example, the burden of Stephens's refutation of Wilensky was to buttress his belief 'that the welfare state is a product of labour organization and political rule by labour parties and thus represents a first step towards socialism' (1979, p. 72; see p. 19 above). Similarly, the purpose of Furniss and Tilton's comparative history of welfare state experience in the US, Britain and Sweden is to demonstrate 'that a democratic majority, backed by a committed labor movement, can capture and employ political power to create a more decent society along the lines of a social welfare state' (Furniss and Tilton, 1979, p. 93). Christopher Hewitt has also argued that social democratic parties can have a profound influence on the narrowing of income inequality in advanced capitalist societies, largely through the mechanism of government redistribution through the welfare state (1977, pp. 450, 460; see also Hicks, 1988).

In the 1980s, Walter Korpi was an influential advocate of the view that (social democratic) politics makes a difference. Writing of the postwar experience of Germany, Austria and Sweden, he and Gøsta Esping-Andersen argue that 'the relative power position of wage-earners has been of central significance for the development towards an institutional type of social policy' (Esping-Andersen and Korpi, 1984). Assessing survey evidence on the emergence of social rights during sickness in eighteen OECD countries since 1930, Korpi finds 'rather unequivocal support for the assumption of the significance of left government participation in the development of social policy'. By contrast, 'while it appears reasonable to assume that the rate of growth of economic resources is of relevance for the opportunities to enact social reforms', he finds 'limited support for this hypothesis'. He concludes cautiously that 'class-based left parties appear to have played a significant role in the development of social rights' (Korpi, 1989, pp. 323–5). Julia O'Connor also claims to have isolated a strong association between left power (in both parties and trade unions) and levels of civil consumption expenditure (J. S. O'Connor, 1988).

There is then some (contested) evidence that 'politics makes a difference'. However, we need also to consider *how* it is that 'politics makes a difference'. Much as we found in discussing the evidence brought to support the industrialism thesis, evaluating data in support of modernization and traditional social democratic theses is problematic. Many of the differences in outcomes are the product of the use of differing indices of welfare effort and comparison across differing time periods. In his magisterial review of the evidence, Esping-Andersen, for example, argues that very little difference can be found in the impact of politics on *levels* of welfare expenditure (a commonly used indicator of welfare effort) but that political forces are crucial in determining differing welfare *policy regimes* (Esping-Andersen, 1990, pp. 35–54; see below, pp. 171–7).

Furthermore, some empirical surveys have found that if politics does matter, it is not necessarily the political impact of social democratic forces that matters most. Castles, for example, identifies the weakness of parties of the right as decisive for the emergence of 'generous' welfare states, while Hicks and Swank argue that '*all* less business-oriented parties, Christian democratic as well as social democratic, centrist as well as labor, prove about equally supportive of welfare expansion' (Castles, 1978, 1982, 1985; Hicks and Swank, 1984, p. 104: emphasis added). Wilensky identifies Catholic rather than left party incumbency as the strongest indicator of welfare expenditure and suggests that *the intensity of party competition* (notably between left and Catholic parties) may itself tend to increase welfare spending effort.[8] In the face of this we have the empirical evidence of Huber and Stephens (2001) and Korpi and Palme (2003) that partisanship is still the crucial variable *even in an era of welfare retrenchment*.

Despite these concerns, we can identify some analytic advances in the modernization and social democratic approaches. Most significantly, they do allow that the processes of transformation that create the modern world are simultaneously industrial/technological and political. Correspondingly, weight is given to the expansion of citizenship and the extension of democracy, and attention is also directed to the ways in which the specifically *capitalist* organization of the production process shapes the circumstances of welfare state emergence. Unfortunately, among advocates of modernization and the more traditional variants of the social democratic thesis, these analytic advances are substantially vitiated by the *form* that this revised assessment takes. Thus they have tended to share with industrialism a Panglossian celebration of progress and the imposition of

---

[8] Wilensky, 1981, pp. 356–8, 368–70; on differential spending effort related to party competition among the individual states of the United States, see Jennings, 1979.

assumptions of 'inevitable' development. Inasmuch as they deal with both historical actors (most notably, the organized working class) and the importance of capitalism, they may be accused of misunderstanding both. Thus, for example, in the influential work of Tom Marshall, the working class is often seen to struggle historically to ensure full political citizenship and to use democracy once achieved to secure social rights under the welfare state. But the very achievement of democracy (and associated welfare state rights) is seen to resolve or at least to accommodate the differences of interest between capital and labour out of which such political struggle might have been seen to arise. The spectre of capitalism, and the deep-seated division of interests it is seen to generate, is raised only to argue that it has been 'tamed' or 'subverted' by the rise of the welfare state.

There are a number of historical objections to this account. First, it is far from clear that the coming of parliamentary democracy does bring the irreversible cessation of class hostilities and a uniform social democratic consensus on the welfare state and the mixed economy. Even where the formal concession of democracy led to the more or less successful incorporation of the working class within the political apparatus of the existing state, this did not lead to the permanent reconciliation of class differences and class hostilities in capitalist societies. Thus it is very uncertain that the idea of 'the class politics that undermines the need for class politics' is justified by actual welfare state experience.

Secondly, whatever the role of the working class in the later *development* of the welfare state, the earliest welfare state measures were generally introduced by liberal and/or conservative elites and not by the representatives of organized labour. Even, for example, in the Scandinavian social democracies, in which the working class welfare state is often seen to be most effectively entrenched, the origins of the welfare state lay with conservative or liberal political forces and often built on a multi-class appeal (Esping-Andersen, 1985; Baldwin, 1990). Similarly, there is plenty of historical evidence of organized labour opposition to welfare state measures, often because these were seen as (1) an attack on the autonomy and integrity of trade unions' own forms of mutual support, (2) a way of depressing wages through welfare subsidization (a repeated argument against family allowances/child benefit), and (3) a form of state control over the workforce (see below, p. 39).

Thirdly, historical experience suggests that the class analysis of social democracy/modernization theorists is not only too optimistic/uniform but also too crude. Early welfare state measures (of social insurance) were generally limited to particular (very suitable or very vulnerable) trades. Disputes over contributory and non-contributory pensions schemes exacerbated differences of interest between the independent/skilled/ 'respectable' working class (who made limited provision for death and sickness through friendly societies) and the residuum of unskilled (and uninsured) workers. Similarly, there have been differences of interest among employers of labour, between large capital-intensive employers with an interest in a healthy, well-educated and 'regular' workforce, and those in the most keenly competitive, labour-intensive markets whose interest was in securing a mass of unskilled labour at the cheapest possible price (De Swaan, 1988; Swenson, 2002; Mares, 2003). Such differences of interest among (and within) both labour and capital continue down to the present.

The historical record also shows that the state may have its *own* interest in the promotion of social policy, not least in the securing of a citizenry fit and able to staff its armies. For example, the concern with 'national efficiency' and the physical incapacity of the British working class to defend the empire against the challenge of the Boers has long been cited as a source of British welfare reforms at the turn of the twentieth century (Thane, 1982, pp. 60–1; Fraser, 1973, p. 133; J. Hay, 1975). This view was echoed by Lloyd George, who argued in 1917 that 'you can not maintain an A-1 empire with a C-3 population' (cited in Gilbert, 1970, p. 15). More generally, there has been a view, longstanding though most recently articulated in a Foucauldian idiom, that social policy is largely about inducing (self-)discipline and (self-)regulation among national populations.

Advocates of the traditional social democratic position certainly have good grounds for stressing the importance of citizenship. The idea of a shared status of all members of the community and especially the *right* to varying forms of provision from the state is seemingly a definitive element of the welfare state and Esping-Andersen insists that 'few can disagree with T. H. Marshall's . . . proposition that social citizenship constitutes the core idea of a welfare state' (Esping-Andersen, 1990, p. 21). Yet Marshall's unilinear model of expanding citizenship, his qualifications notwithstanding, is unsatisfactory (see pp. 24–6 above). In fact, the nature of citizenship has been, and continues to be, much more consistently contested than Marshall allows. The question of who counts as a citizen, whether full citizenship is gender-specific, what is to count as a citizen's entitlement and under what circumstances welfare rights will be granted and by whom continue to be daily concerns of contemporary political life.[9] As we shall see in chapter 3, this is ever more the case when immigration (and its relationship to participation in welfare) becomes increasingly contested. Only the very general process of overall social expenditure growth (often under very varying rules of citizen entitlement) has concealed this continuing struggle over the status of citizenship (Turner, 1986, 1990; Held, 1989).

---

[9] On the feminist critique of conventional conceptions of citizenship, see Pateman, 1988; Lister, 1993; O'Connor, 1996; and the discussion at pp. 70–1 below.

The 'Keynesian revolution' occupies a similarly problematic place in the traditional social democratic account. Even more explicitly than the winning of citizenship, the emergence of Keynesian forms of economic management, which we have seen to occupy a central place in the justification of the social democratic theory of gradual social transformation, has not been a once-and-for-all change in the governance of capitalist economies. In a number of developed welfare states, perhaps most triumphally in the UK, the formal commitment to full employment and government macro-management of demand has long since been abandoned, and with it goes a substantial part of the theoretical justification of the social democratic position. (For a discussion of the more general consequences of this change for a social democratic politics, see C. Pierson 2005b).

These observations on citizenship and the fate of Keynesianism may suggest a need to reorient our understanding of the elements of bipartisanship, consensus and shared citizenship which have been so frequently identified in the postwar period. Certainly, postwar social policy was often institutionally bipartisan and apparently consensual. However, this bipartisanship may have depended in substantial part on the favourable economic climate that made positive-sum resolutions of distributional conflicts a viable policy. Accordingly, this policy may be better understood in terms of the capacity simultaneously to satisfy a number of (differing) constituencies rather than in terms of a straightforward universalization of citizenship or the coming of consensus. Where reforms did not satisfy these several constituencies, political conflict over social policy could still be acute. Just such an argument has been made about the postwar period in Britain and both phenomena may also be seen in the violent conflict over the Swedish social democrats' pensions reform of 1958 (see, on Sweden, Esping-Andersen, 1985; on the UK, Taylor-Gooby, 1985; Pimlott, 1988; Deakin, 1987). Thus it is possible that the universal citizenship *form* may have been the medium for promoting interests with a much more traditional class-based political and economic *content*.

Finally, as Esping-Andersen has pointed out, welfare state measures may only properly be seen as securing the overall interests of social democracy's natural constituency in the (broad) working class inasmuch as they are *market usurping* – that is to the extent that they insulate workers from the discipline of the market.[10] But clearly many welfare state measures, and especially early welfare state social policy, were not market usurping but *market supporting*. Trade unions were, for example, extremely suspicious of the way in which labour exchanges would be used to recruit strike-

---

[10] The issue of whether such market usurpation will prove to be in the *long-term* interests of the working class will depend on the place of the national welfare state in the world economy and other political developments.

breakers or generally to service employers with non-unionized labour. Social welfare provision was, and still is, criticized as a mechanism for depressing wages, and Pat Thane writes of 'widespread suspicion' towards Liberal welfare reforms in the UK before 1914 from a working class which found them to be 'too limited, too "intrusive", and a threat to working-class independence both collective and individual' (Thane, 1984, p. 899; see also Marwick, 1967; Pelling, 1968; J. Hay, 1978a, pp. 16–21). Many early recommendations on work/farm colonies, even those supported by social democratic politicians, were explicitly coercive in intent (Harris, 1977; Gilbert, 1966, pp. 253–65). Terms of entitlement continue to reflect labour market status and often explicitly 'encourage' labour market participation. Thus any straightforward claim that the welfare state is an imposition of working-class interests through the medium of parliamentary democracy, which accordingly attenuates the conflict of (class) interests, 'tames' the excesses of capitalism and promotes a national unity based around common citizenship, is unsustainable.[11]

Several of these weaknesses are confronted by the 'power resources' model. While this approach is still broadly social democratic (premised on the pursuit of a reformist path through legal-parliamentary means), the benign assumptions of an end to class conflict and an irreversible progress towards an ever enhanced citizenship are rejected. This is a social democratic strategy premised on the historical strength of working-class forces in continuing struggle with the powers of capital. A very considerable effort is made to show empirically that the effective strength of working-class forces (articulated through labour parties and trade union organizations) has made a real difference to the patterns of promotion of the welfare state under advanced capitalism.

However, there remain a number of problems with this model. First, while the more naive evolutionism of traditional social democracy is rejected, elements of a Marxist evolutionism persist. Presumptions about the uniformity of workers' interests, the necessary growth in the proportion of the working class, and the weakening of the powers of capitalism in the face of the collective action of the workers underpin several of the strategic claims in the 'power resources' model. However, there are good grounds for doubting that these presumptions about a majoritarian working class with unified interests are true (C. Pierson, 1986, pp. 7–30, 58–83; Przeworski, 1985; Przeworski and Sprague, 1986).

It may also be that the political focus of the 'power resources' model is too narrow. Middle-class support has been crucial to the pattern of welfare

---

[11] There is a case for insisting that it is the capacity of the organized working class to continue to pursue class-based politics that is the basis for the continued capacity of the welfare state to represent a practice that is in the interests of that class.

state development, particularly in the postwar period, and at strategic times in the historical emergence of the European welfare states the attitudes of rural classes have also been a decisive element. Similarly, parties other than the social democrats (especially the confessional parties of continental Europe) have also played an important historical role in the expansion of the welfare state and their position has not always been one of seeking to minimize levels of social expenditure. This suggests that any understanding of the class politics of the welfare state must consider the positions of a number of classes (not just capital and labour) and of a number of parties (not just the social democrats) and that the decisive element in the success of the social democratic welfare state project may lie in the capacity of the working class and social democratic parties to forge long-term, majoritarian *alliances* in support of its decommodifying form of social policy.

A second criticism of the 'power resources' model is that some of its optimistic assumptions about the possibilities for successful social democratic strategies arise from its concentration on experience in a number of particularly favourable Scandinavian and, more especially, Swedish examples. As Lash and Urry have pointed out (1987, p. 10), all of the favourable corporatist/welfare state examples generally cited in support of the social democratic model are actually numerically swamped by the single counterexample of the United States. Still more important is the diminishing 'success' of these social corporatist states in the 1990s (see Gould, 1999). Although the 'death of the Swedish model' has been exaggerated, there is no doubt that its status as the exemplar of social democratic welfare state success has been very seriously compromised (with an unemployment rate which by the late 1990s was almost double that of the US). And this has to be set in the context of a more general process of welfare state retrenchment (now widely recognized in the power resources literature itself).

Three further general criticisms have been raised against the social democratic perspective. First, there are those who insist that the social democrats' exclusive concentration on the politics of class neglects the decisive impact of interest or 'ascribed status' groups or, indeed, of the state apparatus itself. Secondly, there are those who maintain that all the social democratic approaches fail to recognize that the most important aspects of power under the welfare state lie in its gender-specific consequences for women and its 'race'-specific consequences for ethnic minorities. The claims underlying these first two criticisms will be addressed in chapter 3. A third objection to the social democratic approach is that it underplays the extent to which the welfare state, *even under social democratic auspices*, continues to be, in essence, an instrument of social control of the working population in the interests of capital. This perspective of 'social control' will be considered in chapter 2, in which we turn to criticisms of the social democratic welfare state informed by 'the new political economy'.

2
Political Economy and the Welfare State

In the twenty-five years following the Second World War, it was largely the traditional social democratic outlook that defined the prevailing orthodoxy on advanced capitalism and the welfare state. Buttressed by empirical and programmatic work in social administration, sanctioned by bipartisan support for the expansion of state services and underpinned by continuous economic growth, the social democratic prescription for managed capitalism and social amelioration dominated throughout the advanced industrial world. But from the late 1960s onwards, both the social democratic postwar settlement and its comforting assumptions about the reconcilability of advanced capitalism and the welfare state came under increasing challenge from both right and left. In this chapter, we begin to consider the range of critical responses to the postwar social democratic orthodoxy.

The New Right and the Welfare State

Perhaps the most prominent (and successful) opponent of the postwar orthodoxy has been the New Right, which has argued for a strong identity between social democracy and the welfare state, while insisting that both are inconsistent with the moral, political and economic freedom that only liberal capitalism can guarantee. In common with the other theoretical positions outlined in this study, the New Right does not define a unique set of prescriptions for the welfare state. In fact, it is possible to identify at least two distinct 'strands' in New Right thinking: 'a liberal tendency which argues the case for a freer, more open, and more competitive economy, and a conservative tendency which is more interested in restoring social and political authority throughout society' (Gamble, 1988, p. 29; D. S. King, 1987, pp. 7–27). In brief, both elements of the New Right are hostile to welfare state intervention because (1) its administrative and bureaucratic methods of allocation are inferior to those of the market; (2) it is morally objectionable (for both the sponsors and the recipients of state welfare); (3) it denies the consumers of welfare services any real choice; and (4) despite the enormous resources devoted to it, it has failed either to eliminate poverty or to eradicate unjust inequalities of opportunity (Gamble, 1988, pp. 27–60). Indeed, the New Right almost invert the common sense of industrialism, modernization and social democratic approaches to insist that the origins of the present social, economic and political problems of advanced capitalist societies lie not in the failure of markets but in the mistaken pursuit of those market-usurping policies identified with the welfare state.

The more interesting and the more important intellectual challenge of the New Right probably comes from its neoliberal rather than its neo-conservative wing (although in recent years it is perhaps the latter that has had the greater political impact, at least in the US). Those political move-ments and ideologies of the 1980s which identified themselves with the New Right, most notably 'Thatcherism' in the UK and 'Reaganism' in the US, were in practice a potent, if not entirely consistent, mixture of eco-nomic liberalization and renascent conservatism. In defiance of the liber-tarian conclusions drawn by some on the New Right, in the UK and still more prominently in the US, the 'freeing up' of the economy was associ-ated with the traditionally conservative imperatives of strengthening the 'law and order' state, a more aggressively nationalistic foreign policy, the reversal of minority rights, the glorification of 'traditional family life' and an endorsement of the religious and moral crusade of the moral majority (Nozick, 1974; Gilder, 1982; Stockman, 1986; D. S. King, 1987). Some of these conservative elements on the New Right receive fuller attention in chapter 5. Here our attention is more closely focussed upon its neo-liberal aspect.

Underlying most neoliberal assessments of the relationship between capitalism, social democracy and the welfare state is a rehearsal of the sen-timents of Adam Smith's advocacy of liberal capitalism (see pp. 10–11 above). It is recognized that Smith wrote under very different circum-stances and to a quite different agenda and audience than his latter-day admirers. Yet his was a critique of the interventionist (albeit in his time mercantilist) state and a call for limited government (whether or not democratic). He advocated the spontaneously arising market economy as *the* means of securing both optimum individual and social welfare and the surest guarantee of individual liberty. It is just these prescriptions, and the ways in which social democracy and the welfare state have counter-manded them, that lie at the heart of the neoliberal view.

In essence, the argument of the New Right is that the impact of social democracy and the associated welfare state represents a usurpation of the sound principles of liberal capitalism. Its political ideal is to achieve a return to what is understood to have been the social and political *status quo ante*. Thus Milton Friedman insists that 'The scope of government must be limited. Its major function must be to protect our freedom both from the enemies outside our gates and from our fellow-citizens: to preserve law and order, to enforce private contracts, to foster competitive markets' (1962, p. 2). Though government intervention beyond this minimum might sometimes be justified, according to Friedman, it is 'fraught with danger' (1962, pp. 2–3; see also Minford, 1987). Certainly, where we have had economic progress, this has been the 'product of the initiative and drive of individuals cooperating through the free market. Government measures have hampered not helped this development' (Friedman, 1962, p. 200; D. S. King, 1987, pp. 83–4). Correspondingly, Friedman's advocacy of monetarism is at least in part directed at curtailing the counterproductive interventions of social democratic governments (Friedman and Friedman, 1980; Bosanquet, 1983, pp. 5–10, 22–4, 43–61).

Perhaps the most sophisticated philosophical statement of the neoliberal view is that developed by Friedrich Hayek in the three volumes of *Law, Legislation and Liberty* (1982). For Hayek, the liberal 'Great Society' championed by Smith can only be secured on the basis of 'Catallaxy', the neologism Hayek uses to describe 'the special kind of spontaneous order produced by the market through people acting within the rules of the laws of property, tort and contract' (1982, vol. 2, p. 109). Both social democracy and the welfare state seek to undermine this order based on the interlocking of spontaneously emerging markets and are thus inconsistent with the principles of a free and just society.

In fact, Hayek's Smithian liberalism is tempered by a good measure of Burkean conservatism. As in Burke's critique of the French Revolution, Hayek condemns the '*constructivist rationalism*' of all those, from 1789 onwards, who have sought to recast society in accord with some understanding of the principles of Reason (1982, vol. 1, pp. 5, 29–34). Order (and tradition) certainly appeal to Hayek's conservatism but this is the spontaneously generated and in principle unknowable order created by innumerable interactions within a number of interlocking markets – the catallaxy. Indeed, 'it is because it was not dependent on organization but grew up as a spontaneous order that the structure of modern society has attained that degree of complexity which it possesses and which far exceeds any that could have been achieved by deliberate organization' (Hayek, 1982, vol. 1, p. 50). In part, this is an issue of philosophical principle, namely Hayek's belief that every individual should be, in so far as is possible, self-directing. But it also embodies a seemingly compelling sociological argument. As Hayek himself makes plain, in even the most centralized and state-dominated societies, the central political authorities can have only a very tenuous control over the many millions of social decisions made every day within its domain. By contrast, the individual may have a very intimate control as well as an irreducible/irrepressible interest in that much smaller range of *salient* decisions he or she must make in organizing his or her own life. Hayek combines this with something like Smith's own faith in the benevolence of 'the invisible hand' to sustain a distinctive account of the promotion of welfare. Thus, he argues, 'a condition of liberty in which all are allowed to use their knowledge for their purposes, restrained only by rules of just conduct of universal application, is likely to produce for them the best condition for achieving their aims' (1982, vol. 1, p. 55).

Hayek ascribes a correspondingly limited role to the state. The duty of the public authority is not to pursue its own ends but rather to provide the framework within which 'catallaxy' may develop. Those functions for which the state may properly raise taxation are limited to these:

- provision of collective security against the threat of external assault;
- preservation of the rule of law where law is in essence confined to the impartial application of general rules of property, contract and tort;
- provision for (though not necessarily the administration of) those collective or public goods which the market cannot efficiently provide; for example, protection against (internal) violence, regulation of public health and the building and maintenance of roads.

To these duties of the minimal state, Hayek adds the following:

- provision of 'a certain minimum income for everyone', more precisely for 'those who for various reasons cannot make their living in the market, such as the sick, the old, the physically or mentally defective, the widows and orphans – that is all people suffering from adverse conditions which may affect anyone and against which most individuals cannot alone make adequate provision but in which a society that has reached a certain level of wealth can afford to provide for all'. (Hayek, 1982, vol. 3, p. 55)

However, Hayek is insistent that this last duty to relieve destitution is not to be identified with the welfare state. Relief is not a statutory right of citizenship, but needs based and discretionary. Least of all is such relief to be understood as part of an attempt to manufacture 'social justice'.

Hayek's model may be completed by a brief consideration of his views on democracy. Although Hayek would doubtless have considered himself a democrat, he was perhaps still more an advocate of individual freedom, and certainly he was an opponent of the ideas of sovereignty and unlimited government frequently associated with the rise of democracy. 'Only limited government can be decent government,' he insisted, 'because there does not exist (and cannot exist) general moral rules for the assignment of particular benefits' (1982, vol. 2, p. 102). Where parliament is sovereign, governments become the plaything of organized sectional interests. Principles and 'the national interest' are abandoned in the attempt to mobilize a majority-creating coalition of particular interests against the *genuinely* common or public interest.

The welfare state and the political agenda of social democracy are seen by Hayek to be at odds with almost every aspect of this model of the liberal capitalist ideal. First, social democrats set out to adjust the spontaneous order of catallaxy, a project which Hayek depicted as hopeless given the impossibility of adequate centrally organized knowledge of the infinity of market-like decisions. Interventions in the market will *always* have suboptimal outcomes and *always* lessen general social welfare. Secondly, the welfare state represents a break with Hayek's insistence that the law must be confined to rules of 'just conduct of universal application'. Social democracy prescribes particularistic legislation, most notably to confer privileges on its allies in the organized labour movement, and governments under its auspices seek not only to negotiate general and market-usurping agreements between labour and capital but even to intervene on a day-to-day basis in the conduct of particular transactions within the marketplace. Not only is this an invasion of individual freedom and a usurpation of the proper role of the law, it is also bound to fail, given the opacity of the spontaneously generated catallaxy.

Thirdly, the welfare state is also the principle institutional vehicle of the misconceived aspiration for 'social justice' (Hayek, 1982, vol. 2, p. 1). Justice, Hayek insists, is strictly *procedural* and can only refer to the proper enforcement of general rules of universal application without regard to its particular results. No set of human arrangements, no cumulation of particular actions (however unequal its outcomes) can be described as just or unjust. 'The mirage of social justice' which the social democratic welfare state pursues is, at best, a nonsense and, at worst, pernicious and itself unjust. It means undermining the justice of the market, confiscating the wealth of the more successful, prolonging the dependency of the needy, entrenching the special powers of organized interests and overriding individual freedom. Indeed, 'distributive justice [is] irreconcilable with the rule of law' and in seeking to press state intervention beyond its legitimate minimum, the social democrats have been the principal offenders in 'giving democracy a bad name' (Hayek, 1982, vol. 2, p. 86).

Public Choice Theory

Hayek's writings may have become newly prominent in the 1980s but they are certainly not new. His arguments against the welfare state date back more than half a century. But in recent years, this longstanding (and largely philosophical) case has been supplemented with arguments drawn from social science sources and particularly from work in public choice theory. The latter is often seen to give enhanced empirical and logical rigour to the moral and philosophical case against the welfare state.

Public choice theory, located on the boundaries between economics and political science, has traditionally been concerned with collective or non-market forms of decision-making. In the hands of the New Right, it is taken to show that under liberal democratic procedures, collective choice through state actions, beyond that necessary minimum advocated by both Smith and Hayek, will always tend to yield outcomes that are less efficient or desirable than outcomes determined by private choice through markets. Public choice writers sympathetic to the New Right seek to show that the welfare state project is flawed both logically and sociologically.

The great weakness of decision-making procedures under liberal democratic arrangements within which the welfare state has developed is that they encourage both governments and voters to be fiscally irresponsible. The individual making a private economic choice within the market has always to weigh costs against benefits in making a decision. Public choice theorists argue that in the political 'market' both voters and governments are able to avoid or at least to deflect the consequences of spending decisions and thus to seek benefits without taking due account of costs. Within the rules of the liberal democratic game, it is then possible for both governments and voters to act rationally but through their collective action to produce suboptimal or even positively harmful consequences. This, it is suggested, may be shown in a number of ways.

First, it may not be rational for individual voters carefully to consider the full range of a prospective government's public policy, still less to consider the overall consequences of such policies for the 'national interest'. The marginal impact of a single voter's decision is so limited that the opportunity costs of a well-considered decision would be unreasonable (Downs, 1957; Olson, 1982). Under these circumstances, no rational actor will normally press his or her consideration beyond a crude calculation of how the incumbent government has benefited the voter. Given this, it is in the interests of a government seeking re-election to ensure that the pre-election period is one in which as many voters as possible feel that they are prospering under the current regime. Government will then, it is suggested, seek to manage the economy in the run-up to an election so as to lower inflation and unemployment and to maximize incomes (perhaps through lowering personal rates of taxation). In this way, a political business cycle may be established, with governments manipulating economic variables in the prelude to an election. Not only will this give misleading signs to the electors, but it will also undermine the long-term stability of the economy and will tend to increase the state's indebtedness (through an imbalance of spending and taxation). Under circumstances of adversary politics, such fiscal irresponsibility is unlikely to be challenged by the opposition, who are more likely to 'bid up' the electorate's expectations, promising 'more for less' in the attempt to unseat the existing government (Downs, 1957; Alt and Chrystal, 1983).

Clearly in a private economic market such over-bidding would be constrained by the threat of bankruptcy. A corporation that sold goods and services at less than their cost of production would soon be forced out of business. But governments do not face this same constraint (at least in the short and medium term). By increasing the public debt, governments may defer the costs of their present spending on future governments (and/or generations). This may have a damaging effect on the medium-term prospects for the economy – by encouraging inflation, squeezing out private sector investment or whatever – but while this runs against the overall public interest, it is not rational for either particular governments or particular voters to seek to stop it. Indeed, Olson argues that economic growth becomes a 'public good' for most interest groups. It is more rational to seek to extract a greater proportion of the national budget (through political pressure) than to seek to enhance the overall growth of the economy (Olson, 1965, 1982; Rose and Peters, 1978).

In a number of other ways, this logic of collective action can be seen to furnish suboptimal outcomes. Governments seeking to maximize their electoral appeal are driven to support the particularistic claims of well-organized interest groups and to satisfy the claims of special interests. The costs of meeting the claims of the well-organized are discharged on the unorganized generality of the population. The politics of voter trading and political activism tend to lead to an expansion of government beyond that which is either necessary or desirable (Tullock, 1976).

This oversupply of public services is further exacerbated by the nature of the public bureaucracy. First, the public bureaucracy is itself a powerful interest group and public bureaucrats have a rational interest in maximizing their own budgets and departments. Secondly, the public bureaucracy does not normally face competition, or indeed any of the economic constraints of acting within a marketplace. Where costs are not weighed against benefits and where the utility maximization of bureaucrats is dependent on the maximization of their budgets, the public choice theorists insist that there will be a chronic tendency for the public bureaucracy to oversupply goods and services (Niskanen, 1971, 1973; Tullock, 1976). This problem becomes still more acute when the monopolistic powers of the public bureaucracy are strengthened by an expansion of white collar trade unionism, as happened, for example, in the much expanded British civil service in the period after the Second World War (Bacon and Eltis, 1978).

This complex is seen broadly to describe the political circumstances of the modern welfare state. Under liberal democratic and adversarial political arrangements, and without some sort of constitutional constraint on the action (and spending) of governments, politicians, bureaucrats and voters *acting rationally* will tend to generate welfare state policies which are suboptimal, and indeed, in the long run, unsustainable.

The New Right and the Welfare State: A Summary

The case of the New Right against the welfare state, which, in the hands of its academic advocates, often took an abstract and technical form, achieved its prominence in the era of Thatcher and Reagan largely as a response to a series of social and political problems in the advanced capitalist world of the 1970s. Accordingly, further comment on these New Right theses is deferred to the more appropriate context of chapter 5. Here we can conclude our consideration of the general New Right case, by briefly summarizing the main substantive claims to which it has given rise:

- *The welfare state is uneconomic*   It displaces the necessary disciplines and incentives of the marketplace, undermining the incentive (of capital) to invest and the incentive (of labour) to work.
- *The welfare state is unproductive*   It encourages the rapid growth of the (unproductive) public bureaucracy and forces capital and human resources out of the (productive) private sector of the economy. Monopoly of state provision enables workers within the public sector to command inflationary wage increases.
- *The welfare state is inefficient*   Its monopoly of welfare provision and its creation and sponsorship of special/sectional interests lead to the inefficient delivery of services and a system which, denuded of the discipline of the market, is geared to the interests of (organized) producers rather than (disaggregated) consumers. Generally, as governments extend the areas of social life in which they intervene, so policy failures mount.
- *The welfare state is ineffective*   Despite the huge resources dedicated to it, welfare state measures fail to eliminate poverty and deprivation. Indeed, they worsen the position of the poorest by displacing traditional community-based and family-based forms of support and entrap the deprived in a 'cycle of dependence'.

- *The welfare state is despotic*   It constitutes a growth in, at best, the enervating hand of bureaucracy and, at worst, social control of individual citizens and, in some cases, whole communities, by an overweening state. In many such cases the victims of state control and manipulation are those same deprived citizens whom it is claimed the welfare state exists to assist.
- *The welfare state is a denial of freedom*   Its compulsory provision of services denies the individual freedom of choice within the welfare sector, while its heavy and progressive tax regime can be represented as 'confiscatory'.

Thesis 5

The welfare state is an ill-conceived and unprincipled intrusion on the welfare-maximizing and liberty-maximizing imperatives of a liberal market society. It is inconsistent with the preservation of freedom, justice and real long-term welfare

---

Marxism, Neo-Marxism and the Welfare State

A second general account of the irreconcilability of capitalist and welfare state imperatives, and thus a rejection of the social democratic orthodoxy, has come from the Marxist and neo-Marxist left. It is a much cited paradox of this Marxist analysis of the welfare state and welfare capitalism that it seems to share much in common with the politically quite opposed New Right. This is not perhaps so surprising, given the status of Marx's definitive study of *Capital* as 'a critique of political economy'. Just as Marx took the work of the classical political economists and sought to press their premises to radically new conclusions, so have more recent Marxist writers found much to endorse in the New Right's morphology of the problems of welfare capitalism, while seeking quite different explanations pressed to very different conclusions. What they share is a common belief that the 'steady state' welfare capitalism of traditional social democratic analysis is untenable. Both have sought out contradictions within the welfare state/welfare capitalism, the one to label them 'the excesses of democracy/socialism', the other to style them 'the contradictions of capitalism'. In essence, the impasse of social democracy and the welfare state is seen to lie in the impossibility of reconciling the imperatives of capitalism with the requirements of authentically democratic arrangements or the furnishing of 'genuine' social welfare.

Twentieth-Century Marxism and the Welfare State

In chapter 1, we saw that the essence of Marx's view was that even if limited social reform could be forced by organized labour, the securing of widespread state welfare for the majority of the population was inconsistent with the demands of capital accumulation. Down to the Second World War, mainstream classical Marxists saw little reason to amend this account of welfare provision under capitalism. Though these were the years in which many formative welfare states emerged, provision was seen to be minimal and in the 1930s rising unemployment and falling benefits were seen to express the dominance of the (crisis) logic of capital over the wishful thinking of welfarist social democrats. By contrast, in the halcyon years of social democracy after 1945, it was the social democrats who had little time for 'outmoded' Marxist analyses of (a now transformed) capitalism. Marxism, with its outdated appeal to the class war, belonged to a bygone era of working-class poverty, mass unemployment and class privilege. While postwar societies were not egalitarian, under the impact of Keynesian economics and extensive social welfare provision, systematic differences of class no longer carried their prewar resonances. Meanwhile the Marxist left, demoralized by the experience of the Hungarian uprising (of 1956), the (limited) exposure of Stalinism and the seemingly uninterrupted growth of the postwar economy, increasingly directed its attention towards alienation and the cultural consequences of capitalism. Marcuse's *One Dimensional Man* depicted organized capitalism as a system of total administration in which the working class was lost as the revolutionary agent of social change. Even opposition was now co-opted within an all-embracing system of structured irrationality (of which the welfare state was an important component). Consciousness of the need for radical change was confined to marginal groups on the periphery of society – students, ethnic minorities and *déclassé* elements. The provision of welfare to the working class became not an avenue for their gradual advance towards socialism but the means by which workers were controlled, demoralized and deradicalized. According to Marcuse, 'the prospects of containment of change . . . depend on the prospects of the welfare State . . . [as the embodiment of] a state of unfreedom' (1972, pp. 51–2).

However, by the end of the 1960s – especially under the impact of the events loosely and graphically associated with 1968 – the image of unproblematic postwar social democratic consensus began to crack. A period of uninterrupted political and industrial unrest also saw a re-emergence of academic interest in Marxist and other radical/socialist thinking. It is from this period that we can date the emergence or possibly renaissance of Marxist theories of the (welfare) state.

Neo-Marxist Analysis of the Welfare State

Although others, and most notably Antonio Gramsci, might lay claim to initiating Marxist study of the welfare state, the origins of this renaissance are widely seen to reside in the much rehearsed debate between Ralph Miliband and Nicos Poulantzas (Gramsci, 1971; Miliband, 1969; Poulantzas, 1973, 1978). These more recent accounts have instituted a number of changes from classical Marxist thinking on the state. Without entering on this extended debate here, we may note the following significant amendments in more recent accounts:

Proposition 1
The state enjoys *relative autonomy* from the capitalist class; the possibility of the state acting in the general interests of capital is dependent on its distance from particular capitals.

Proposition 2
The state articulates the general needs of capital accumulation – and this may involve paying an *economic* price for securing the *political* compliance of non-ruling class interests.

Proposition 3
The state is not straightforwardly unitary; it is, as Poulantzas has it, 'constituted-divided' by the same divisions that characterize capitalist society more generally.

Neo-Marxism I: The Welfare State as Social Control

In fact, (neo-)Marxist responses to the welfare state have been remarkably varied. We have already seen that advocates of the power resources model have interpreted the welfare state (under specified conditions) as a strategic element in the transition to socialism. Others drawing on propositions 1 and 2 above, continue to regard the welfare state as predominantly an instrument for the social control of the working class, acting in the long-term interests of capital accumulation. Within the broadly neo-Marxist camp, this is the view that is perhaps closest to the classical Marxism of Marx, Engels and Lenin. It confronts quite explicitly the traditional social democratic perspective of a benign and progressive welfare state, but also challenges the claims of the 'revisionist' power resources model.

We have seen that one of the core claims of the classical Marxist position was that in any epoch, the state mobilizes exclusively the interests of a single ruling class. Thus, in contrast to the social democratic view (and proposition 3 above), it is insisted that, under capitalism, 'the functioning and management of state welfare remains part of a *capitalist* state which is fundamentally concerned with the maintenance and reproduction of capitalist social relations' (Ginsburg, 1979, p. 2). Above all else, the welfare state is involved in securing the production and reproduction of labour power under capitalist forms. The benefits of the welfare state to the working class are not generally denied, but they are seen to be largely the adventitious by-product of securing the interests of capital. Here there is characteristically an echo of Marx's commentary on an earlier series of reforms, the Factory Acts, which, while a gain for the working classes thus protected, arose from the 'same necessity as forced the manuring of English fields with guano' – that is the need to preserve from total exhaustion the sole source of future surplus value (Marx, 1973a, p. 348).

Thus, Norman Ginsburg maintains:

> From the capitalist point of view state welfare has contributed to the continual struggle to accumulate capital by materially assisting in bringing labour and capital together profitably and containing the inevitable resistance and revolutionary potential of the working class . . . the social security system is concerned with reproducing a reserve army of labour, the patriarchal family and the disciplining of the labour force. Only secondarily and contingently does it function as a means of mitigating poverty or providing 'income maintenance'. (1979, p. 2)

This principal thesis is defended through a number of more specific rebuttals of the social democratic position:

- Social provision under the welfare state is characteristically geared to the requirements of capital, not the real needs of the working population.
- Many welfare policies were originated not by socialists or social democrats but by conservative or liberal elites. Their intention was to manage/regulate capitalism and to discipline its workforce, not to mitigate the social hardship of the working class.
- Social policy has long been recognized by these elites as the 'antidote' to socialism. As British Conservative Prime Minister Arthur Balfour insisted in the 1900s, 'social legislation . . . is not merely to be distinguished from Socialist legislation, but it is its most direct opposite and its most effective antidote' (cited in Marshall, 1975, p. 40).
- Changes in social welfare regimes reflect the changing accumulation needs of capital: for example, (1) the shift from extensive to intensive exploitation of labour (and the correspondingly greater need of a healthy, docile, disciplined and educated workforce); (2) the need for

fit men to staff the armies of the imperialist capitalist nation-states (and of women to replace them in the sphere of industrial production); (3) the rise (and perhaps the fall) of mass production and scientific management.

- The funding of welfare state measures has often been regressive and/or associated with an extension of the tax base; at best, welfare state spending has been redistributive within the working class or across the life cycle of the average worker.
- The compulsory state management of welfare has deprived the working class of the self-management of its own welfare (through friendly societies and trade unions); the *form* of welfare services has characteristically been bureaucratic and anti-democratic.
- Social legislation has often enhanced the intrusive powers of state professionals in the everyday life of individual citizens and concentrated surveillance and discretionary power in the hands of agents of the state.
- The ameliorative impact of state relief and the ideology of a welfare state in which each member of the community is guaranteed a certain minimum of welfare provision has demobilized working-class agitation for more radical economic and political change.

Thesis 6

The welfare state is a particular form of the developed capitalist state. It functions to secure the long-term circumstances for the continued accumulation of capital

Commentary: Neo-Marxism I: The Welfare State as Social Control

A number of commentators have complained that it is extremely difficult to 'operationalize' Marxist theses on the welfare state (Pampel and Williamson, 1988, p. 1450; Korpi, 1989, pp. 315–17). However, there is a good deal of historical evidence to support the social control thesis. First, welfare state measures often developed in tandem with a traditional Poor Law whose intent was explicitly coercive (as in the UK down to 1948). Secondly, the conditions placed on state benefits (a record of regular employment, 'willingness to work' clauses, a qualifying period and cut-off points for payment of benefits) are often oriented not to the meeting of recipients' needs but rather to the requirement not to undermine the dynamics of the labour market. This has become increasingly clear in recent years given the more or less general emphasis on active labour market policies and the trajectory from welfare to work. Thirdly, the administration of benefits by the state has placed considerable discretionary, investigative and directive powers in the hands of state officials. Thus Piven and Cloward argue that the intent of welfare provision in the US has always been one of 'regulating the poor', allowing for more generous provision at times when mass mobilization (rather than mass need) pressed on the prevailing order, but then reimposing tighter labour market disciplines on recipients (by moving them off welfare rolls) once the immediate threat of disorder has been demobilized. This, for example, was their verdict on the New Deal social security reforms:

> The first major relief crisis in the US occurred during the Great Depression. By 1935, upwards of twenty million people were on the dole. But it would be wrong to assume that this unprecedented volume of relief-giving was a response to widespread economic distress, for millions had been unemployed for several years before obtaining aid. What led government to proffer aid . . . was the rising surge of political unrest that accompanied this economic catastrophe. Moreover, once relief-giving had expanded, unrest rapidly subsided, and then aid was cut back – which meant, among other things, that large numbers of people were put off the rolls and thrust into a labour market still glutted with unemployment. But with stability restored, the continued suffering of these millions had little political force. (Piven and Cloward, 1971, p. 45)

Further support for the social control thesis may be found in the evidence of early working-class hostility to the state provision of welfare. Such hostility (from trade unions and friendly societies) can be understood not simply as the conservatism of the 'respectable' working class, but rather as a fear that the state would replace working-class self-administration with forms of social welfare that would serve the interests of capital. There is further historical evidence that many early social work/public health initiatives – for example, the activities of Charitable Organization Societies on both sides of the Atlantic or the introduction of schools' medical services – were immediately concerned with the production of a literate, docile, 'regular' and 'fighting fit' workforce. According to Elizabeth Wilson, 'the literature of social work *is* the ideology of welfare capitalism' (E. Wilson, 1977, p. 28; Ginsburg, 1979; Taylor-Gooby and Dale, 1981; Langan and Lee, 1989). Again, much of the earliest US welfare legislation was concerned with rehabilitation which would bring the economically inactive off benefits and into work. Often states' welfare legislation was commended precisely because of the financial benefits which would accrue to business and taxpayers. Meanwhile, the severest punitive measures were reserved for those who could not or would not respond to their 're-education' and remained unemployable (see, for example, Katz, 1986).

Yet, despite all this evidence, it is difficult to sustain the argument that the growth of the welfare state was exclusively or even preponderantly in the interests of the capitalist class. It is certainly true that early public welfare measures were parsimonious, often introduced under conservative/ dual monarchy regimes and with an explicitly anti-social democratic or anti-trade union intent. Yet the more liberal reforming regimes were often driven by a radical/social democratic wing, they were a response to new working-class electors and they frequently sought to outmanoeuvre the electoral appeal of social democratic parties by offering public welfare for the working classes. Similarly, while early public welfare measures often had a coercive and disciplinary element, they still represented an improvement in the basic circumstances of many members of the working class. Thus, for example, even though early pensions were minimal and means tested, this represented an improvement on reliance on the Poor Law and the workhouse. Again, while there were, for example, attempts to restrict welfare to non-unionized labour, state management of welfare was probably less antagonistic to labour than was the administration of welfare by employers (though less in the working-class interest than self-management through trade unions or friendly societies). Where such measures were introduced on a social insurance rather than a public assistance basis, an (albeit circumscribed) *right* to public welfare was also established. While such early gains were often extremely limited, they were not generally conceded without a struggle. While parliamentary democracy and the welfare state might have come to constitute part of the apparatus for the political incorporation of the working class and the deradicalization of labour, the view that accordingly such measures were willingly embraced by enlightened and sophisticated conservative elites proves to be historically quite exceptional.

Contemporary fears among elites (and the pattern of early take-up of social insurance) also suggest that social insurance might indeed lessen the stranglehold of the market on the working class. Even very limited compensation for unemployment or sickness did lessen the drive for workers to return to the market to undergo the disutility of labour. Thus although public welfare has often been fiscally regressive (based on a payroll tax and [re]distributing benefits to the better-off and longer-lived), inasmuch as programmes were based on (or subsidized by) general tax revenues this could be expected to have a mildly redistributive effect. Similarly, fears that the expenditure incurred could lead to a fiscal crisis of the state can, in fact, be retraced to the very origins of the public welfare system. Indeed, the escalating cost of earlier systems of public assistance was one of the major spurs to welfare reform – in Britain, for example, both in the 1840s and again in the 1900s.

One response to this evidence is to suggest that such improvements as the working class did enjoy under the welfare state were simply the adventitious benefits of capital's interest in a more productive source of surplus value. In this sense, the evidence is but a vindication of Marx's understanding of the contradictory logic of capitalism. The capitalist class could not have a healthier, better educated, reliable (and thus more profitable) source of surplus value without improving the health, education and housing of the working class. It may also reflect the importance of the working class as a source of consumption under difficult circumstances for the valorization of capital. Yet this does not lessen the material improvements secured by the working class, and it was the case that these services were generally being provided by the state rather than in a potentially more coercive and partisan way by the owners of industry themselves. Furthermore, the *unintended* consequences of welfare state legislation might significantly strengthen the defensive powers of the working class. The experience of the early introduction of sickness insurance in Britain was of a greater than expected take-up and of a lower return to work by recuperating workers (Gilbert, 1966). As we shall see in chapter 5, the ways in which social insurance (even if self-financed) was to distort the labour market was to become a very major concern of those who argued that the postwar welfare state was undermining the very bases of the capitalist economy.

Neo-Marxism II: Contradictions of the Welfare State

This view of the welfare state as primarily the instrument of capitalist social control continues to attract some support. More typically, however, the renaissance in neo-Marxist thinking has followed proposition 3 above and concentrated on contradictions *within* the welfare state itself. It has also become increasingly oriented around the apparent *crisis* experienced in the welfare state after twenty-five years of seemingly unproblematic growth in the immediate postwar period. Indeed, it is difficult to isolate a *general* statement of this (neo-)Marxist view from the context of a perceived *crisis* of the welfare state. This is most clearly the case with James O'Connor's path-breaking work on the *Fiscal Crisis of the State*, which is considered in some detail in chapter 5 (O'Connor, 1973, 1987). It is also a concern of Ian Gough's classic study of *The Political Economy of the Welfare State*.

Locating the welfare state in terms of the overall structure of welfare capitalism, Gough is profoundly critical of those social democratic accounts of welfare which have sought to isolate economy and polity or to reduce welfare to the study of discrete social problems and particular institutions. He himself defines the welfare state 'as the use of state power to modify the reproduction of labour power and to maintain the non-working population in capitalist societies' (Gough, 1979, pp. 44–5). Such modification is effected through the taxation and social security systems, regulation of the provision of certain 'essentials' (for example, food and housing) and the provision of certain services in kind (most notably, health and education). He views the development of this welfare state as essentially *contradictory*. Thus it 'simultaneously embodies tendencies to enhance social welfare, to develop the powers of individuals, to exert social control over the blind play of market forces; and tendencies to repress and control people, to adapt them to the requirements of the capitalist economy' (Gough, 1979, p. 12). On the one hand, welfare state institutions are seen to be consonant with the interests of capital. They represent a response to changes undergone in capitalist development – for example, periodic unemployment, technological change, the need of a skilled and literate workforce – and to the new requirements these changes generate in the area of social policy. On the other hand, the origins of the welfare state lay in organized working class struggle – and the ameliorating response of organizations of the ruling class to the threat this was seen to pose. This means that the welfare state cannot be seen as straightforwardly 'functional for capital' – as simply a means of exercising social control over the working class and subsidizing capital's profit-making. At least a part of the prodigious growth of the postwar welfare state may be seen as a response to the defensive economic strength of the organized working class and the labour movement. Yet, at the same time, 'paradoxically . . . it would appear that labour indirectly aids the long-term accumulation of capital and strengthens capitalist social relations by struggling for its own interests within the state' (Gough, 1979, p. 55).

The welfare state, then, is a 'contradictory unity', exhibiting both positive and negative features for both capital and labour. Correspondingly, the long-term consequences of the welfare state for the continued accumulation of capital are themselves ambivalent. Although the welfare state may serve to subsidize some of the costs of capital, its strengthening of the defensive powers of the working class may in the long run undermine the reproduction of suitable conditions for profitable capital accumulation. The welfare state's institutionalization of income support and full employment will tend to strengthen the defensive power of the organized working class and thus the capacity of labour to protect real wage levels and to resist attempts to raise productivity. Under the (perhaps consequent) circumstances of sluggish economic growth, it will prove ever more difficult to finance the growing state budget without increasing inflation or further weakening growth or both. For the funding of the welfare state could be neutral for capital accumulation only if the whole of the tax burden of funding it could be met within the household sector and thus preponderantly by the broad working class. However, in reality, the distribution of the burden of taxation between capital and labour – and indeed the scale and distribution of welfare services themselves – is itself a matter of class struggle and reflects the prevailing balance of social forces. Under these conditions, the circumstances for long-term capital accumulation may be imperilled. The outcome is likely to be inflation, a slow-down in economic growth and, for developed welfare states operating in a world market, the potential loss of international competitiveness.

The Welfare State as 'the Crisis of Crisis Management': Offe

Perhaps the most developed account of the welfare state as the contradictory and contested product of continuing capitalist development within the neo-Marxist or, more properly, 'post-Marxist' literature is that developed by Claus Offe. Offe follows classical Marxism in arguing that the '"privately regulated" capitalist economy' is innately crisis-prone. However, this crisis is not best understood as predominantly *economic*. In fact, the welfare state emerges as an institutional/administrative form which seeks to 'harmonize the "privately regulated" capitalist economy with the [contradictory] processes of socialization this economy triggers' (Offe, 1984, p. 51). The welfare state is that set of political arrangements which seeks to compromise or 'save from crisis' what classical Marxism had identified as the central contradiction of capitalism – that between social forces and private relations of production. The welfare state arises then as a form of systemic crisis management.

For Offe, the structure of welfare capitalism can be characterized in terms of three subsystems, as in figure 2.1. According to his account, the economic subsystem of capitalism is not self-regulating and has dysfunctional consequences for the legitimation subsystem. The state has to intervene in and mediate between the other two subsystems to secure, on the one hand, continued accumulation, and on the other, continued legitimation. Correspondingly, the state under welfare capitalism is to be seen as a form of crisis management – and for twenty-five years following the Second World War a remarkably successful one. But this process of reconciliation under the welfare state proves in the long run to be impossible because the welfare state is subject to a particular crisis logic of its own. Three manifestations of this underlying contradiction of the welfare state are of particular importance:

1   *The fiscal crisis of the welfare state*   The state budget required to fund strategies of recommodification tends to grow uncontrollably and to become increasingly self-defeating, occasioning (through high taxation and welfare provision) both a 'disincentive to invest' and a 'disincentive to work'.

2 *Administrative shortfall* The welfare state repeatedly fails to live up to its own inflated programmatic-administrative claims, a failure variously attributed to the ineffectiveness of the indirect instruments of public policy, to struggles *within* the state and to the external imperatives of public accountability, democratic representation and short-term political expediency.

3 *Legitimation shortfall* Under these circumstances of fiscal crisis and administrative shortfall, state intervention is seen to be increasingly particularistic and ad hoc and this undermines the political norms of 'equality under the rule of law', leading to a shortfall of mass loyalty/legitimacy.

This makes the focus of Offe's analysis *the crisis of crisis management* (Offe, 1984, pp. 57–61).

Under advanced capitalism, Offe argues, *economic* contradictions of capital accumulation increasingly express themselves in a *political* crisis of the welfare state. Offe's economic subsystem is characterized by the production and exchange for profit of privately owned commodities. The success of this capitalist economy based on private ownership is indispensable to the long-term viability of the welfare state, both because it is

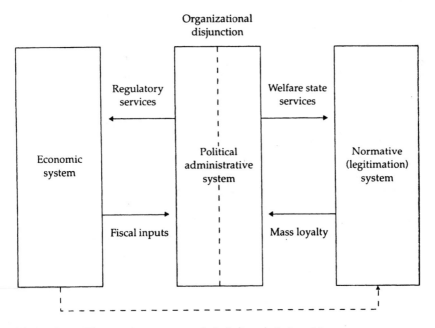

Figure 2.1 Three subsystems and their interrelationship
Source: Offe, 1984, p. 52.

the ultimate source of that state's fiscal viability (through taxation and borrowing), and because consequently it is the basis of mass loyalty and legitimacy for the state (through the funding of welfare services, the securing of 'full employment' and so on). The key problem for the crisis management strategy of the welfare state is that, in practice, 'the dynamics of capitalist development seem to exhibit a constant tendency to paralyse the commodity form of value', and thus to imperil the state's primary source of revenues (Offe, 1984, p. 122).

Unregulated, it is suggested by Offe, the development of the capitalist economy tends systematically to exclude elements of labour power and capital from productive exchange (through the underemployment of labour or the underutilization of capital). The state cannot itself generally restore effective and profitable commodity exchange by intervening directly in the accumulation process, as this would both undermine the normative basis of the private-exchange capitalist economy and engender the risk of an (anti-nationalization) capital investment strike.[1] Since the state is prevented from intervening directly in the economy, it has to proceed indirectly, through essentially Keynesian means, to re-establish the conditions under which capital and labour will be drawn into profitable commodity exchange, through regulations and financial incentives (corporate tax concessions, special development areas, interest-free industrial loans, subsidizing energy costs), public infrastructural investment (training and retraining, recruitment services, subsidized transport facilities), and the sponsoring of neo-corporatist arrangements (between trade unions and employers). Offe calls this strategy 'administrative recommodification'. The intention is to promote the fuller utilization or *commodification* of both capital and labour through indirect, administrative means. Its vitiating weakness is that, in practice, it promotes a process of *decommodification* – that is, it undermines the circumstances for the fuller utilization of capital and labour. Thus the strategies which are supposed to encourage *more* effective commodity exchange in fact place ever greater areas of social life *outside* the commodity form and *outside* the sphere of market exchange. The principal contradiction of the welfare state then is that strategies of *re*commodification effect a widespread process of *de*commodification (Offe, 1984).

Similar issues have been raised by Claus Offe's distinguished countryman, Jürgen Habermas. He argues that the nature of this crisis in the developed capitalist state is a crisis not so much of capitalism as of the reactive aspirations and strategies of its opponents. Sociologists of all persuasions have tended to present *abstract labour* as the key explanatory variable in

---

[1] Corporatism may represent a partial attempt to realize such a policy. Elsewhere, Offe discusses the nature of state interventions of this kind (Offe and Wiesenthal, 1985).

industrial societies, and the utopia that has inspired most socialists is that of 'a labor-based social organization of free and equal producers'. But, Habermas insists, within the advanced capitalist societies, labour no longer enjoys this definitive centrality nor can production and growth any longer provide the basis for a utopian view of a future society. Thus the 'utopian idea of a society based on social labor has lost its persuasive power'. The great import of this discovery is that, for Habermas, it was precisely this utopia of 'free and equal producers' which inspired the development of the welfare state. Since the mid-1970s such a model has been rapidly losing its authority. What Habermas calls the 'new obscurity' (the incapacity of progressive forces to decide how or whither we should progress) 'is part of a situation in which a welfare state program . . . is losing its power to project future possibilities for a collectively better and less endangered way of life' (Habermas, 1989a, pp. 53–4).

'The welfare-state compromise and the pacification of class antagonisms' were to be achieved by 'using democratically legitimated state power to protect and restrain the quasi-natural process of capitalist growth'. The status of employee was to be complemented by social and political citizenship, on the presupposition 'that peaceful coexistence between democracy and capitalism can be ensured through state intervention' (Habermas, 1989a, p. 55). For a period following the war this strategy was successful within the expanding economies of advanced capitalism, but from the early 1970s it became increasingly problematic, not least because of contradictory elements within the welfare state itself.[2]

The first of these contradictions turned on the familiar question of the reconcilability of capitalism and democracy and the incapacity of the state to intervene directly to organize the accumulation process. Accordingly, Habermas argues, the more successful the welfare state is in securing the interests of labour, the more it will come to undermine the conditions for its own continuing success and the conditions for its long-term viability. For those voters on whom the social democrats or 'welfare state parties' relied in the postwar years, and who benefited most from the development of the welfare state, may increasingly move to protect themselves against the more underprivileged and excluded.

Habermas also identifies a second and less familiar contradictory principle within the welfare state. The pioneers of the welfare state directed themselves almost exclusively towards the taming of capitalism, as if the state power they used to effect such control was itself neutral or 'innocent'. But while their interest lay in the emancipation of labour, the day-to-day practice of the welfare state has increased state control over the

---

[2] Though Habermas does recognize other extrinsic sources of difficulty for the welfare state from the mid-1970s (Habermas, 1989a).

individual worker. In the promotion of welfare legislation programmes, 'an ever denser net of legal norms, and of governmental and para-governmental bureaucracies is spread over the daily life of its potential and actual clients'. Habermas concludes:

> In short, a contradiction between its goal and its method is inherent in the welfare state project as such. Its goal is the establishment of forms of life that are structured in an egalitarian way and that at the same time open up arenas for individual self-realization and spontaneity. But evidently this goal cannot be reached via the direct route of putting political programs into legal and administrative form. (1989a, pp. 58–9)

In part because of its former successes in securing the basic needs of the mass of the population, the welfare state is subject to increasing discontent and defections among a more affluent population dissatisfied with the bureaucratic and alienating way in which its 'services' are delivered.

Thesis 7

The welfare state is a particular form of the developed capitalist state. It embodies the essentially contradictory nature of developed capitalism and is chronically liable to the logic of fiscal and administrative crises

Post-Fordism and the Decline of the Keynesian Welfare State

In the end, the 'crisis' of the welfare state failed to resolve itself in quite the dramatic way that Offe and others had anticipated. Rather, welfare states appeared to be subject to a process of what has come to be called '*structural adjustment*': a series of gradual but deep-seated reforms which were designed to make social policy more consonant with a quite new (international) political economy, and which were often identified with the process of 'globalization' (and discussed below). Perhaps the most sustained effort to understand these changes from within a broadly neo-Marxist theoretical framework has come from those working under the rubric of *post-Fordism* (see Burrows and Loader, 1994). Broadly speaking, Fordism describes that form of capitalism (and its attendant social and political institutions) which predominated in the West in the period between the end of the Second World War and the end of the 1960s. This was the epoch of full (male) employment, sustained economic growth and 'managed' capitalism. The welfare state under Fordism was a response to both the accumulation needs of capital (including mass *consumption* as an important component in the valorization of capital) and the defensive strength of the organized working class. For a time, it facilitated not only the class basis for mobilization behind the welfare state (the massification of collective labour) but also the corporate basis (in the rise of organized labour and organized capital) and the institutional basis (with the rise of the interventionist state). The social and economic turbulence of the late 1960s and early 1970s, however, was an expression of the exhaustion of this Fordist regime (and its characteristic welfare state form) as a framework for sustainable capitalist economic growth. Stability (security plus predictability), which had been a positive feature in the immediate postwar years, had descended into rigidity or, to use a much favoured medical analogy, sclerosis. The institutions of Fordism and the Keynesian Welfare State, which had once secured the grounds for capital accumulation by sustaining effective demand and managing the relations between capital and labour, had now become a barrier to further economic growth. The crisis of Fordism was thus about finding and institutionalizing a new social and economic regime (a *post*-Fordist regime) which could restore the conditions for successful capitalist accumulation and thus economic growth.

The watchword of post-Fordism is *flexibility*. At the global level, flexibility can be seen in the deregulation of international markets, the abandonment of fixed exchange rates and the introduction of new financial institutions which give (especially financial) capital much greater international mobility, freed from tutelage to particular nation-states. In the world of industry, Fordist mass production of standardized goods, typified by the assembly line and the minute division of semi-skilled labour, increasingly gives way to batch production of diversified products, a growth in small-scale service industries and increased 'flexibility in the use of machines, materials, and human beings as well as in the inter-firm relations of production' (Albertsen, 1988, p. 348). The demands of batch production and 'niche marketing' taken together with the production possibilities afforded by the application of new technologies favour a 'demassification' of the workforce. At its simplest, employment becomes polarized between a 'core' of well-paid, secure and qualified wage-earners with polyvalent skills and a 'periphery' of poorly paid, casualized and unskilled workers who may move in and out of a category of still more marginalized 'welfare dependants'. There is a growth in subcontracting, in 'non-standard' employment and in work within the 'informal' economy (with its attendant lack of rights). Most significantly, the division in the workforce between a skilled employed core and an unskilled and partially employed periphery, and the prospect of 'jobless growth', mean that those 'who are most desperately dependent on the welfare state's provision of transfers and services are, however, politically most vulnerable' (Offe, 1987, pp. 529–34). The 'core' working class no longer has any reason to adopt the material interests of this disadvantaged 'surplus class' as its own. Meanwhile, trade unions, especially at the national level, lose much of the power that they exercised when industry was based on the typically union-ized semi-skilled worker of Fordist mass production.

Two changes in the general transition towards post-Fordism are seen to be of especial importance in recasting welfare state policy. First, there are the ways in which 'flexibilization' of the *international* political economy has undermined the pursuit of Keynesian policies at a *national* level. Thus the deregulation of international financial institutions has tended to weaken the capacities of the interventionist state, to render all economies more 'open' and to make national capital and more especially national labour movements much more subject to the terms and conditions of international competition. Inasmuch as the Fordist welfare state truly was a *Keynesian* welfare state, those changes in the international economy which have precipitated a decline of Keynesianism may be seen to have had a very material effect on the welfare state. The prospects for sustain-ing long-term corporatist arrangements within particular nation-states (including the institutionalization of a 'social wage') will seem even less promising in a deregulated international economy. For many of its spon-sors, the commitment to sustain full employment through government-induced demand was an indispensable element in the welfare state regime. Yet it is unclear now that *any* government can redeem this pledge and in so far as the deregulation of the international economy and its conse-quences lie outside the scope of even the most powerful governments, it represents a challenge to national welfare state settlements, *irrespective* of the varying political aspirations of national governments.

A second challenge to the bases of the traditional welfare state comes from changes in the labour process and the organization of employment associated with flexibilization under post-Fordist imperatives. Changes in patterns of employment and corresponding class formation bring with them modification in both the patterns of dependency and the patterns of political support within a post-Fordist welfare state. It has been argued for some time that, partly as a result of the growth of the welfare state itself, the advanced industrial societies in which Fordism was most effectively entrenched have seen the emergence of a new line of political cleavage between those dependent for their consumption on the public and private sectors respectively (Dunleavy, 1980). The post-Fordist epoch is one in which the political power base of the public sector is increasingly out-powered and out-voted by the interests of the private sector. There is a consequent erosion of the basis of political support on which the Fordist welfare state was built. For other commentators, it seems likely that divi-sions in the workforce between 'core' and periphery' will accelerate the transition from a 'one nation' welfare state built around the objective of providing 'a high and rising standard of benefit . . . for all citizens as of right', towards a 'two nations' or 'Americanized' welfare state, in which there is 'a self-financed bonus for the privileged and stigmatising, disciplinary charity for the disprivileged' (Jessop, 1988, p. 29; 1991, pp. 151, 154; Lash and Urry, 1987, pp. 229–31). At worst, it may lead to a wholesale residualization of state welfare, as the securely employed middle classes defect from public welfare, leaving the state to provide residual welfare services for an excluded minority at least possible cost to a majority who are now sponsors but not users of these public services.

A third aspect of post-Fordist reform is the greater subservience of social policy to the imperatives of economic competitiveness (and, in its neo-Marxist variants at least, to the interests of global capital). In Jessop's account, for example, the attempt to install a distinctive post-Fordist social policy is summarized in terms of a transition from the Keynesian Welfare State (KWS) towards a *Schumpeterian Workfare State* (Jessop, 1994). Under this new formation, the state's social policy interventions are directed towards the twin goals of sponsoring innovation and technological know-how among its 'own' players in an open international market economy (the element loosely identified with Schumpeter) while sublimating social protection ever more explicitly to the needs of 'competitiveness' and a transformed labour market (workfare in intent if not always in practice). In Jessop's words, 'it marks a clear break with the KWS as domestic full employment is de-prioritised in favour of international competitiveness and redistributive welfare rights take second place to a productivist re-ordering of social policy' (1994, p. 24). Similarly, Phil Cerny's account (1990, 1995) identifies a general move from 'the welfare state to the competition state', with 'a shift in the focal point of party and governmental politics from the general maximisation of welfare within a nation . . . to the promotion of enterprise, innovation and profitability in both private and public sectors' (1990, p. 179). In fact, these arguments about post-Fordism and the welfare state are properly seen as part of a still broader account of fundamental changes in the character of welfare states arising from the multiple processes of *globalization*. As such, I defer further discussion to chapter 7. We have also, though, to consider criticisms of the social democratic orthodoxy that have their origins in the political theory of the 'new social movements' and it is to these that we turn next.

Thesis 8

Changes in the global political economy are undermining traditional forms of national social policy and moving us increasingly 'from the welfare state to the competition state'

3
New Social Movements and the Welfare State

In the Introduction, I indicated that recent years have seen the emergence of a distinctive critique of the social democratic welfare state from the perspective of several new social movements. These have generally been concerned with those costs and consequences of welfare provision which have escaped the vision of the political economists. In this chapter, I consider the distinctive contributions of the feminist, anti-racist and green critiques of welfare state arrangements. In the final section of the chapter, I look at the claims of those who are sceptical about *all* of those generalizing theories of welfare state development discussed so far and who insist on a much closer examination of the individual historical records of a range of quite differing welfare states.

Feminism and the Welfare State

The burgeoning of distinctively feminist writing on social policy over the last thirty years cannot be seen to define a single and unified perspective on the welfare state.[1] There are, however, a number of shared features of feminist accounts of welfare state development which help to distinguish them from all of the 'mainstream' approaches so far considered. First, feminist writers concentrate on the gender-specific consequences of the welfare state. Secondly, they broaden their evaluation of welfare beyond the formal or monetarized economy, to consider production and reproduction within the domestic sphere (as well as criticizing the ways in which

---

[1] For comprehensive surveys, see Sainsbury, 1994; O'Connor, 1996; Orloff, 1996.

the divisions between public and private are constituted). Thirdly, they register that the welfare state is largely *produced* and *consumed* by women, though typically under the control of, and in the interests of, men. There is disagreement as to whether the welfare state is primarily to be explained in terms of *patriarchy* (the systemic oppression of women by men) or *capitalism* (the systemic oppression of labour by capital), but characteristically feminist approaches have represented the welfare state as organized in the interests of men and of capital, at the expense of women. Recent years have seen a growth in empirical and comparative investigations of the role of women within welfare state regimes. Indeed, a good deal of recent feminist work on the welfare state has been articulated around a critique of the emergent (and gender-blind) literature of comparative welfare state regimes. A further feature of more recent feminist work on the welfare state, despite what remains a prevalently critical tone, has been an investigation of the ways in which a reformed social policy might, and occasionally has secured the social and political interests of women.

One of the earliest systematic feminist critiques of social policy (dating from the 1970s and 1980s) emerged from a Marxist-feminist perspective which represented the welfare state as an expression of *both* patriarchal and capitalist oppression.[2] Such analyses begin from the recognition that, left to themselves, markets are unable to secure the circumstances for the successful long-term accumulation of capital. Particularly within advanced capitalism, the state must intervene in the economy and society to guarantee conditions for sustained capital accumulation. It is in this context that the development of the welfare state must be understood. For the welfare state describes all those state interventions which are required to ensure the production and reproduction of labour power in forms which will sustain capitalism's profitability. However, given the (ideological) imperatives of maintaining the family, in which labour power is reproduced, as a 'private' sphere, the state typically intervenes 'not directly but through its support for a specific form of household: the family household dependent largely upon a male wage and upon female domestic servicing' (M. McIntosh, 1978, pp. 255–6). Thus the profitability of capitalism is sustained not just through the state-sanctioned oppression of labour under the wage contract, but also through the oppression of women within the state-supported form of the 'dependent-woman family' (Weir, 1974).

This state-sponsored family form is promoted through a range of taxation and benefit provisions (differential arrangements for men and women, and for single and married women) and omissions (the absence of

---

[2] For a classification of feminist approaches to the welfare state, see Williams, 1989, pp. 41–86; Orloff, 1993. Of course, these criticisms of the welfare state did not begin with the second-wave feminists. See, for example, Rathbone, 1986.

statutory nursery places or collective cooking/laundry facilities). It secures the interests of capital in three main ways:

1   It lowers the costs of the reproduction of labour power. A major determinant of the wage costs of capital is the reproduction (on a day-to-day and generation-to-generation basis) of labour power. These costs are substantially cut where they can be displaced on either the state (public education, public health care), or on women's unpaid domestic labour (cooking, washing, childcare, care of dependent relatives).
2   It provides employers with a 'latent reserve army of labour'. Married women are a source of potential cheap labour (given the prioritization of the male 'family wage') to be drawn into employment in times of labour scarcity and to be redeployed towards their 'natural' role in the home when jobs are scarce.
3   Where 'caring'/reproduction services are performed within the waged sector of the economy, the definition of such employment as 'women's work' enables it to be provided at comparatively low cost.

A number of important qualifications have been appended to this briefly outlined position. First, it has been suggested that such accounts tend to underestimate the specific impact of *patriarchy*. It is argued that greater weight must be given to the way in which the welfare state serves the interests of (especially white and skilled) working-class *men*. Some commentators have suggested that the welfare state has an *economic* cost for capital (in privileging male wages) but that this is outweighed by the *political* benefits of the gender division of interests within the general category of wage labour which it sustains (Barrett, 1980, p. 230). Secondly, greater attention has been directed towards the *ideological* construction of women's subordination under welfare state capitalism. The capacity of the welfare state to organize the interests of capital in the ways indicated relies on pre-existing forms of oppression of women by men which the state is able to shape and exploit but not to create. More weight is given to the deep-seated ideology of men and women's 'natural' roles, which are seen to be crucial in underpinning the structures of patriarchal capitalism. Greater attention is thus directed towards the specifically *patriarchal* aspects of women's oppression under the welfare state. Thirdly, there has been a re-evaluation of the nature of women's work in the welfare state. Women do not function straightforwardly as a reserve army of labour. In fact, the dependent-female, male-waged household is increasingly untypical in modern economies, while labour markets are heavily sex segregated, so that expanding women's employment does not typically mean supplementing or replacing a male workforce.

Finally, it is argued that while the expansion of the welfare state has often meant the replacement of women's unpaid labour in the home with women's underpaid 'caring' work in the public sector, state provision of such services *can* represent a strengthening of women's position (Quadagno, 1990, p. 27; see also Balbo, 1987, p. 204). It does, for example, represent the recognition of a public/state responsibility for those forms of care which were previously defined as exclusively a private (and woman's) responsibility. The welfare state has afforded an avenue of (otherwise blocked) career mobility for some women. It has offered (albeit very limited) childcare provision and healthcare services. These are not to be exhaustively understood as securing the long-term interests of capital, but rather as forms of provision which constitute a 'second-best' strategy for both women *and* capital. According to Brenner and Ramas, 'the welfare state is a major arena of class struggle, within the limits imposed by capitalist relations of production. Those limits can accommodate substantial reforms.' Yet this establishes a context in which women have to choose 'between a welfare state which assumes the male-breadwinner family and no state help at all' (Brenner and Ramas, 1984; Rein, 1985).

Sheila Shaver has argued of this Marxist-feminist paradigm that, in general, 'Marxism's categories were too little questioned, and feminism's too superficially applied.' She called for a more historical approach grounded in 'the day-to-day legislative and bureaucratic politics of the welfare state', recognizing that the structure of the welfare state is simultaneously 'gendered' and 'classed' (see Shaver, 1989, pp. 91–3). This is reflected in a more general shift in the focus of recent feminist writing on the welfare state. There has, for example, been a wealth of new and detailed historical writing on women and the welfare state (see Skocpol 1992; Pedersen, 1993; Gordon, 1994) which shows women to have been very actively involved (albeit not from a position of strength) in the generation of early social policy regimes. There has also been a major growth of case studies and cross-national surveys which show that not all welfare states are the same in their treatment of women (see Lewis, 1992; Sainsbury, 1994; Hill and Tigges, 1995; O'Connor, 1996; Daly and Rake, 2003; Christopher et al., 2002; Geist, 2005). This has reinforced the emphasis of Hernes, grounded in Scandinavian experience, on the positive opportunities for working towards a 'woman-friendly state' (1987, p. 15). In general, there has been a shift away from a narrow focus on the position of women as an issue within the welfare state towards much more extensive evaluations of social policy regimes which are understood to be profoundly and comprehensively gendered (Lewis, 1992; Orloff, 1993, 1996; Geist, 2005).

The newer literature has also developed a more nuanced reading of the salience of key welfare terms such as 'dependence', and above all 'care', whose ambiguous meaning is seen to have a very clearly gendered inflection (see Fraser and Gordon, 1994; Maclean and Groves, 1991; Daly and Lewis, 2000; Daly and Rake, 2003; Pascall and Lewis, 2004). Indeed, the category of 'care' or 'social care' both directs attention to an aspect of welfare much neglected in more traditional analyses (including the work of 'power resources' theorists) and illustrates a crucial area in which this welfare experience is different for women. In Daly and Lewis's account, care is seen to be a central practice in all human welfare. It is about securing the personal well-being of the variously defined dependant – but in a context which is defined by non-contractual relationships, personal ties of obligation, commitment, trust and loyalty. In Daly and Lewis's account, social care constitutes 'the activities and relations involved in meeting the physical and emotional requirements of dependent adults and children, and the normative, economic and social frameworks within which these are assigned and carried out' (2000, p. 285). It is above all about the well-being – psychological as well as physical – of the elderly and the very young. It has long been, as Daly and Lewis observe, 'a woman-specific concept' (2000, p. 283). Although care crosses many boundaries (of state and market, of formal and informal support, of paid and unpaid labour), its focus has been the work of women in (and sometimes beyond) the family. This is, in the end, how most welfare is delivered.

The concept of care gives us a different lens through which to view the (comparative) experience of welfare states. It brings to light previously unseen aspects of the real-world provision of welfare. It allows us to take a different view of the (often neglected) responsibilities of welfare states. It enables us to see how the welfare experience of men and women differ systematically and points to the areas where reform is required (both within and across public and private spheres) if women are to achieve parity of status (and well-being) with men (see, for example, Christopher et al., 2002; Geist, 2005). Finally, it directs our attention to what Daly and Lewis identify as an emergent 'crisis of care':

> Demographic and financial factors have acted as pressures increasing the demand for care whereas the social factors, in particular changing norms about family and kin responsibilities and the role of women, have contributed to a transformation of the conditions under which care has been traditionally organised. All of these together have acted to effectively decrease the supply of care at a time when the demand is rising. (2000, p. 288)

A concern with reclassifying the category of 'care' has often gone together in the feminist literature with a reconsideration of the key welfare category of 'citizenship'. An essential term in traditional welfarist advocacy (above all in Marshall), citizenship is seen by critics such as Pateman (1988) and Lister (1993, 2001) to be profoundly gendered. Classically, citizenship has been seen overwhelmingly to belong in a public domain which has itself been predominantly populated by men. Indeed, the individual with which classical liberal theory has concerned itself is already gendered: 'the public character of civil society/state is constructed and gains its meaning through what it excludes – the private association of the family' (Pateman, 1988, p. 236). Under more contemporary forms of social citi-

zenship, so Pateman argues, a similar logic of exclusion obtains. In societies based on market economies, 'paid employment has become the key to
citizenship' (1988, p. 237). Access to the more generous system of contributory social rights, as well as self-esteem, seems to turn on one's record
in employment. But the work that has counted towards citizenship is paid
work in the public sphere of the formal economy. Under the Beveridgean
welfare state in the UK, for example, women were quite explicitly given a
secondary status and welfare rights which derived from their presumed
marriage to a male breadwinner. Beveridge recognized that 'housewives
as mothers have vital work to do' (1942, p. 53) – but it would largely
be as unpaid carers and mothers in the home. Even in an economy which
looks less and less the way that Beveridge imagined it to be, women's
practical experience of welfare citizenship (because of differing patterns
of employment, lower lifetime earnings, greater responsibility for dependants and so on) is different from that of men (Lister, 1993). According
to Pateman, 'if an individual can gain recognition from other citizens as
an equally worthy citizen only through participation in the capitalist
market, if self-respect and respect as a citizen are "achieved" in the public
world of the employment society, then *women still lack the means to be
recognized as worthy citizens* (1988, pp. 246–7, emphasis added). The universalization of social citizenship, then, cannot simply be about expanding the number who enjoy its status but must also be about changing the
character and nature of social citizenship itself. This is acutely the case
where the nature of women's involvement in the world of paid work is
changing rapidly, as it has in many developed welfare states over the past
twenty years, and where women and families face a series of so-called
'new' social risks – including single parenthood, irregular employment and
rising indebtedness. (On the incidence and consequences of 'new' social
risks, see, for example, Bonoli, 2005, and the discussion in chapter 7.)

   The precise configuration of the feminist view of the welfare state continues to develop. What this work seems unquestionably to have established,
however, is (1) that the domestic sphere of production and reproduction in
which most welfare is secured has been systematically ignored in more
traditional 'mainstream' accounts; and (2) that the more public systems
of formal economic and state welfare cannot be understood except in
the context of their relation to welfare within the family-household system.

Thesis 9

The welfare state is comprehensively constituted-divided by gender.
It is heavily dependent upon arrangements outside the formal
economy and/or public provision through which women provide
unwaged/low-waged welfare services

Commentary: The Feminist Critique of the Welfare State

There is a good deal of evidence to support the broad bases of the feminist argument and one of the clearest indicators of the gendered structure of inequality under the welfare state is given by the differential vulnerability of men and women to poverty. While poverty has nowhere been eliminated under the welfare state, its incidence and distribution have altered. In preparing his Report for Britain in the 1940s, Beveridge found that the insufficiency of wages to support children explained up to a quarter of all poverty (Beveridge, 1942, p. 7). Thirty years later, over half of the lowest quintile group of income by family type were pensioner households. While low pay and pensioner status remain important sources of poverty (especially for women), these causes of poverty have been in part attenuated by economic and social policy changes. What these changes have in their turn exposed, particularly over the last twenty years, is a process of the *feminization of poverty* (Pearce, 1978; Bane, 1988; Goldberg and Kremen, 1990). While some commentators insist that 'it is not so much that women are more likely than before to be poor, but that their previously invisible poverty is becoming increasingly visible', it is possible to identify at least a *statistical* feminization of poverty in recent years (Glendinning and Millar, 1987, p. 15).

This feminization of poverty is especially clear in the case of lone female parents and their children. According to the US Bureau of the Census (1996), more than half of all poor families in the US in 1995 were female-headed, a figure that had increased from a little over a third in 1970. According to the Bureau, US poverty rates generally declined through much of the 1990s but rose again sharply after 2000. In 2003, more than a quarter of female-headed households were living in poverty (with rates that were substantially higher for those families headed by black and Hispanic women), compared with a rate in the general population of about one in ten. Lone parent families headed by a woman were twice as likely to be living in poverty as those headed by a man (US Bureau of the Census, 2003, pp. 9–13). Looking at a wider range of international examples, Christopher et al. (2002) found that women's poverty rates are generally higher than men's, but that the degree of this greater impoverishment differed widely and that in one case (Sweden) women were actually *less* vulnerable to poverty than men. In Sweden, absolute levels of poverty were low for both women and men (at 2 and 3 per cent respectively). As in the US, lone mothers were especially vulnerable to poverty. The OECD (2005) reports that across its member states poverty rates for single parent families (overwhelmingly headed by women) averaged 32.5 per cent, ranging from 9 per cent in Sweden to 49 per cent in the US.

Measures of *persistent* poverty (that is those whose poverty episodes last more than twelve months) also show women to be more vulnerable than men (Daly and Rake, 2003, pp. 102–3).

While the poverty and welfare status of lone mothers has attracted particular attention in recent years, not least because of the 'explosive' growth in this family form especially among blacks in the US, elderly women and especially lone elderly women have continued to be a group particularly vulnerable to poverty. In general, women live longer than men but have lower lifetime earnings and have generally accumulated fewer pension entitlements during their working lives. While in continental Europe single person female-headed households have an income around 90 per cent of total mean income, in the UK and the US female income is much lower – around three-quarters of the average – and women are much more substantially dependent on means-tested payments (reflecting the ways in which working lifetime inequalities in employment and earnings tend to be reflected in pension entitlements). Experience of poverty in old age varies widely. In the US, almost half of all women aged sixty-five or over have incomes at or below 125 per cent of the poverty level (cited in Gunnarsson, 2002). According to Daly and Rake (2003, p. 112) as many as a third of women over sixty-five in the UK are vulnerable to poverty (at 60 per cent of median income). In Sweden this figure falls to 10 per cent and in the Netherlands to 7 per cent.

In the most basic area of income maintenance, the welfare state has probably failed women more comprehensively than any other group (although in the US race is at least as important an indicator of disadvantaged welfare status). At the same time, it is important to see that not all welfare states have been the same and that some have been quite successful in addressing women's disadvantaged position (at least so far as income is concerned). Sweden, for example, not only has very low rates of poverty and a low differential between men and women; it also does an enormous amount of work of redistribution between initial market-generated incomes and post-tax, post-transfer incomes. 'Ironically,' as Christopher et al. note, 'the state is most friendly to women (compared to men) when the sex gap in poverty was smallest to begin with' (2002, p. 232). In any case, the failure of the welfare state to meet the needs of women cannot simply be explained in terms of inadequate levels of benefits. Provisions that are apparently 'gender neutral' will have a strongly gender-differentiated effect when the working and income lives of men and women vary systematically. Fully to make sense of welfare state 'failure', we must connect this to the evidence supporting several other claims in the feminist critique.

In fact, *formal* inequality of welfare rights for men and women has tended to recede (but certainly not disappear) over the past ten to fifteen years, especially within the European Union. There has been a movement away from taxation and social security provision based on the (male-headed) *family* towards a system based on the individual (male or female). (Although the tendency to measure poverty at household level probably leads to an underrecording of real levels of intra-household poverty for many women.) Some formal differences do remain (for example, unequal pensionable ages and differential rights to parental leave) but, in practice, these differences are probably much less important than the consequences of applying 'gender neutral' rules to social and economic institutions which are themselves strongly sex segregated. As we have seen, women's lower lifetime earnings and intermittent employment patterns mean that they are much less likely than their male counterparts to have access to occupational pensions or contributory social security benefits in old age. There is still a significant gender gap in relation to lifetime earnings (with women earning 15 per cent less than comparable men across the EU, 22 per cent less in the UK: Eurostat, 2005b). However, as we shall see, the welfare state does more than simply 'reproduce' existing patterns of sexual (and racial) inequality. It also reconstitutes and reorganizes the process of impoverishment and patterns of inequality.

A further major element in the feminist critique concerns the very unequal distribution of (especially unpaid) caring and domestic labour. This was originally presented under the rubric of a Marxist-feminist critique, in which women's unpaid domestic labour was seen – both in the social reproduction of the workforce and in caring for unwaged dependants – to subsidize economic costs which would otherwise have to be met by capital, through the direct provision of services, increased taxation or an increase in workers' wages. It has long been recognized that housework – principally 'cleaning, shopping, cooking, washing up, washing, and ironing' – has been work that is overwhelmingly unpaid and done by women. Though difficult to quantify, a number of studies have estimated housework to be in excess of fifty hours per week in an average household (Oakley, 1974; Hartmann, 1981; Piachaud, 1984). A second aspect of such unpaid domestic labour is the work of caring for dependants – the sick and disabled, the elderly and, perhaps above all, children. (The British Social Attitudes Survey in 1991 (Jowell, 1991) found that 60 per cent of women looked after children when sick compared to 1 per cent of men!) Because much of such care is informal and within the private or domestic sphere, it is difficult to establish how much care is being given by how many carers. Overall, women are more likely to be carers than men (17 per cent compared with 12 per cent) and spend more time in the provision of care (41 per cent of women spent over fifty hours a week caring for someone living with them compared to 28 per cent for men) (Corti and Dex, 1995).

Attempts to redirect welfare provision from the state to 'the community' have intensified the demands on women to provide unpaid care. According to Finch and Groves,

Both demographic change and the 'restructuring' of the welfare state have been grafted on to a pre-existing situation in which women have been defined as the 'natural' carers and also as the dependants of men. These alleged characteristics of women make them especially attractive as potential providers of unpaid care, in the private domain to which they have traditionally been assigned. (1983, p. 5)

State policy is particularly explicit in regarding the provision of childcare as 'women's work'. Drawing on a series of presumptions about the 'natural' dispositions of motherhood, the welfare state has often been quite explicit in affording differential status to mothers and fathers (for example, in rights to paid and unpaid leave from work, in the payment of children's allowances and in the right to claim unemployment benefits). The clearest, if indirect, measurement of the differential costs of childcare for men and women can be seen in their differing patterns of participation in paid employment. As Graham observes, 'caring for young children is typically a full-time and unpaid job and most women withdraw from full-time paid work to do it' (1987, p. 223). Throughout the developed capitalist economies, male labour force participation rates have fallen over the past twenty to thirty years, while female participation rates have increased (OECD, 1985a, pp. 12–13). Yet labour force participation rates of women (though not men) with (especially young) dependent children are still low (often reflecting a paucity of childcare provision). Across the twenty-five members of the EU in 2003, among women aged 20–49, 75 per cent of those without children worked, with just one-fifth of these working part-time. Among the same age group of women *with* children participation fell to around 60 per cent, with a third working part-time (Eurostat, 2005a).

For most women then, childrearing implies economic dependency, whether on a male partner's income or, failing this, on the state. Lone parenthood and dependence on state benefits are, as we have seen, major and growing sources of poverty. In 1994 more than a million lone parents were reliant on income support (Oppenheim and Harker, 1996). Nor are the disadvantages to women of their responsibility for childcare confined solely to dependence and loss of present earnings. First, because of the characteristic break in career which childrearing entails, most women who return to full-time employment do so on less advantageous terms than their male peers who have had no break in employment. Secondly, many forms of welfare provision, especially retirement pensions, are based on long-term contributions while in paid work. This includes not only public entitlements, but also, for example, rights under increasingly important private or company pension schemes, which are much less generally available to those with intermittent or part-time work records. In summary:

the differential distribution of the rewards received from entitlement programs reflects their eligibility rules. Although these are technically gender-
neutral, they are modelled on male patterns of labor force participation. By
rewarding continuous attachment to the labor force, long years of service,
and high wages, these rules disadvantage women whose shorter and more
irregular work histories make it more difficult for them to obtain full benefits. (Quadagno, 1990, p. 14)

These disadvantages are further exacerbated by the tendency of many
women (especially those with continuing responsibility for dependants) to
return to work on a part-time basis. Although there is significant international variation, part-time work is disproportionately carried out by
women. While such partial employment may enable women to reconcile
their caring and domestic responsibilities with paid employment – and,
indeed, women have mobilized politically precisely to enable them to
return to pre-existing employment on a part-time basis – a number of disadvantages can flow from part-time employment. Not only is remunera-
tion lower, but part-time workers also tend to receive lower rates of pay,
enjoy less security of employment and prospect of promotion and have
weaker welfare and employment rights. It often means working anti-social
hours (as, for example, in much hospital-based nursing). It also helps to
explain a pattern in which women's average earnings continue to be, as we
have seen, significantly lower than those of men. Because of a lack of
state provision of childcare, many women wishing to return to work are
forced to make 'ad hoc' arrangements, often with (female) relatives or
friends. Where such work is paid, especially within the 'informal' childcare
economy (for example, the work of unregistered childminders), it is carried
out by women on low wages with few welfare or employment rights
(Jackson and Jackson, 1979).

Once again, we need to be careful not to generalize too readily from
UK experience and to recognize that there have been some real (if limited
advances) over the past ten to twenty years. As Pascall and Lewis note,
'part-time work may be a strategy for bringing women into the labour
market and shaking traditional assumptions about women's roles (as
recently in the Netherlands) or for marginalising them (as in the UK)'
(2004, p. 381). The introduction of 'daddy leave' (a period of paid leave
after childbirth that can only be taken by fathers) represents one (small)
attempt to reallocate the responsibility for care. Geist (2005) is able to
report a growing division in the domestic economy of caring between
different welfare state regimes, with 'social democratic' and 'liberal'
regimes showing a greater propensity to share caring responsibilities, while
more 'conservative' welfare states retain this as almost solely the (unpaid)
responsibility of women. (On differing types of welfare state 'regimes', see
below, pp. 171–7). Of course, even in the most 'progressive' regimes, this
still leaves women to undertake the lion's share of domestic work.

This leads on to a final element in the feminist critique, that is the claim that women, in part because of their dependent status and their domestic responsibilities, offer employers a potential pool of cheap and adaptable labour. In fact, any straightforward version of the 'reserve army' thesis is probably unsustainable, because the very pronounced sex segregation of the labour market means that women's labour is not usually directly replacing the work of men. This does not however mean that women are not a source of cheap labour. Whatever its salience in the wider economy, in terms of employment *within* the welfare state, women are the principal and comparatively cheap source of labour power. Thus the nursing profession, which is often seen to replicate women's 'natural' and 'caring' role in the home within paid employment, is almost 90 per cent female. Ancillary workers, responsible for much cleaning and catering work in Britain's National Health Service, are predominantly female and disproportionately drawn from ethnic minority populations (Williams, 1989, p. 170; Beechey and Perkins, 1987, pp. 86–90; Cook and Watt, 1992). Similarly, the teaching of young children is predominantly a female profession (with the partial exception of Germany). In both health and education, however, women are still systematically underrepresented in the more senior and decision-taking levels of the profession. At the same time, the public services may offer a (rare) opportunity for career advancement. Women are strongly represented in the senior levels of Sweden's extensive public services, for example, while their numbers at the highest level of Sweden's private sector remain discouragingly low.

At this point, three provisional conclusions seem in order. First, there is plenty of evidence that backs up the feminist critique of existing welfare state arrangements – though we have to read this in the broader context of differing working lives, different caring responsibilities and differing lifetime needs. At the same time, thirty years of feminist pressure to reform has had an impact (albeit internationally a highly variable one) on welfare state arrangements. Especially where they have found an ally in sympathetic social democratic governments, feminists have had some success in pressing their agenda for welfare state reform (on the importance of a 'sympathetic' political context, see Huber and Stephens, 2001). It follows from this that welfare states are not all of a kind. Both in their structures and, more crucially, in their outcomes, welfare state experiences vary. And this is a variation not simply of scale, but also of kind.

The 'Anti-Racist' Critique of the Welfare State

In the non-institutional politics of the new social movements, a parallel has frequently been drawn between the disadvantaged position of women and the disadvantaged position of ethnic minorities. Such a parallel can and, to a very limited extent, has been applied to discussions of the welfare state (Williams, 1989, 1993; Cook and Watt, 1992). The anti-racist critique may be less clearly delineated and less fully elaborated than the critical positions adopted by feminist writers. However, as Jill Quadagno makes clear (1994, pp. 3–15) in the US, at least, 'race' is crucial to any understanding of the politics of the welfare state (see also Block et al., 1987; Murray, 1984; Moynihan, 1965). In an influential study, Martin Gilens answers his own question in *Why Americans Hate Welfare* (1999) with the simple suggestion that a (white) majority, ill-informed by a partisan media, hate welfare because they see it as a program that gives resources to an undeserving minority which is presumed to be predominantly black.

> Racial attitudes stand out as a key factor in understanding white Americans' opposition to welfare. Not only is the perception of blacks as lazy the second most powerful indicator of welfare spending preferences, but it is the most important influence on the perception that welfare recipients are undeserving (which is itself the most powerful predictor of welfare spending preferences). (Gilens, 1999, p. 96)

In this way, 'simple' racial prejudice among white people against black people is an important constituent of the latter's disadvantaged position within the welfare state. But individual racist attitudes cannot exhaustively explain the levels and persistence of disadvantage. In seeking a more systemic explanation, and paralleling the discussion of 'patriarchy' and 'capitalism' in the feminist critique, there is some disagreement among commentators as to whether the disadvantages experienced by ethnic minorities under existing welfare state arrangements are primarily to be explained in terms of the interests of the majority community, or else by the interests of international capital. However, there is widespread agreement with the core proposition that ethnic minorities face a 'double process' of disadvantage under the welfare state. First, their economically and socially less privileged position tends to make them more reliant on provision through the welfare state. Secondly, this welfare state on which they are peculiarly dependent treats them on systematically less favourable terms than members of the majority community. This core claim has been developed in a number of directions.

First, ever since its inception, the welfare state has been underpinned by a conception of nationhood and it has been counted as one of its strengths that it institutionalizes and strengthens claims based on the equality of citizenship. However, not all those living within a given national territory have counted equally as 'members of the nation' or as citizens, and not everybody has enjoyed the same rights of access to the welfare state. In fact, some sort of residence qualification for relief is a commonplace of public welfare which long predates the coming of the welfare state (Webb and Webb, 1927; De Swaan, 1988). Thus a whole series of disqualifications from access to the welfare state have been enacted against migrant workers, their families and their descendants. These divisions have been reinforced where the immigrant community can be further identified by differences of colour, language or religious background. Among those who see the welfare state as a form of class compromise, it has been argued that this compromise may represent a rapprochement between capital and a white, male, metropolitan and organized working class, secured largely at the expense of other groups of workers (at home or abroad). As we shall see shortly, some have argued that the current welfare state needs to be reconstructed along more 'nationalistic' lines if it is to continue to secure majority support.

This claim dovetails with a second, that immigration has served as a source of cheap labour – to be employed (albeit intermittently) either by capital or indeed within the welfare state itself. Here again, ethnic minority and immigrant workers are seen to parallel the role feminists attribute to women as a 'reserve army of labour', introduced in times of labour scarcity to do poorly paid work and to act as a constraint on rising wages. Similarly, and particularly for black women, those areas of a highly segregated labour market to which they most readily gain access are in low-skilled 'caring' or 'servicing' occupations. Indeed, Williams, writing of employment in the National Health Service in the UK, insists 'that the racist image of the *Black woman as servant* is as strong as that of *carer* in the acceptance of Black women in domestic, nursing and cleaning roles' (Williams, 1989, p. 72; Carby, 1982, p. 215). Bhavnani (1994, pp. 78–9) reports that black women in the NHS are overrepresented in ancillary and lower nursing grades and within the less prestigious areas (of mental health and geriatrics). Because of their lower levels of sanctioned skills and of unionization, their lack of accumulated employment rights and political clout, in periods of economic downturn ethnic minorities are subject to differentially high levels of unemployment. Just as for both state and employers the 'ideal' solution to the problem of unemployment in the case of women was to define them out of the workforce, so the 'optimum' solution in the case of migrant workers may be to repatriate them. Where this is not possible, these displaced workers are still more likely than others to find themselves dependent on the residual provision of state benefits.

A further parallel with the feminists' argument is to be found in the role attributed to ethnic minority labour in reducing the costs of the reproduction of labour power. First, immigrant workers may not enjoy the same rights to housing, unemployment benefit and health care as 'indigenous' workers. Secondly, immigration laws may explicitly seek to exclude from citizenship or indeed from residence dependent relatives of the immigrant worker. Thirdly, the costs of education and training of the immigrant worker will generally have been met by his or her country of origin, while the 'guest' worker approaching retirement age may be 'encouraged' to 'go home'. Fourthly, immigrant workers are especially likely to find themselves deployed in the 'informal' or 'black' economy, where wages are low and social and employment rights non-existent.

Critics also argue that the welfare state itself performs a role in the reproduction of these disadvantages of ethnic minority labour. An educational system in which ethnic minorities systematically underachieve or a system of housing allocation in which ethnic minorities are confined to the poorest quality public stock are seen to reinforce across generations disadvantages which were originally experienced by an immigrant population. Finally, it is argued that access to more generous forms of welfare provision – for example, social security in the US or earnings-related pensions in the UK – is tied to an individual's previous employment record. This 'achievement' oriented welfare state is constructed around characteristically white and male patterns of permanent, full-time and (more or less) continuous employment. Even within a gender-blind and colour-blind welfare system, characteristic differences in economic opportunities and earnings for women and blacks means unequal rewards from the welfare state.

Clearly, there are important similarities between the feminist and anti-racist critiques of the welfare state. But there are also substantial differences. For example, the ideology of 'promoting healthy family life' may have very different, if similarly unattractive consequences for white women and black men. Again, the patterns and consequences of exclusion of women and ethnic minority men from the employed workforce may be quite different. Perhaps the single most important issue raised in this context is the status of ethnic minority women. Thus Williams writes of a black feminist critique of other schools of feminism arising from 'the use of the concept of "patriarchy", from the omission of Black women's struggle against slavery, colonialism, imperialism and racism in the writing of feminist history (or "herstory"), and from the tendency to see racial oppression and sex oppression and the struggles against them as parallel but separate forms' (1989, p. 70). Williams argues that 'Black women have a qualitatively different experience of the welfare state compared with white women' and if ethnic minority women are 'doubly disadvantaged' within the welfare state, this does not straightforwardly represent a process of *reinforcement*, but rather a *reconstitution* of their experience (1989, pp. 78–9).

Thesis 10

The welfare state is a characteristic form of the developed capitalist state securing the interests of capital and of white people (and especially men), at the expense of ethnic minorities (and especially women)

Commentary: The 'Anti-Racist' Critique of the Welfare State

Turning to the evidence which is cited in support of the 'anti-racist' perspective, we can again identify important similarities with (as well as some significant differences from) the feminist critique. The first point to note is that while *ethnicity* is seen as an appropriate way of describing people's differing and largely self-ascribed cultural identities, '*race*' is widely rejected as a spurious and largely ideological term. Claims that 'races' and 'racial differences' have some biological basis, and even that they form some sort of evolutionary hierarchy, are denied. The rhetoric of race – of, for example, 'the British race' or 'the white races of South Africa' – is seen simply as a device for mobilizing prejudice in the interests of one (often ethnically diverse) group over others.

Characteristically, the idea of 'race' is associated with 'insiders' and 'outsiders' or members and non-members. Historically, it was perhaps most often used in the context of imperialism and colonialism to justify the dominance of a (generally white-skinned) minority over an (often brown- or black-skinned) majority. Within the welfare state, it is more typically a majority population that constitutes the 'insiders' and a minority or minorities that make up the 'outsiders'. Such accounts rest on an extremely selective history. In fact, the whole of human history is marked by patterns of migration and many of the most developed industrial societies (and among them, some of the most developed welfare states) are largely immigrant societies (Australia, New Zealand, Canada and the United States, for example).

The experience of these immigrant societies demonstrates that it is not always the indigenous population that successfully sustains the claim to constitute the 'true' basis of the nation. Thus in North America and Australasia, the *truly* native population was effectively marginalized by more powerful incomers. The US, as is well known, was itself made up of successive waves of immigration. Following the English and other northern Europeans, the Irish, southern and eastern Europeans, and Hispanics found themselves to be successively and temporarily the newest and the most economically and socially disadvantaged sections of the US population. This history of successive waves of immigration was itself entwined with the forced importation of black Americans and their subsequent and continuing struggle for formal and substantive equality. This experience of the American blacks also illustrates the ways in which the dynamics of population in the welfare state have been affected by *internal* migration (as, for example, in their shift from southern agriculture to northern industrial cities). Though less dramatic and less long-distance, migration has been and continues to be an important element in the histories of the developed welfare states of Western Europe (Grammenos, 1982, pp. 30–2; S. Paine, 1974, pp. 5–36; Piore, 1979; Rosenblum, 1973; Skellington, 1996). In 1995, immigration accounted for nearly 75 per cent of the total increase in the population of the European Union, with only Ireland and Portugal reporting net emigration (Eurostat, 1996b, p. 7). This situation has been greatly extended and complicated by the growth of the European Union, especially the most recent expansion (in 2004) to include much poorer (and lower waged) economies in east-central Europe (IOM, 2004). For perhaps the first time, we are seeing substantial movements of labour *within* the European Union. As we shall see in the closing paragraphs of this section, immigration, especially the spectre of illegal immigration, has fuelled an intensive debate about the compatibility of large-scale migration and extensive or 'solidaristic' welfare states.

In practice, the experience of racism in the welfare state is not, of course, confined to immigrants or ex-immigrant populations, as the experience of Maoris, Aborigines and native Americans attests. (Indeed, the aboriginal peoples of Australia have a health and welfare status which is vastly inferior to that of the rest of the population; Jones, 1996, pp. 9–10.) Yet this has been the principal focus of the anti-racist critique and it is an experience which makes their claims particularly clear. Furthermore, it is a part of the disadvantaged experience of non-immigrant ethnic minorities to find themselves *treated like immigrants*. Correspondingly, the focus here is on the immigrant experience of the welfare state.

A crucial background condition for this immigrant experience is the fact that welfare states have always been *national* institutions based on some conception of *national* citizenship (for a useful discussion, see Miller, 1995). While we have seen that welfare as the right of a citizen has something to commend it as an alternative to welfare as the charitable relief of the destitute pauper, it clearly marginalizes the position of those resident in a national territory but not enjoying the full rights of citizenship. Exclusion from full citizenship is a frequent concomitant of immigrant status and exclusion from full citizenship will often mean exclusion from full participation in the welfare state (Freeman, 1986, p. 51). Correspondingly, formal differences in *legal* status are perhaps more important in the anti-racist than in the feminist critique. Of course, exclusions from access to the welfare state on the basis of citizenship are not necessarily racist, nor are they necessarily unjustified, if one understands the welfare state to be funded by the accumulated efforts and abstinence from immediate consumption of a given national population.[3] However, if the ways in which citizenship is granted and withheld, or the ways in which welfare rights are implemented, are themselves racist, this qualification is nullified.

---

[3] For an interesting discussion, see Carens, 1988.

In practice, different types of migrant, enjoying different legal statuses, are differentially excluded from rights of access to the welfare state (Hammar, 1990). The most disadvantaged group in this sense is likely to be made up of illegal immigrants. As workers, illegal immigrants tend to be almost wholly without employment rights. Normally, they have no rights to the provision of health care or to housing, no rights to welfare protection or pensions and no entitlement to social provision for their dependants. Living under constant threat of deportation, they remain largely on the sufferance of their employers and often find themselves 'superexploited' in intermittent work on low wages, under poor and unregulated conditions, often, for example, in the building trade or in domestic service (Grammenos, 1982, pp. 17–18; OECD, 1985a, pp. 101–5). There are clear indications that, as official migration to the developed countries has been increasingly restricted over the last twenty years, illegal immigration may have been rising (Maillat, 1987, p. 55). The extent of this growth is, in its nature, hard to quantify. In the UK, where there is no official government estimate of the number of illegal immigrants, current estimates vary between 123,300 and 1 million (Levinson, 2005). The fact that it is so difficult to give accurate estimates of the number of illegal immigrants makes it very hard to refute the claims of those who are inclined to see the arrival of migrants as a series of 'floods', 'waves' and 'tides'. It is clear that the political salience of illegal immigration has risen steeply over the last five or six years.

Rather less marginal is the position of 'official' migrant workers. Facing a labour shortfall in a period of sustained economic growth in the 1950s and 1960s, a number of European countries sought to supplement their labour supply by 'inviting in' migrant workers from less developed countries. Those countries with an extensive colonial past (for example, the Netherlands and the UK) tended to turn to their former colonies, sometimes because such workers were seen to be cheaper to the host country than immigrants from extracolonial sources (Joshi and Carter, 1984, p. 58). Others, such as (the former West) Germany, took workers from the less developed areas of southern Europe (initially from Italy, later from Yugoslavia and Turkey). While such migrant workers enjoyed certain welfare rights (for example, limited access to housing and health care, and the statutory protection of health and safety legislation), they did not enjoy the same rights as indigenous workers. They did not, for example, enjoy the same entitlement to unemployment benefit or, very often, the right to bring in dependants with the same rights of access to housing, education and health care as the dependants of indigenous workers. Nor did they always enjoy the same rights on *leaving* the workforce (Brubaker, 1989, pp. 155–60). As Grammenos points out, while migration before 1945 was largely 'one way', in the postwar period migration more commonly took the form of 'rotation' (Grammenos, 1982, pp. 30–1). Under such 'two-way migration', workers (ideally young, skilled, educated and free of dependants) work temporarily in the host economy, meeting pressing labour demands and leaving when the labour market slackens. West Germany's '*Gastarbeiter*' or 'guest worker' system, largely based on temporary Turkish migrant labour, has often been seen as the archetypal expression of this system. The warmth of the welcome for such visiting workers, as for other 'guests', is contingent on the recognition that their stay will be temporary and, as Freeman points out, 'the problem with the guest-worker system from the point of view of the host state is that it tends to break down' (Cashmore and Troyna, 1983, p. 52; Grammenos, 1982, p. 30; Freeman, 1986, p. 60). The idea of a 'two-tier' welfare state continues and in recent years a number of states (the US, UK, Australia and Denmark among them) have tightened the regulations under which immigrants may be eligible for welfare support (see Soroka et al., forthcoming).

A third category of migrant worker is defined by those accepted for permanent settlement and/or incorporation into full citizenship. Formally, such a group may enjoy full equality with members of the indigenous population. However, where welfare practice is discriminatory, this formal equality of citizenship may not result in actual equality of treatment or of condition. Thus, as has been the experience of those with Afro-Caribbean and Asian backgrounds in both the US and the UK, formal equality of citizenship has not ended discriminatory practices in the provision of health, housing or personal social services. Perhaps most importantly, it has not ended discrimination in what is for most people the single most important source of welfare – that is, the labour market. Fully to appreciate this, we need to move on to consider how racism is said to service the interests of the welfare state capitalist economies.

In discussing the feminist critique of the welfare state, we saw how women's subordinate position was said to serve the capitalist economy in three ways: (1) by providing a source of cheap labour, (2) by providing a 'reserve army' of labour to be drawn in and out of active participation in response to the changing needs of the labour market, and (3) by reducing the costs of the reproduction of labour power. We can trace these same elements in considering the anti-racist critique of the economic consequences of existing welfare state arrangements.

Occasionally, the welfare state has been seen to be directly complicit in securing the supply of cheap labour within a racist regime. Writing of attempts at reform in the US in the 1970s, Jill Quadagno argues that for 'more than a century, blacks had been excluded from welfare in the South because the welfare system was an instrument of social control, a part of the local racial caste system' (1990, p. 24). Both Alston and Ferrie (1985) and Quadagno (1988a, 1988b, 1990, 1994) argue that the structure of the welfare state in the American south from the 1930s to the 1970s was principally shaped by the interests of white southern planters in the preservation of a poor and dependent black population. When federally supported old age assistance was first introduced in the 1930s, the white southern Democrats who controlled the southern political machine resisted all attempts to increase the levels of support to poor southern black families, and thus fended off the threat to the availability of the black population to perform low-paid and irregular work. In the cotton belt of the south, average monthly benefits were systematically lower than in the north and west (standing in 1938–9, for example, at $7.06 in Mississippi, $21.79 in New York and $30.54 in California). Rates were lower for blacks than whites throughout the cotton belt south, and within this region lower in the cotton counties than the non-cotton counties (Quadagno, 1988a, pp. 244–5). Through their control of the local welfare state, 'southern land-holders . . . were able to prevent the payment of significant benefits to their tenants, croppers, and wage workers under the Social Security Act, and thereby assured themselves a continued supply of cheap, loyal labor' (Alston and Ferrie, 1985, p. 117).

Although this particular form of the racial welfare state in the southern US was eventually to be rendered obsolete by changes in agricultural technology, black migration and black political empowerment, Quadagno identifies much the same process at work in the south in the 1970s. Reviewing President Nixon's unsuccessful welfare reform proposals aimed at securing a guaranteed annual income for the working poor (the Family Assistance Plan), a reform which promised significantly to raise the wages of black workers in the south and threaten its traditional low-wage economy, Quadagno found 'the Southern power elite' to be among its most vocal and committed opponents. As Georgia Representative Phillip Landrum protested: 'There's not going to be anybody left to roll these wheelbarrows and press these shirts' (Quadagno, 1990, pp. 23–5).

More usually, the 'complicity' of the welfare state in the supply of cheap labour is less direct. It is a process which is particularly well illustrated by the experience of immigrant labour. In fact, the long-term economic consequences of immigration for the receiving countries have been much discussed (see, for example, S. Paine, 1974, pp. 12–23). Some have suggested that, in the longer term, immigration may detract from capital accumulation by delaying technological innovation or increasing social infrastructural costs. Yet the predominant economic view, and certainly the motivation of those welfare states which encouraged migration in the 1950s and 1960s, was that the importation of migrant workers (especially on a temporary basis) would improve circumstances for capital accumulation. Under conditions of near full employment, there is likely to be a shortfall in the availability of indigenous labour, which will put upward pressure on wages and lead to difficulties in filling lower paid and unskilled jobs. Under these circumstances in the 1950s and 1960s, many of the Western European welfare states turned to migrants as a source of comparatively cheap labour to fill unskilled positions. For the migrants themselves, coming from less developed countries with high unemployment and much lower wages, there was clearly an economic incentive to take what were, by Western European standards, poorly paid and unattractive jobs. In the host countries, under conditions of near full employment, the use of such immigrant labour was not only in the interests of capital but also of native workers. Migrants were not competing with native workers, but, in fact, creating more skilled jobs for nationals by filling those unskilled positions which were needed to support higher levels of general economic activity. Thus migrant workers were generally introduced to perform unskilled jobs at low wages and heavily concentrated in particular sectors of a highly segregated labour market (Maillat, 1987). In West Germany, in 1968, for example, while the national average male wage was DM 5.81 per hour, the rate for male migrants from southern Europe was DM 4.51 per hour (cited in S. Paine, 1974, p. 99). Such disadvantages are not confined to temporary migrants. Evidence from the Commission for Racial Equality (CRE, 2005c) shows that in the UK working age adults from ethnic minorities are more likely than white people to be vulnerable to unemployment. People of Pakistani and Bangladeshi descent fare particularly badly and are just under four times more likely than white people to earn less than 40 per cent of national average income. In the US, in 2004, the median annual income of two-parent families with children stood at $63,195 for whites, $52,645 for blacks and $40,675 for Hispanics (US Bureau of the Census, 2005). From several countries there is evidence of 'an ethnic minority labour market which seems to be in some respects quite different from that of white workers' (C. Brown, 1984, p. 293). The picture is not uniform, with 'the position of minority ethnic groups . . . becoming more differentiated both *between* and *within* minority groups', but these populations are still overrepresented among less skilled and lower paid occupations and underrepresented (with the partial exception of some Asian men) in professional and managerial positions (Oppenheim and Harker, 1996, pp. 123–4). According to the CRE (2005c), in the UK Census of 2001, 52 per cent of male Bangladeshi workers were reported to be working in the restaurant industry (compared with only 1 per cent of white males), while one in eight male Pakistani workers was a taxi driver or chauffeur (compared with a national average of one in a hundred).

In turning to the status of migrants and ethnic minorities as a 'reserve army of labour', we again find a pattern of disadvantage which is rather different from that experienced by women. First, that migrant labour should act as a reserve pool of labour, to be taken up in times of heightened activity and stood down in periods of economic recession, is not seen as a regrettable economic 'accident'. It has, from time to time, been entrenched as *an element of governments' economic policy*. The intention of bringing in temporary migrant labour is precisely to meet a *temporary* excess of labour demand. When demand no longer exceeds supply, the policy imperative is to shed labour by returning migrants to their countries of origin. This policy intention (however flawed its realization) was quite clear in the Western European welfare states following the economic downturn of the early 1970s.[4] In West Germany new restrictions were placed on rights of entry for dependants of foreign workers; in France family reunions were suspended for a time in the late 1970s (Grammenos, 1982, p. 29). In the UK rules governing right of entry and entitlement to state support have been repeatedly tightened, most recently in respect of those seeking political asylum (see CRE, 2005d). In practice, the effects of recession on migration, integration and repatriation have often been very different from those that governments of the 1970s had anticipated (Hammar and Lithman, 1987). But they have done little to lessen the economic marginality of immigrant workers. Maillat concludes:

> In the final analysis, the differences in the unemployment rates of nationals and foreigners are indicative of the insecure nature of the jobs held by foreigners. Reasons for this vulnerability of foreign workers relate to their concentration in sectors in crisis, the high proportion of unskilled workers among them, their lack of any real negotiating power, and the fact that they are often the first in line in the event of redundancies. (1987, p. 51)

This disadvantage in terms of employment also extends to resident ethnic minority populations. In the UK in the mid-1990s, a period of falling unemployment, levels of joblessness were more than twice as high among blacks as among whites. Among those under twenty-five, male unemployment for black and other ethnic minority populations was running at 37 per cent, compared with 18 per cent in the equivalent white population (Oppenheim and Harker, 1996, pp. 115–6). In 2002, the ethnic minority employment rate for Great Britain was 59 per cent, which compares with an overall employment rate of over 75 per cent. In ethnic community populations, the average rate of unemployment was roughly twice what it was among whites (CRE, 2005d). In the US in 2005, when unemployment among the white male population had slipped below 5 per cent, and the overall rate stood at 5.2 per cent, the rate among blacks still stood at 10.3 per cent (US Bureau of Labor Statistics, 2005).

The problems of migrants and ethnic minorities are further aggravated by their generally lower levels of formal qualifications and acquired skills, their lack of accumulated employment and welfare rights and, in the case of migrants, the unwillingness of state and employers to invest in a 'temporary' resource.

---

[4] Despite governments' policy intentions, the effects of recession in terms of migration, integration and repatriation have often been perverse (Hammar and Lithman, 1987).

A third element indicated in the anti-racist critique is the role of immigrant and ethnic minority workers in lowering the reproduction costs of labour. Here again, for migrant labour at least, this is a conscious intention of various governments' economic policy. The preponderance of the young, single, healthy and economically active among migrants means that they make very limited demands on the most expensive elements of the welfare state – health, education and pensions. There are also elements of transfer income, for example, unemployment benefit, from which they may be effectively excluded. At the same time, migrants help to finance the welfare state through direct and indirect taxation. Although migrant and ethnic minority populations are often represented as a drain on welfare state resources, Grammenos argues that they may be very substantial net contributors to the public exchequer. He cites evidence for (West) Germany, which shows 'that savings on child-rearing and education resulting from immigration come to at least 19 per cent of net investment for the period 1969 to 1973' (1982, p. 31). Grammenos also argues that the fact that 'the host country receives young healthy workers without having to educate them or support them as children' led to savings in (West) Germany in the period 1957–73 which 'would have generated additional capital of 27.721 billion DM at 1973 prices' (1982, p. 37; Blitz, 1977, p. 496). The economic consequences of a permanently settled immigrant population are less clear-cut. The demographic make-up of this population will be different from that of the established population. In time (as the immigrant community ages), one would expect it to make greater demands on the social infrastructure. However, in the UK experience, the comparative growth of the (ex-)immigrant population and its historically high levels of labour force participation challenge the popular claim of the later 1970s that ethnic minorities are a drain on both the productive economy and the welfare state (see Golding and Middleton, 1982). In fact, a defraying of the costs of labour power may occur very directly through the dependence of the welfare state on the low-paid labour of (especially women) workers from the ethnic minority population (see above, p. 77).

One final element in the anti-racist critique concerns the ways in which the welfare state itself *reproduces* the disadvantages of ethnic minority populations. In part, this simply echoes the observation made by the feminists (pp. 75–6 above) and by Jill Quadagno that a welfare state which relates entitlements to previous labour market performance militates against all those, notably women and ethnic minorities, whose lifetime's earnings and employment are below the white male average. In part, it concerns racial discrimination on the part of those officials responsible for allocating public housing, adjudicating claims for benefits or making decisions about the educational destinations of children. Although patterns of welfare inequality are complex, and differ in important ways between different ethnic minority populations, evidence of unequal welfare outcomes is clear.

In the UK, the 1985 Committee of Inquiry into the Education of Children from Ethnic Minority Groups, established by the government under the chairmanship of Lord Swann, echoed earlier findings in identifying systematic educational underachievement among the West Indian school population (Swann, 1985; Brown and Madge, 1982). The Swann committee cited evidence showing that low examination performance among sixteen-year-old working-class children stood at 20 per cent among white children and 21 per cent among Asians, but rose to 41 per cent among West Indians. It also noted that while 1 per cent of West Indian pupils went on to full-time degree courses in further education, this compared with a figure of 5 per cent among Asians and 'all other leavers' (Swann, 1985, pp. 60–2). The committee argued:

> A substantial part of ethnic minority underachievement . . . is the result of racial prejudice and discrimination on the part of society at large, bearing on ethnic minority homes and families, and hence, *indirectly*, on children. [The rest] . . . is due in large measure to prejudice and discrimination bearing *directly* on children, within the educational system, as well as outside it. (Swann, 1985, pp. 89–90)

Nearly two decades on from Swann, the picture is more complex. Evidence suggests that many Asian pupils are significant 'overachievers' compared with the rest of the school-age population, but Afro-Carribean pupils (especially boys) are more likely to be permanently excluded from school for bad behaviour and have been underrepresented among those going on to university. The Commission for Racial Equality points out that there is significant variation in the educational performance of differing groups *within* the Asian population (CRE, 2005a). Thus Indian and Chinese pupils outperform other groups throughout their school careers, while Bangladeshi and Pakistani pupils perform less well than white pupils throughout compulsory schooling.

The provision of housing is another area of the welfare state which reflects an ethnically divided access to resources and reveals a pattern of disproportionate disadvantage among ethnic minorities, as deprivations based on social class and economic status are reinforced by patterns of discrimination. Patterns of household tenure among different ethnic groups are complex (with much higher levels of owner-occupation in the Asian population). Asians are now as likely to be in detached or semi-detached houses as are whites (about 80 per cent), but these levels are still much lower among Bangladeshi and Caribbean families. Although the general incidence of overcrowding has declined in the past decade, it is still very significant for Pakistanis and Bangladeshis (CRE, 2005b). Data from the Office of the Deputy Prime Minister show an overrepresentation of ethnic minority groups among homeless households. According to 2002 data, while ethnic minority groups comprise 8 per cent of the population, they represent 22 per cent of the households accepted as homeless by local authorities (CRE, 2005b).

Explanations of these patterns are very varied and not all support the claims of the anti-racist critique. Yet it is possible to identify a very broad agreement about the existence of *prima facie* evidence of discrimination and inequality along ethnic lines within the welfare state.

It is worth drawing attention here to the peculiar position of ethnic minority women. This population is seen to be disadvantaged in terms of both feminist and anti-racist critiques of the welfare state. Thus Cook and Watt insist that 'Black women in Britain have to face . . . the dual oppressions of racism and sexism which impinge on their opportunities and consign them to low-paid and lower-status jobs' (1987, p. 69). A 1985 OECD study, *The Integration of Women into the Economy*, found that immigrant women were often the single most economically disadvantaged group in the population. Typically, they have 'more dependants but fewer family resources; they have a greater need for gainful employment but run a higher risk of unemployment' (OECD, 1985a, p. 92). However, this 'double disadvantage' is not simply cumulative. Thus, for example, while black women are disadvantaged economically both as blacks and as women, the nature of this disadvantage is also shaped by the fact that they are married to (economically disadvantaged and more marginally employed) black men or, particularly in the US, that they are disproportionately likely to be at the head of (frequently impoverished) single parent families (W. J. Wilson, 1987). This may yield distinctive patterns of, for example, employment participation or welfare dependency. Correspondingly, the experience of black women under the welfare state is something other than the cumulative consequence of being black and being female (Cook and Watt, 1992). The pattern of incomes provides one illustration of this. In 2002, men from ethnic minority backgrounds in the UK were earning on average about 72 per cent of the income of white men; women from the same ethnic groups were earning about 43 per cent of the income of white men and around 87 per cent of the average income of white women (DTI, 2004).

In recent years, increasing attention has come to be focused on the relationship between immigration, globalization and the sustainability of existing welfare regimes. Drawing on a number of the themes we have already established, this literature has queried whether increased levels of immigration under circumstances of globalization are consistent with a more extensive or 'solidaristic' welfare state. In essence, the argument has been that extensive welfare states (of the kind characteristically seen in continental and northern Europe) rely on some sort of national consensus, an agreement to pool social risks within a group in which participants feel some minimal sense of mutual identification (a sort of 'delimited' altruism). In Soroka et al.'s summary:

Immigration has the potential to raise powerful challenges to the political legitimacy of the welfare state. Immigration can unsettle historical conceptions of community, which define those who are 'us', recognized members of existing networks of rights and obligation, and those who are 'strangers' or 'others' whose needs seem less compelling. According to many commentators, the growing presence of newcomers, especially ethnically distinct newcomers, may erode the sense of social solidarity on which welfare states are constructed. (Soroka et al., forthcoming)

This challenge is often seen to have reached a new intensity with the 'moral panic' that has surrounded increases (real or imagined) in levels of immigration and (illegal) asylum-seeking. It is often combined with an attack on what are seen to be established liberal presumptions about the benign character of multiculturalism – and a call for more emphasis on the integration of existing immigrants and numerical restrictions on the numbers of future migrants (see Goodhart, 2004). It is sometimes suggested that what Martin Gilens found in the US – an unwillingness to fund an extensive welfare state in a racially divided society – may present a warning, or at least a challenge, for much larger 'multicultural' welfare states in Europe (see, for example, Alesina and Glaeser, 2004).

Theoretically, there are a number of possibilities here. Increased immigration could be associated with *increased* social expenditure (and therefore a net cost to the welfare state). Given that immigrants generally have lower (recognized) skills and competences, are poorer and more vulnerable to unemployment, they may push up social costs. In so far as they are generally younger, and more likely to have small children, they may push up the cost of child-related programmes. On the other hand, immigrants may *reduce* social spending. If they are younger, they will generally make fewer calls on the welfare state's most expensive programmes – in health care and pensions. They will increase tax revenues. Yet, if the thesis of the critics is right, the identification of particular welfare programmes with immigrant populations (even if they are not the principal or even very extensive users) may in itself be enough to mobilize political support for parties of the moderate or indeed the far right – who will tap into this public sentiment to engineer a more general assault on social welfare.

The conclusions of Soroka et al.'s (forthcoming) survey are somewhat ambiguous. They conclude that there is a real immigration impact on the size of welfare states. They estimate that 'the typical industrial society might spend 16 or 17 per cent more than it does now on social services had it kept its foreign-born percentage where it was in 1970'. On the face of it, this is a very significant impact. But they also argue that 'the effect seems wholly political' – that is, it is not driven by 'real' demographic changes but by the response of (largely mainstream) parties to popular sentiment (which they may, of course, have had some part in mobilizing). Keith Banting draws the following conclusions:

First, Western democracies with large foreign-born populations have not had more difficulty in sustaining and developing their welfare states than other countries. However, second, the extent of social change does seem to matter: countries in which immigrant communities grew rapidly experienced lower rates of growth in social spending in the last three decades of the twentieth century. Third, despite the worries of some critics, the adoption of robust multiculturalism policies does not systematically exacerbate relations and erode the welfare state. (2005, p. 111)

Whatever the real patterns of causation, there can be little doubt that the question of immigration is likely to feature prominently in the politics of welfare over coming years – and that at least a part of the story that will be told by politicians keen to maintain the fabric of existing welfare provision will concern maintaining the 'integrity' of existing welfare nation communities, which, in its turn, is likely to favour a 'constrained' pattern of immigration. For those who maintain the integrity of the 'anti-racist' critique, this is likely to look like little more than a further twist in the long-established political practice of 'blaming the victims'.

The Green Critique of the Welfare State

In so far as we may speak of a single green perspective on the welfare state, it is principally to be derived from a characteristic concern with the harmful consequences of unsustainable economic growth and bureaucratized welfare services. While there is a conservative wing to the green perspective, which argues against the welfare state and in favour of traditional (and sometimes pre-democratic) forms of religious, community and family life, the mainstream green critique of the welfare state can be seen as an attack 'from the left'. Broadly, green commentators identify the welfare state with the political programme of traditional social democracy, and see both as inevitably implicated in the logic of advanced capitalism. In varying ways and to differing degrees, they reject all three (Dobson, 1995).

We may summarize this green critique of the welfare state under two major headings: the welfare state and the logic of industrialism; and the welfare state as social control.

The welfare state and the logic of industrialism

The welfare state is embedded in an industrial order which is itself premised on economic growth. We have seen that such economic growth was a core component of social democratic strategy under the Keynesian welfare state. It was the engine of economic growth that was to fund the welfare state, which in turn would adjust patterns of distribution in society so as to offset the inegalitarian consequences of growth under capitalist forms. For the greens, this perspective of open-ended growth is untenable: 'an economy and society premised and organised on the basis of ever increasing levels of economic growth is impossible ("unsustainable") within the finite ecological parameters of human societies' (Barry, 1998). Theirs is a protest 'not against the failure of state and society to provide for economic growth and material prosperity, but against their all-too-considerable success in having done so, and against the price of this success' (cited in Poguntke, 1987).

According to Jacobs (1996), the 'dominant model' of economic growth underpinning improving social welfare no longer works. In part, this is an expression of familiar green arguments about the environmental 'limits to growth' (global warming, poisoning of the oceans, loss of biodiversity) but there is also an insistence that economic growth no longer generates improvements in the quality of life for most people. Rising Gross National Product (GNP) is not an index of improving well-being for the general population (indeed, the index of Sustainable Economic Welfare, which many greens prefer, has been moving steadily *downwards* over the past twenty years).

> Raising the rate of economic growth, given its current patterns, will not improve people's well-being. These patterns are generating the social costs – inequality, crime, environmental degradation, insecurity, the decline of public services and public goods – which are reducing people's perceived quality of life. (Jacobs, 1996, p. 83)

The trade-off between inequality and efficiency on which the social democratic view of the welfare state was premised (that economic inequality is justified *if* it both promotes economic growth and allows the state to compensate the losers through welfare redistribution) no longer works. We live in societies of rising income inequality in which the poorest have been left behind. The existing welfare state is not a viable long-term political arrangement because the costs of economic growth (on which it relies) are too severe for the natural and human environment, and are eventually counterproductive.

Greens also insist that the welfare state is one of the most important sites of the dominance of technological rationality or technocracy in contemporary societies. Rejection of the attempt to subjugate all forms of human and social conduct to the logic of rational domination has a long history in the New Left/Western Marxism. Retraceable at least to the writings of Horkheimer and Adorno is the view that the attempt to dominate and exploit nature (which industrialism has represented) will always enjoin the subjugation and exploitation of humankind-in-nature. It was Marcuse who described the welfare state as a 'state of unfreedom' built on 'technological rationality' and 'administered living' (1972, pp. 51–2). For the greens, the welfare state is inextricably involved in surveillance, control and the creation of social capital, to the detriment of the human(e) development of the population it administers.

This subservience to both economic growth and technical rational domination is to be understood as a part of the logic of developed capitalism. Gorz, for example, follows more traditional Marxists in arguing that the two main functions of the institutions and policies of the welfare state are 'the production of order' *and* 'the production of the right type of demand' needed for capitalist development (1985, p. 14). The welfare state, even if it emerges in response to the mobilization of the working class, is a way of discharging the social costs of capitalist development on the general public. It also serves to represent collective problems and needs as individual ones, which may be responsive to marketable goods and services. For most greens, real social needs could be met more efficiently through greater public provision (preventative rather than curative health care, public rather than private transport), but this is not consonant with the interests of capital. The welfare state has also to respond to the surplus production of social need that is generated by capitalist forms of industrial organization (for example, nervous disorders and alcoholism generated by the stress of work under capitalist imperatives). The welfare state is a part of capitalism which is itself unavoidably tied to the corrupt logic of economic growth. Neither is consistent with the support of sustainable and humane forms of social life.

Green commentators also charge that the social democratic commitment to the welfare state as a compromise based on the encouragement of capitalist economic growth means 'bracketing out' a whole range of radical issues (including socialization of production, workers' control, quality of life, the planned use of resources) which were a part of the traditional ideological baggage of pre-welfare state socialism. Its commitment to and association with the capitalist welfare state makes social democracy an impossible vehicle for radical social change. Finally, the welfare state represents a national rather than a global response to the problem of reconciling general social welfare with economic growth. As such, it depends on displacing the dysfunctions of economic growth on the less developed countries, offering a national political solution which makes global problems of welfare still more severe. The lack of real social security is expressed not only in the scale of absolute poverty across the globe (especially in sub-Saharan Africa) but also in attendant problems of military conflict, displacement of populations and international drugs trafficking which redound on the developed world (see Jacobs, 1996, pp. 41–64).

The welfare state as social control

The greens' critique of the welfare state is also intimately concerned with its implications for the exercise of 'micro-power' or social control by the state over the individual. Thus the history of the rise of the welfare state is simultaneously the history of the rise of the 'disabling professions' (Illich, 1977). In reducing the citizens of the democratic state to the clients of the welfare state, welfare institutions, under the guise of the 'helping' or 'caring' professions, exercise ever greater control over the personal lives of individuals. Far from 'enabling', welfare state professionals – doctors, social workers, teachers, housing administrators – much more characteristically 'disable' their clients, stripping them of the competence (and often the legal right) to make their own decisions and making them increasingly dependent on the state and its paid professionals. For Lasch, 'the expansion of welfare services presupposed the reduction of the citizen to a consumer of expertise' (1978, p. 224). According to Illich, 'industrial welfare systems . . . incapacitate people's autonomy through forcing them – via legal, environmental, and social changes – to become consumers of care' (1978, p. 41). Pluralistic self-reliance, focused on communal and individual initiatives grounded in native knowledge and competences, is displaced by the legalized monopoly of standardized state management of state-defined needs in a subject and dependent clientele. As a consequence, the welfare state is necessarily anti-democratic. What should properly be the subject of choices made by individuals or collectivities becomes the province of professionals, whose credentials are state certified and whose interventions are state legitimized. Choosing to give birth at home or without medical supervision, building one's own home to one's own specifications, educating one's own children at home in one's own way are all choices/forms of self-help proscribed by the state. Furthermore, even the best intentioned and 'enabling' of welfare state interventions are undermined by their bureaucratic form. Even where the welfare state is predominantly the product of working-class agitation to counterbalance the despotic control of capital, it cannot avoid itself becoming a form of domination over its subject population. Typically, the greens insist that 'the conflicts and contradictions of advanced industrial societies can no longer be resolved through étatism, political regulation and the proliferating inclusion of ever more claims and issues on the agenda of bureaucratic authorities' (Offe, 1985–6, p. 4). In so far as social welfare is a response to real needs – and not simply to the 'false needs' created by the requirements of industrial capitalism – these can only be satisfactorily met by small scale, cooperative, 'bottom up' self-production/self-management.

Thesis 11

The welfare state is a particular form of the industrial capitalist state. Even under social democratic auspices, it is vitiated by the logic of unsustainable economic growth and alienating bureaucratic forms

In practice, green parties often stand for a quite extensive, as well as an extensively reformed, welfare state, built around the idea of universalism. The UK Green Party, for example, builds its welfare strategy around the idea of a citizen's income (sometimes called a basic income) – an income paid to all citizens unconditionally and universally – and the phasing out of means-tested benefits. It commits to a shorter working week, more investment in pre-school childcare, a substantial increase in Child Benefit and an upgrading of the (affordable) housing stock. This would be funded by the introduction of eco-taxes, a Land Value Tax and increases in inheritance tax and income tax (Green Party, 2005). We shall return to an evaluation of the core element in this green perspective – the idea of a citizen's income – in the closing chapter.

The Historical Uniqueness of Welfare States' Development

All of those positions considered thus far have tended to identify one or more mobilizing principles underlying welfare state development. But I have already observed that not all commentators are persuaded that the development of welfare states can be most effectively explained in terms of these kinds of metatheoretical principles. In particular, and in response to the accounts of both left and right, criticism has increasingly been directed towards (1) the persistent functionalist or derivationist elements in such accounts; (2) the dominance of society-centered over state-centred explanations; and (3) the dominance of class to the exclusion of other social forces in understandings of the generation of social policy. In a variety of ways, such critics have called for a greater concentration on the *historical uniqueness* of particular welfare states' development and an emphasis on multiple sources of social policy initiatives. In the final sections of this chapter, I turn to a brief assessment of this theoretically more sceptical approach.

Interest group politics and the welfare state

Given this theoretical scepticism, those who, for example, stress the importance of interest group activity in the emergence of welfare states do not represent this as the definitive guiding principle of welfare state development. Nor do they seek to isolate some particular social force/social movement as the prevailing fact of such evolution. Indeed, in contrast to the major positions already outlined, they insist on (1) the independent importance of the political processes through which welfare state policies emerge; (2) the importance of existing state formations for the structure of (early) welfare states; and (3) the historically unique configurations of social and political forces which shaped welfare state development in different countries. Advocates of this position[5] do not argue that the process of welfare state development is wholly indeterminate (and that industrialization, urbanization and democratization have no independent effect on the emergence of welfare regimes), but they do maintain:

- that prevailing accounts give too much weight to such determining societal prerequisites;
- that a more accurate understanding of the substantial differences between welfare states requires a closer investigation of their particular and peculiar historical circumstances;
- that many existing accounts overstress the salience of social class as a source of welfare state development, to the neglect of other social forces – based, for example, on age or gender structures – and other social groups – for example, professional associations, civil servants and veterans' organizations;
- that the competing social forces at the fount of the welfare state must be understood to have been mobilized and accommodated within the comparatively new medium of mass democratic political organization.

The intent of the interest group politics approach is above all a procedural or methodological rather than a substantive one, calling for a clear interrogation of the historical record to be used to discipline the rather grander generalizations of some other approaches. However, a number of substantive claims can be identified with this perspective.[6] Among the most important of these are:

- that economic and demographic change affect the structure of group resources and demands for welfare spending and that the existence of democratic institutions facilitates the realization of these group interests;
- that non-class, ascriptive groups (notably, the retired and the aged) are central to the growth of the welfare state;
- that democratic political procedures (voting participation and electoral competition) are important for explaining the translation of group demands into higher spending;

---

[5] Pampel and Williamson, 1988, 1989; Pampel and Stryker, 1990; Weir et al., 1988b; Baldwin 1990; Skocpol, 1992.
[6] Piven and Cloward, 1971, 1977, 1985; Block et al., 1987; Ashford, 1986a, 1986b; Ashford and Kelley, 1986; Gilbert, 1966, 1970; Berkowitz and McQuaid, 1980; J. Hay, 1975, 1978a, 1978b; R. Hay, 1977; Mommsen, 1981; Ritter, 1985; Lash and Urry, 1987; De Swaan, 1988; Hennock, 1987; Skocpol, 1980; Ullman, 1981; Foot, 1975; Klein, 1983; Gale Research Co., 1985; P. Pierson, 1994.

- that where (working-) class organization is poorly developed, mobilization for public welfare measures is likely to be by other subaltern social forces, for example, by the unemployed or ethnic groups;
- that sectoral interests (for example, those of agriculture), professional interests (doctors) and business interests (private insurance companies) may have a decisive effect in shaping the particular character of welfare legislation;
- that within any given broadly defined group, there may be a diversity of interests for and against the welfare state. Thus, for example, differing levels of the medical profession may have differing attitudes to compulsory health insurance (Britain in 1911); differing groups of workers may have differing attitudes to state provision of welfare (where, for example, trade unions offer health insurance as a collectively bargained 'fringe benefit') (US in the 1930s); employers in monopoly and competitive sectors of the economy may also have quite differing approaches to, and interests in, the state provision of welfare (Germany in the 1930s); or attitudes may change through time (employers in the UK and Germany in the late nineteenth and early twentieth centuries).

State-centred approaches to the welfare state

Again, what have been labelled 'state-centred' approaches to welfare state development do not generally deny the salience of the sorts of issues raised in the major theoretical positions outlined above. They recognize the importance of industrialization, urbanization, democratization and class interests. However, they do insist that all these influences are mediated in practice by the independent effects of state organization. That is, the relationship between the 'macro' causes of welfare state development and actual social policies and practices is shaped by the differing configurations of historically unique nation-states. Characteristically, Theda Skocpol, one of the leading advocates of 'bringing the state back in', criticizes both pluralist and Marxist accounts of social change and welfare state development as being too *society* centred. What are required are 'state-centred accounts of comparative historical development' (Skocpol, 1985; see also Nordlinger, 1981).

This point is pursued by Douglas Ashford in *The Emergence of the Welfare States*. He insists that 'the many forms of the contemporary welfare state are the manifestations of the complex and diverse compromises forged by political leaders and administrative officials over many years.' Thus 'political, institutional and even constitutional issues affected the transition from liberal to welfare state as much as economic and social realities' (1986b, pp. 2, 3–4).

Abram De Swaan is still more explicit:

> Social security was not the achievement of the organized working classes, nor the result of a capitalist conspiracy to pacify them . . . The initiative for compulsory, nationwide and collective arrangements to insure workers against income loss came from reformist politicians and administrators in charge of state bureaucracies. (1988, p. 9)

The perspective of the welfare state emerging fully formed and wholly determined from a set of pre-existing social prerequisites is a misconception based on historical hindsight. The growth of the welfare state was 'a gradual and often uninformed process propelled as much by ambitious politicians and rather visionary civil servants as by an abstract notion of a crumbling social order or of fears of major social unrest' (Ashford, 1986b, pp. 3–4).

To see the (welfare) state as simply a response to the needs of capital or else as the product of industrialization is inadequate. What is required is an account of the process by which social issues move on to the policy agenda, what policy proposals are accepted, which rejected (and why), and how and by whom such policies are implemented. Correspondingly, state-centred accounts tend to stress *the growth of states' competence*. The growth of the state's capacity to act is a subtype of the more general evolution of bureaucratic forms of organized action. Thus, to an extent, the development of the welfare state is a product of the expanded techniques of information processing, communication and surveillance which make the nation-state (and, especially important in the welfare field, the overcoming of localism) possible (Berkowitz and McQuaid, 1980).

Such accounts also stress the independent importance of the state's *learning capacity*. This is an approach most fully developed by Hugh Heclo. Reviewing the varying sources of social policy development, he concludes that 'while parties and interest groups did occasionally play extremely important parts, it was the civil services that provided the most constant analysis and review underlying most courses of government action.'

Furthermore, the politics of such social policy initiatives is not best understood as the exercise of power but rather through the idea of 'politics as learning'.

> Governments not only 'power' . . . they also puzzle. Policy-making is a form of collective puzzlement on society's behalf; it entails both deciding and knowing. The process of making pension, unemployment, and superannuation policies has extended beyond deciding what 'wants' to accommodate, to include problems of knowing who might want something, what is wanted, what should be wanted, and how to turn even the most sweet-tempered general agreement into concrete collective action. (Heclo, 1974, p. 305)

The principal agency and location of this political learning process has been the public bureaucracy.

The general tenor of this state-centred approach is effectively summarized by Skocpol and Ikenberry:

> the ideas for modern social insurance and welfare policies came from domestic experimentation and transnational communication, and they were put into effect by sets of political executives, civil administrators, and political party leaders who were looking for innovative ways to use existing or readily extendable government administrative capacities to deal with (initially key segments of) the emerging industrial working class. Pioneering social insurance innovations, especially, were not simply responses to the socioeconomic dislocations of industrialism; nor were they straightforward concessions to demands by trade unions or working-class based parties. Rather they are best understood . . . as sophisticated efforts at anticipatory political incorporation of the industrial working class, coming earlier (on the average) in paternalist, monarchical-bureaucratic regimes that hoped to head off working-class radicalism, and coming slightly later (on the average) in gradually democratizing liberal parliamentary regimes, whose competing political parties hoped to mobilize new working-class voters into their existing political organizations and coalitions. (1983, pp. 89–90)

State-centred accounts of social policy development have tended to criticize prevailing explanations for their neglect of the (indeterminate) process of policy formulation and the (uncertain) practice of policy implementation. Correspondingly, they do not themselves produce a firm list of expectations to which the actual history of all welfare states can be expected to correspond. They do however recognize important similarities between actual welfare states and these tend to be addressed in terms of (1) the international diffusion of social policy patterns (as part of the social policy 'learning' process); (2) the similarity of bureaucratic development; and (3) the ubiquity of the challenges to which social policy must respond. But a greater emphasis is placed on the *uniqueness* of differing welfare states,[7] particularly around:

- the nature of state-building (federal/absolutist past, imperialism, period of state formation);
- the nature of the civil service and its reform (period at which formed/reformed; meritocratic or appointed/nepotic);
- the nature of the state (period at which democratized; federal or unitary);

---

[7] Orloff and Skocpol, 1984; Quadagno, 1984, 1987, 1988b, 1994; Skocpol, 1980, 1992; Weir et al., 1988a; Orloff, 1988; Skocpol and Amenta, 1986; Amenta and Skocpol, 1989; Amenta and Carruthers, 1988; Baldwin, 1990; P. Pierson, 1994; Leibfried and Pierson, 1995.

- the relationship of the state to powers in civil society (incorporation or isolation; attitude to organized labour and/or organized capital).

> **Thesis 12a**
>
> The (partially indeterminate) development of welfare states must be understood in a comparative and historical context. Among the most important sources of this development are the actions of interest groups, nationally unique political configurations and varying patterns of state organization

State-centred approaches to welfare state retrenchment

More recently, this approach has been extended and amended to focus on explaining processes of welfare state retrenchment (or its absence). This is a position most strongly identified with the work of Paul Pierson (1994, 1996, 1998, 2000). The puzzle that Pierson addresses is why, in the face of so many calls for retrenchment and so many pressures on existing welfare institutions, there have been so few really substantial reductions in the size of developed welfare states. The essence of the answer lies in the very large communities of political support that have built up behind welfare state programmes over the past half century or more: 'maturing social programmes produce new organised interests, the consumers and providers of social services, that are usually well placed to defend the welfare state' (Pierson, 1996, p. 178). He draws attention to a pattern of *path dependency* in which programmes, institutions and practices, once firmly established, become extremely difficult to reverse. Existing commitments and expectations 'lock in' policy-makers. This helps to explain why it is so difficult to introduce pension policy changes, despite the seeming imperative for reform: 'once in place, such systems may face incremental cutbacks, but they are notoriously resistant to radical reform' (1996, p. 317). This means that, in sum, the 'new' politics of the welfare state should be seen less as a politics of 'retrenchment' than a 'politics of permanent austerity'. The politics of welfare in hard times becomes less about claiming credit for expansion and more about avoiding blame for retrenchment. Under these circumstances, the general explanations of welfare state *expansion* (especially those associated with the idea of *power resources*) will prove an increasingly unreliable guide to likely welfare state development. For this, we need to look at context-specific and historically unique welfare state configurations in which political actors seek, within the limits set by established interests and institutions, to manage a series of internal and external challenges without grave loss of support. We return to this approach in much more detail in chapter 6.

Thesis 12b

The (partially indeterminate) development of welfare states must be understood in a comparative and historical context. In an epoch of 'permanent austerity', political actors seek to manage decrementalism in a way that avoids the loss of support within a context in which the scope for reform is severely limited by historically established practices and constituencies of interest

Conclusion

Both interest group and state-centred approaches are concerned less with the generic development of *the* welfare state than with the historically unique development of differing welfare states. Indeed, if we are to make an informed evaluation of the multiplicity of theoretical claims outlined in these opening chapters and of the likely prospects for change in the future, it is essential to consider these historical patterns of welfare state development. It is to just such a consideration that we turn in chapter 4.

PART II
Origins and Development of the Welfare State

4
From the Beginning to the 'Golden Age', 1880–1975

For many people, the welfare state is a product of the period immediately following the end of the Second World War. In the Anglo-Saxon world, it is widely identified with the (partial) implementation of the recommendations of Sir William Beveridge's celebrated Report on Social Insurance in the first years of the postwar British Labour government. The very term 'welfare state' is widely associated with Archbishop Temple's wartime contrast between the *power state* of Nazi Germany and the *welfare state* which was to be the ambition and promise of postwar Allied reconstruction (Temple, 1941, 1942; Zimmern, 1934).[1] This common understanding may well be justified inasmuch as most of the developed capitalist world saw a quantitative and, at times, qualitative leap in the public provision of welfare in the twenty-five years following the war. Yet, while the world was profoundly altered by the experience of world war, after 1945 as after 1918, there were important elements of continuity with the prewar order, not least in the provision of public welfare. In recent years, there has been a growing recognition that if we are to understand the experience of the 'Golden Age' of the welfare state after 1945 and the epoch of 'crisis' after 1970, we need to consider their common origins in a much earlier period of public welfare innovation. Correspondingly, this chapter offers a synoptic reconstruction of the history of the welfare state which runs from its origins in the last third of the nineteenth century through to the period of its much accelerated growth after 1945.

---

[1] Ashford (1986b) attributes the first use of 'welfare state' to A. Zimmern (1934). It is sometimes suggested that the term 'welfare state' was already in common usage in the UK by the late 1930s. For a differing explanation, see Hayek, 1960, p. 502.

Before the Welfare State

In fact, welfare states are little more than a hundred years old and mass social democratic movements little older. Significantly, welfare states tended to emerge in societies in which capitalism and the nation-state were both already well established and these pre-existing economic and state formations have themselves prescribed the limits of subsequent welfare state development. Capitalism in its many forms has a relatively long history, stretching across several centuries and touching, if not penetrating, almost every quarter of the globe. This longevity and ubiquity of capitalism has often been seen to predominate over the comparatively modern and (territorially limited) influence of welfare administered through the state. A similar logic applies to the relationship between the welfare state and pre-existing state forms. Usually, the welfare state was a product of already existing (nation-) states, which were themselves intimately related to the rise of capitalism. Accordingly, prior elements of state formation (territoriality, monopoly over the legitimate use of violence, underwriting of the rule of law) have often been seen to predominate over the commitment to welfare even within the more highly developed welfare states.

While it is the case then that most welfare states emerged under (liberal) capitalism and its corresponding state forms, this does not define the first or original relationship between state, economy and welfare. Pre-capitalist societies subscribed to quite different views of the responsibility for social welfare. In fact, the theorists of nascent liberal capitalism had considerable success in sustaining the belief that the laws of capitalism corresponded with the laws of nature and chimed with men's 'natural instincts'.[2] The brilliance of these accounts should not however blind us to the fact that liberal capitalism was not naturally given but historically created and often, if not universally, historically imposed. Taking up this argument, C. B. Macpherson insists that the premodern notions of 'fair prices', 'fair wages' and 'just distribution' – sustained by the external sanction of church or state – themselves arose as a defence of the pre-existing order against the novel encroachment of market relations. They endorsed the subjugation of economic relations to social and political ends *under which all previous human societies had operated*. Similarly, the medieval idea of a 'Christian duty to charity', while more honoured in the breach than in the observance, reflected a view of the nature of welfare which was quite different from the maximizing individualism of the advocates of liberal capitalism. Furthermore, if we move forward to the early capitalist period itself, it was not the views of Adam Smith but those of the mercantilists,

---

[2] Definitively in Smith, 1976a, 1976b; though Smith famously had his reservations about this belief.

of whom he was so critical, that defined the prevailing view of state, economy and welfare. Under this mercantilist doctrine, the state was seen to have an active role to play in the promotion of national prosperity and a responsibility for the labouring poor, as the principal source of this national wealth. This, as seen, for example, in the Elizabethan reform and codification of the Poor Law, expressed itself in an almost modern disposition to coercion and control (Webb and Webb, 1927; Fowle, 1890; Fraser, 1981). Thus the liberal capitalist view of an extremely limited entitlement to public welfare did not arise primordially from the state of nature but had, as Gaston Rimlinger and before him Karl Polanyi noted, itself to be created and sanctioned by the 'liberal break' in states' practice (Rimlinger, 1974; Polanyi, 1944). That is, the non-intervention of the state under liberal capitalism did not arise from a preordained 'state of nature' but had consciously to be created by the state's *disengagement* from previous patterns of intervention in the securing of social welfare (albeit that the premodern state and its interventions were wholly different from their modern counterparts).

Nor did the 'minimal' nineteenth-century state 'stand off' from involvement in the economy and the provision of welfare. Victorian Britain, sometimes depicted as the very essence of laissez-faire liberal capitalism and the 'night-watchman' state, saw the implementation of a wide range of measures on the control of factory work, the quality of housing, the securing of public health, the provision of public education, the municipalization of basic services and compulsory workers' compensation following industrial accidents (Roberts, 1960; Mommsen, 1981; Ensor, 1936; Evans, 1978). Even the definitively liberal US made federal provision in the nineteenth century not only for public education but also for the public support of the blind, dumb, insane and insane/indigent, as well as for public Boards of Health (Trattner, 1988; Katz, 1986). Other states with a more paternalistic and activist state tradition saw still more and more intrusive public regulation of welfare. Thus the prelude to Bismarck's innovative welfare legislation in a newly unified Germany was a tradition of (sometimes compulsory) welfare and insurance legislation in nineteenth-century Prussia.[3] Again, states with a colonial background were often developmentally precocious in their welfare legislation. This in part explains the rapid and early development of the welfare state in Australia and New Zealand (Castles, 1985).

In practice, most of the developed capitalist countries considered here have institutional arrangements for the provision of public welfare dating

---

[3] See J. Tampke, 1981, pp. 72–5; Rimlinger, 1974, pp. 102–15; Ritter argues that 'the 1854 law on miners' provident societies was of central importance in influencing the design of Germany's later social insurance legislation of the 1880s' (1985, pp. 17–21).

back several centuries. Most had legislated some form of Poor Law, under which specified (generally local) public authorities were charged with the responsibility for raising and disbursing (often under pain of some civic penalty for the recipient) limited funds for the relief of destitution (Webb and Webb, 1910– ; Bruce, 1968; Henriques, 1979; Samuelsson, 1968, pp. 129–30; Axinn and Levin, 1975; Fowle, 1890). The concern of these earlier states was primarily with the maintenance of public order, the punishment of vagrancy and the management of the labour market, rather than the well-being of the poor.[4] With the increasing spread of industrialization, a number of nineteenth-century states provided for the maintenance of public health, the regulation of conditions of employment and limited public education. These states also showed a growing interest in the day-to-day surveillance and management of their national populations (Giddens, 1985, pp. 172–97; Mitchell, 1975; Foucault, 1975).

Origins of the Welfare State

Abram De Swaan has argued that 'the development of a public system of social insurance has been an administrative and political innovation of the first order, comparable in significance to the introduction of representative democracy' (1988, p. 149). Yet for all its importance, it was an innovation that was both gradual and rather mundane, and there are considerable difficulties in defining with any precision the dates at which national welfare states became established. The implementation of some measure of public control over welfare is hardly a sufficient criterion for such a definition and few would want to characterize even the most developed of these nineteenth-century capitalist states as welfare states. But identifying a point along a continuum of expanding public provision as *the* threshold of the welfare state is itself somewhat arbitrary. A substantial difficulty is that those traditional accounts through which 'the welfare state' moved into common usage have tended to describe it in terms of that state's *intentions*, that is, as a state principally concerned to realize the welfare aspirations of its subjects (see, for example, Hall, 1952). One obvious objection to this approach is that such an aspiration *cannot* be taken to define the intention or purpose of the welfare state. A still more fundamental objection is that attributing a global *intentionality* to the state and seeking to define it in terms of this intention is itself unsustainable

---

[4] Graphically, Fowle declared that 'in England, France, Spain, and the German Empire, we read the same dismal tale of whipping, branding, the pillory, burning the ear, cropping the ear, couples chained together to cleanse sewers, long terms of imprisonment, and, finally, death itself, in hundreds every year in every country' (1890, p. 43).

(Weber, 1968, vol. 1, p. 55). At the same time, there is clearly a qualitative difference between a comparatively tiny nineteenth-century bureaucracy devoting a few hundred thousand pounds each year to the provision of poor relief and a modern state directing as much as half of its massively enhanced expenditure to the provision of social welfare. While offering no definitive resolution, this study locates the origins of the welfare state around three sets of criteria:

1 *First introduction of social insurance* This is a widely used indicator of welfare state development. Although very modest by contemporary standards, in both breadth and depth of coverage, these are the programmes which have developed into the major institutional (and financial) elements of the welfare state. They entail the recognition that the incapacity to earn a living through contingencies such as old age, sickness or unemployment is a normal condition in industrialized market societies and that it is legitimately the business of the state to organize for collective provision against the loss of income arising from these contingencies (Flora and Heidenheimer, 1981a; Flora, 1986; see also the reservations of C. Jones, 1985).

2 *The extension of citizenship and the depauperization of public welfare* The legitimization of social insurance means also a change in the relationship of the state to the citizen and of both to the provision of public welfare. First, the interest of the state in public welfare is extended beyond the traditional concerns with the relief of destitution and the maintenance of public order (albeit that these remain major elements in even the most developed welfare states). Secondly, the provision of social insurance is increasingly seen as a part of the assemblage of rights and duties which binds the state and the (expanding) citizenry. Thirdly (and correspondingly), the receipt of public welfare becomes not a *barrier* to political participation but a *benefit* of full citizenship.[5] Simple indices of this extension of citizenship are the dates of the inauguration of male and universal suffrage and the date at which the receipt of public welfare ceases to be a bar to full citizenship (that is, no longer entails disenfranchisement).

3 *Growth of social expenditure* One of the most important aspects of the developed welfare state is the sheer quantity of public spending it commands. Throughout the twentieth century (at least until the 1970s), the welfare state commanded a sometimes rapidly growing proportion of a much enhanced national product. Clearly there is no critical threshold figure at which the welfare state may be said to have begun, but as an indicator of this important quantitative aspect of welfare

---

[5] On the importance of claims to welfare as rights, see Goodin, 1988.

state development, we may take a social expenditure of 3 per cent of GNP as a notional indicator of the *origins* of the welfare state. It may be useful to compare this threshold with the date at which social expenditure exceeds 5 per cent of GNP.

The Birth of the Welfare State: 1880–1914

Cross-national evidence of these developments is varyingly approximate. We may be reasonably certain about dates for the extension of suffrage and for the first introduction of various measures of social insurance. However, these last cover programmes which vary considerably in range, expenditure and funding criteria, and this may mask important differences in the social and political impact of seemingly similar initiatives. Of these differences, perhaps the most important was whether provision was tax

Table 4.1   Year of introduction of social insurance (OECD countries)

	Industrial accident	Health	Pension	Unemploy- ment	Family allowances
Belgium	1903	1894	1900	1920	1930
Netherlands	1901	1929	1913	1916	1940
France	1898	1898	1895	1905	1932
Italy	1898	1886	1898	1919	1936
Germany	1871	1883	1889	1927	1954
Ireland	1897	1911	1908	1911	1944
UK	1897	1911	1908	1911	1945
Denmark	1898	1892	1891	1907	1952
Norway	1894	1909	1936	1906	1946
Sweden	1901	1891	1913	1934	1947
Finland	1895	1963	1937	1917	1948
Austria	1887	1888	1927	1920	1921
Switzerland	1881	1911	1946	1924	1952
Australia	1902	1945	1909	1945	1941
New Zealand	1900	1938	1898	1938	1926
Canada	1930	1971	1927	1940	1944
USA	1930	–	1935	1935	–

These categories include schemes which were initially voluntary but state-aided as well as those that were compulsory.
Sources: Flora, 1987a, pp. 144, 210, 433, 559, 627, 777; Flora, 1987b, vol. 1, p. 454; Flora and Heidenheimer, 1981a, p. 83; Dixon and Scheurell, 1989, pp. 151, 245, 192.

Table 4.2 Welfare state innovators: first introduction of major welfare state programmes

	First	*Second*	*Third*
Industrial accident insurance	Germany (1871)	Switzerland (1881)	Austria (1887)
Health insurance	Germany (1883)	Italy (1886)	Austria (1888)
Pensions	Germany (1889)	Denmark (1891)	France (1895)
Unemployment compensation	France (1905)	Norway (1906)	Denmark (1907)
Family allowances	Austria (1921)	New Zealand (1926)	Belgium (1930)
Male suffrage	France (1848)	Switzerland (1848)	Denmark (1849)
Universal suffrage	New Zealand (1893)	Australia (1902)	Finland (1907)

Sources: Flora, 1987b, vol. 1, p. 454; Flora and Heidenheimer, 1981a; Dixon and Scheurell, 1989.

funded or contributory. These figures may also conceal the extent to which a society's commitment to the public redress of the consequences of market disutilities is represented by alternative policies (for example, public works or retraining rather than unemployment compensation). However, these cautions having been sounded, the figures do reveal a striking historical pattern.

In the thirty years between Germany's initiation of health insurance in 1883 and the outbreak of war in 1914, all the countries cited, with the exception of Canada and the US, had introduced some state-sponsored system of workmen's compensation. Even within the US, considerable advances were made towards the end of this period in individual *states'* provision (Axinn and Levin, 1975, p. 131; Reede, 1947; Kudrle and Marmor, 1981).[6] In the same period, eleven of the thirteen European countries had introduced measures to support health insurance and nine had legislated for old age pensions (as had Australia and New Zealand). Although compensation for unemployment was generally the last of the four initial measures of social insurance to be introduced, by 1920 ten of

---

[6] Kudrle and Marmor (1981) cite evidence that about 30 per cent of the US workforce was covered by workmens' compensation legislation by 1915.

Table 4.3   The expansion of citizenship

	Male universal suffrage	Universal adult suffrage
Belgium	1894	1948
Netherlands	1918	1922
France	1848	1945
Italy	1913	1946
Germany	1871	1919
Ireland	1918	1923
UK	1918	1928
Denmark	1849[a]	1918
Norway	1900	1915
Sweden	1909	1921
Finland	1907	1907
Austria	1907	1919
Switzerland	1848	1971
Australia	1902[a]	1902[a]
New Zealand	1879[b]	1893[b]
Canada	1920	1920
USA	1860[b]	1920

[a] with significant restrictions.
[b] largely restricted to Europeans/whites.
Sources: Flora, 1987b, vol. 1; Mackie and Rose, 1982; Taylor and Hudson, 1983.

the European countries had acknowledged some form of state responsibility for protection against the consequences of unemployment. What table 4.2 also shows is that for most countries family allowances belong to a 'second generation' of welfare legislation. Only a third of the states cited had legislated for family allowances by the outbreak of the Second World War.

Turning to *the expansion of citizenship*, there is a strong correspondence (though, as we shall see, no straightforward causal link) between the coming of *male* universal suffrage and the earliest development of social insurance. In the quarter century between 1894 and 1920, eleven of the seventeen countries achieved (more or less) universal male suffrage. Notably, those that had achieved full male suffrage earlier (including Germany, France, Denmark and New Zealand) were also among the most precocious of welfare innovators. We might also note that New Zealand, which was 'a generation early' in extending the vote to women (while restricting this right to Europeans), was also 'a generation early' in introducing family allowances. It is also towards the end of this period that we

Table 4.4 The growth of social expenditure

	Social expenditure 3%+ of GDP	Social expenditure 5%+ of GDP
Belgium	1923	1933
Netherlands	1920	1934
France	1921	1931
Italy	1923	1940
Germany	1900	1915
Ireland	1905	1920
UK	1905	1920
Denmark	1908	1918
Norway	1917	1926
Sweden	1905	1921
Finland	1926	1947
Austria	1926	1932
Switzerland	by 1900	1920
Australia	1922	1932
New Zealand	1911	1920
Canada	1921	1931
USA	1920	1931

Sources: Flora, 1986, 1987a, 1987b; Mitchell, 1975; Taylor and Hudson, 1983; US Department of Commerce, 1975, part 1, p. 340; Urquhart, 1965; Commonwealth Bureau of Census and Statistics (Australia), 1910– ; New Zealand Census and Statistics Office, 1882– .

see the abolition of rules disenfranchising those who had been in receipt of public welfare. As late as 1894, universalization of the suffrage in Belgium explicitly excluded 'les mendiants et vagabonds internés dans une maison de refuge . . . par decision des juges de paix' (beggars and tramps confined to refuges . . . by decision of justices of the peace) (Orban, 1908, p. 24). However, many countries extending their suffrage in the early twentieth century reversed this disqualification of paupers from voting. The enfranchisement of paupers was effected during this period in, for example, the UK (1918), Norway (1919) and Sweden (1921) (Flora, 1987b, vol. 1; Rawlings, 1988, p. 98). This is an important indicator of the transition from public welfare as an *alternative* to citizenship to public welfare as one of the *rights* of citizenship. As we shall see later, this evidence does not however justify the unqualified claim that it was democratization that created the welfare state.

Dates for *the growth of social expenditure* in this early period must be approached with especial caution. Differing national criteria in defining 'social expenditure', differences in the calculation of national income, difficulties in aggregating national and subnational expenditures and the unreliability and paucity of figures before 1945 mean that these expenditure thresholds must be seen to be very approximate. Certainly they should not be taken to define some international sequence of rising expenditure. Yet the overall figures do give compelling expression to the modest but consistent growth in social expenditure throughout this period. With the possible exception of Germany and Switzerland, it appears that none of these countries had reached social expenditure levels of 3 per cent by 1900. Yet by 1920 more than half had reached this threshold, and by 1930 all had passed the 3 per cent figure. Indeed, about a third of these states passed the 5 per cent threshold during the 1920s and most of the others were to follow in the early and middle years of the 1930s (years in which increasing demands on social insurance funds had often to be met from a *falling* national product under circumstances of depression).

Welfare States 1920–1975: The Epoch of Growth

In fact, this experience of the expansion of social budgets in the interwar years helps to isolate the most consistent and remarkable feature of the welfare states in the whole of the period down to the mid-1970s – that is, the ubiquitous dynamic of *sustained growth*. By the 1970s, all of the welfare states we are considering were quite different from what they had been at the end of the First World War. Much else in the advanced capitalist societies had changed with, and sometimes because of them. This period also saw growth in the number of welfare states beyond Western Europe and North America. This process began in Latin America in the 1920s and progressed through the Maghreb and Central America in the 1940s to the newly industrialized states of the Far East in the 1950s and beyond (see figure 4.1). The core institutions of the welfare state are now so commonplace that we are perhaps inclined to forget the sheer scale of the transformation wrought between 1920 and 1970. The pace of growth varied between differing phases, differing programmes and different countries, and here, as elsewhere, caution is required in talking about the generic experience of *the* welfare state. Yet so substantial and striking are the developments of this period that at least some generalizations are warranted.

The growth of the social budget

First, there is the sheer scale and ubiquity of growth in the social budget. In 1914, only seven of the countries in table 4.4 had reached social expenditure levels of 3 per cent of GNP. By 1940, nearly all had reached social

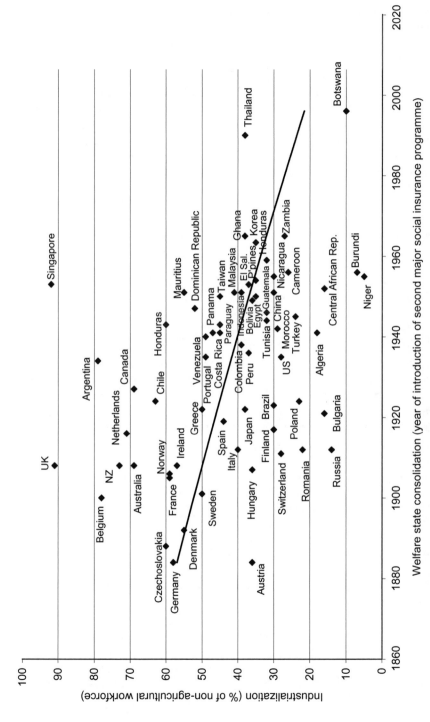

Figure 4.1 Industrialization and the consolidation of welfare (global)

expenditure levels in excess of 5 per cent. In the early 1950s, this figure ranged between 10 per cent and 20 per cent. By the mid-1970s, among the European welfare states, between a quarter and something more than a third of GNP was devoted to social expenditure. Even the most 'reluctant' welfare states saw a wholesale transformation of their public budgets. In the US, total social expenditure rose from 2.4 per cent of GNP in 1890 to 20.2 per cent in 1981. Even in Japan, where an exceptional proportion of welfare is organized and delivered through private corporations, the social budget expanded from 1.4 per cent of GDP in 1890 to 16.2 per cent in 1985 (Flora, 1986, vol. 1, p. xxii; Maddison, 1984; Minami, 1986, pp. 332ff; Oshima, 1965, pp. 368–71; OECD, 1985b, 1988a; US Bureau of Statistics, 1975). By 2000, the largest Latin American welfare states had reached expenditure levels around 20 per cent (ECLAC, 2003).

Much of the remarkable overall growth in public expenditure in the twentieth century can be attributed to the growth of the social budget and this rapidly growing proportion of national wealth devoted to social welfare must be set against the background of a sevenfold increase in average per capita output in the major developed economies over the past hundred years or so (Maddison, 1984, p. 59).

Incremental growth and demographic change

A substantial source of this remarkable and general growth in the social budget was the maturing of rights and claims as pensions legislated in the 'take-off' period came 'on-stream'. This was substantially an incremental and inertial development which was the more pronounced because of certain *demographic changes* which were common to most of the advanced capitalist societies. The most important of these changes were the continuing increase in life expectancy and the decline in mortality rates. For example, life expectancy at birth of females rose between 1900 and 1967 from the age of 49.4 to 74.1 (England and Wales), from 47 to 75 (France) and from 46.6 to 73.5 (West Germany). Crude annual death rates fell in the same countries between 1900 and 1950 from 18.2 (per thousand) to 12.5 in England and Wales, from 21.9 to 12.7 in France and from 22.1 to 10.5 in West Germany (Winter, 1982; Mitchell, 1975, pp. 104–24). What did constitute an authentically *political* intervention was the common practice of introducing (contributory) pensions *before* sufficient premiums had been collected to fund these on an actuarially sound basis. The electoral call for 'pensions now' was a powerful one, even in the characteristically insurance-minded US (Quadagno, 1988a; Fraser, 1973, p. 213; Rimlinger, 1974, p. 234).

It is likely that the severest demographic challenge to the welfare state lies in the future, but the growing aged population in advanced capitalism has certainly hugely extended the costs of the welfare state not just in the provision of pensions, but in those other costly areas where the elderly are disproportionate users of services, as in public health provision. The proportion of the population aged sixty-five or over in the OECD countries rose from 9.7 per cent in 1960 to 12.7 per cent in 1985, and is projected to increase further to 18.0 per cent by 2020 (OECD, 1988a, p. 11). Meanwhile, Heikkinen notes that 'the use of [health and social] services among the aged is 3–4 times that expected on the basis of proportion of the population' (1984, p. 162).

In fact, the demographic structure of the several welfare states has varied. For example, the disproportionately youthful structure of the early twentieth-century New Zealand and Australian populations (as 'new', immigrant-based nations) afforded unusually favourable circumstances for their early expansion. In other countries, notably in France, social policy initiatives have been related to the demographic consequences of the Great War (especially in the number of war pensions and later in the structure of natalist policy).[7] But overall, the number of aged in the population has grown throughout the industrialized world as life expectancy has increased. In the 1880s, only 5 per cent of the population was over sixty-five. One hundred years later, the elderly constituted some 13 per cent of the population and a still higher proportion of the electorate (Heikkinen, 1984, p. 162; OECD, 1984, pp. 3–6). Still more importantly, the ratio of the economically inactive to the economically active section of the population (out of whose productive labour 'pay-as-you-go' pensions must be funded) is rising and set to continue to rise. Dependency ratios (the proportion of people aged 0–14 years plus the proportion of people aged 60 years and over to the proportion aged 15–59 years) actually *fell* in Western and Northern Europe in the 1980s because of the declining numbers of young people. But the World Bank (1994) has estimated that the old age dependency ratio is likely to rise across the OECD from around 19 per cent in 2000 to 37 per cent in 2030. The UK Treasury has estimated that whereas there were 2.3 economic contributors to each pension claimant in the UK in 1985, by 2025 this number will have fallen to 1.8 contributors to each pensioner (Heikkinen, 1984, p. 169; DHSS, 1985, p. 15). Overall, the OECD has estimated that the old age dependency ratio will double by 2040 (OECD, 1988a, p. 35).[8]

Sequential growth of welfare state programmes

Most of the welfare states considered here have also expanded their social welfare provision in terms of a broadly shared sequence. Certainly, there

---

[7] The First World War saw losses of approximately 1.3 million among the French population and an equally large 'birth deficit' (McEvedy and Jones, 1978, p. 56). See also C. A. McIntosh, 1983, esp. pp. 43–57; Ashford, 1986b, pp. 112–13; Dyer, 1978; Glass, 1940.
[8] This demographic challenge to the welfare state is extensively discussed in chapter 7.

have been differences between 'early' and 'late' adopters in terms of the comparative stage of industrialization at which social welfare was introduced, the sorts of funding regimes established and the generosity of initial coverage. There is some disagreement as to whether the spread of the welfare state is best explained in terms of *prerequisites* (with state welfare initiatives being a response to endogenous national developments) or *diffusion* (a process of international imitation of welfare state innovators). In the period before 1908, the spread seems to have been from less industrially developed and more authoritarian regimes towards the more developed and democratic. In the period between 1908 and 1923, the principal determinant of innovation appears to have been geographical proximity to an existing welfare state rather than the level of industrial development. After 1923, there is a tendency for countries to adopt welfare state measures at a lower level of their own economic development (with the notable exception of the US). Paralleling the pattern of the spread of industrialization, 'late starters' have tended to develop welfare state institutions *earlier* in their own individual development and under *more comprehensive* terms of coverage. Nonetheless, many of the late starters are still radically incomplete in terms of the four major programmes identified in the earliest Western European welfare states (Collier and Messick, 1975, p. 1301; Schneider, 1982; Alber cited in Flora, 1986, vol. 1, p. xxiv; Alber, 1982; Kuhnle, 1981; C. Pierson, 2005a).

Wherever welfare states have emerged, the *order* of adoption and expansion of programmes has been broadly similar. We can identify three sequential patterns. In terms of *programmes*, workmen's compensation for industrial accidents was generally the first measure to be adopted. This was followed by sickness and invalidity insurance, (old age) pensions and finally unemployment insurance. Though some provision for maternity occurred quite early, family allowances were generally introduced rather later and were widely viewed as an 'endowment of motherhood' rather than as insurance against the contingency of having children. Secondly, *coverage* also followed a shared pattern. Initially, coverage was limited to workers in particularly strategic industries or in peculiarly dangerous occupations. Mining, for example, was often one of the first industries to be covered (Tampke, 1981, pp. 72–3). Legislation was subsequently extended to cover all industrial workers, thence to rural/agricultural workers, and so to dependants and survivors of insured workers. Latterly, coverage was extended to the self-employed and thence characteristically to the generality of the population (or at least to all those recognized as citizens) without further discriminating criteria. (The pattern was rather different in Latin America, where it was groups of government workers – civil servants, teachers and especially army officers – who were first in line for pension provision, often on preferential terms; see C. Pierson 2005a).

Thirdly, there were broadly similar patterns in the *expansion* of programmes. Earlier extensions tended to be built on broadening the criteria of eligibility (making for more beneficiaries) and legislating for more generous benefits. Characteristically, later enhancements were built on the less restrictive application of definitions of eligibility, and from the late 1950s and 1960s onwards on the transition from flat-rate to earnings-related benefits. There was also a general tendency for programmes to proceed from voluntary to compulsory provision.

The Periodization of Welfare State Growth

In fact, it is possible to think of not just a sequential but indeed of a shared historical pattern in the development of welfare states, at least within advanced capitalism. Clearly this is not a uniform pattern. The US lacked basic federal provisions for social insurance down to 1935 and still lacks comprehensive measures for health care or family allowances. Some welfare states emerged early and then 'stagnated' (Australia), some developed early and expanded before 1940 (New Zealand), while others were marginal before the Second World War but expanded rapidly after 1945 (for example, Finland). Yet a significant historical pattern may be identified.

1918–1940: 'Consolidation' and Development

The period between the wars has often been described as a rather uneventful one for the welfare state, falling between the extensive innovations of the preceding twenty-five years and the period of remarkable growth immediately after 1945. Hamilton characteristically describes this period in the British experience as one of 'steady and purposeful social advance' (cited in Bruce, 1968, p. 255).

Yet more recent commentators have tended to see the 1920s and 1930s as the seed-bed of postwar welfare state development. For Douglas Ashford, this was the period in which serious obstacles to 'the complete nationalization of social policy' were removed, making the expansion of the welfare state after 1945 comparatively uncontentious:

> First, the liberal refuge of private or charitable assistance proved totally inadequate. Second, the private insurers learned . . . that many serious social problems exceeded the capacity of actuarially sound insurance. Third . . . professional groups were gradually co-opted into national social security programmes. Fourth, the agricultural sector first received the protection of the state . . . before substantial aid went to urban dwellers. (Ashford, 1986a, p. 107)

In Britain, Sweden and the US, for example, this is seen as the decisive epoch in establishing the institutions and practices of that more interventionist form of government in which the postwar welfare state was grounded. It also saw governments facing new choices about the macro-management of the economy and the possibility of the active and interventionist pursuit of full employment. Thus Middlemas, in his study of *Politics in Industrial Society*, argues that it was in the interwar years that a new system of 'managerial collective government', built on the negotiation and compromise of the interests of the state, organized capital and organized labour, first emerged in the UK. This was a system oriented around the amelioration of class conflict and the avoidance of systemic crisis through, among other means, the promotion of social policy (Middlemas, 1979).[9] As we shall soon see, in both Sweden and the US, the Great Depression of the early 1930s triggered new forms of government intervention in social and economic life, new relationships between state, employers and trade unions, and a process of political realignment which established new political forces at the heart of the state (Korpi, 1979, 1983; Weir and Skocpol, 1985).

Certainly in terms of coverage and cost, the interwar welfare state often dwarfs provision in the period of innovation. As the figures for social expenditure indicate, while the period between 1880 and 1920 is properly understood as the epoch of *legislative* innovation in the welfare state, it is only after 1920 that the *fiscal* consequences of these initiatives become clear. Many of the early systems of social insurance offered, like Lloyd George's old age pensions in the UK, extremely modest benefits designed for 'the very poor [and] the very respectable' (Thane, 1982, p. 83).[10] Many programmes, notably those in Germany, envisaged a strictly limited financial involvement by the state, expecting benefits to be drawn from the premiums of potential beneficiaries or their employers (Alber, 1986, pp. 40–1). However, the growth of social expenditure in the 1920s and the early 1930s is what we might have expected as the legislative innovations of the pre-1914 period yielded to the maturing of insurance and pension claims in the postwar age. In fact, this tendency for innate or incremental growth of social expenditure – growth not through legislative or executive initiative but through the maturing of pension rights or demographic change – has been a marked feature of the whole period of the welfare state.

---

[9] Although primarily concerned with the UK, Middlemas comments that his 'propositions have an importance not only for modern Britain, but most western industrialized societies' (Middlemas, 1979, p. 23).

[10] New Zealand's innovative old age pensions, for example, cost £197,292 in 1900 rising to £362,496 in 1910 (New Zealand Census and Statistics Office, 1882– : *Year-Book* for 1919).

In many countries, this process was accelerated by the consequences of the Great War. First, it led to a major expansion of pension, health, housing and rehabilitation demands from those millions incapacitated or bereaved as a consequence of the armed conflict. In Australia in 1922, for example, war pensioners outnumbered old age and invalid pensioners in a proportion of more than two to one.[11] Secondly, it conditioned politicians, bureaucrats and taxpayers to new levels of public expenditure, from which there was no wholesale retreat once the immediate demands of wartime had passed (the 'displacement effect' described by Peacock and Wiseman, 1961, pp. 52–61). Thirdly, it necessitated new forms of governmental control and administration, which were again not to be abandoned in the postwar epoch (Middlemas, 1979, p. 19).

The late 1920s and early 1930s also saw what might be described as the first 'fiscal crisis of the welfare state'.[12] The depth of the economic recession of the early 1930s occasioned the earliest major cuts in social welfare provision and demonstrated (1) that it was impossible to sustain actuarially sound social insurance under circumstances of profound economic recession; (2) that demand for social expenditure (especially unemployment compensation) was inversely related to the capacity of the economy to fund it; and (3) that to respond to this problem by cutting social expenditure would simply intensify rather than alleviate these economic problems. The scale of the difficulties of the 1930s also probably dealt the final death blow to the belief among the governing classes that the provision of social welfare or even the relief of destitution could be satisfactorily met from voluntary or charitable sources.

The US: The New Deal

The 1930s was also a decisive period in the development of two of the most widely differing and frequently contrasted welfare state regimes – those of Sweden and the US. In comparative typifications of welfare state development, these two examples are often recorded as the most

---

[11] In 1922, in Australia, there were 225,372 war pensioners, 110,278 claiming old age pensions and just 5,182 invalid pensioners. We shall see below (pp. 122–3) that the early American welfare state was largely made up of Civil War veterans. Germany, France and the UK lost a total of 3.75 million soldiers in the 1914–18 war. (*Official Year Book of the Commonwealth of Australia*, 1923; McEvedy and Jones, 1978, p. 34.)

[12] In the UK, the 1931 May Committee Report 'compounded of prejudice, ignorance and panic' recommended a cut in public expenditure of £120 million, including a 20 per cent cut in unemployment benefit. In Australia, old age, invalid and some war pensions were reduced under the terms of the Financial Emergency Act, 1931. (A. J. P. Taylor, 1965, pp. 287ff; *Official Year Book of the Commonwealth of Australia*, 1932, p. 30.)

developed (Sweden) and the least developed (US) welfare states and, given the centrality of this opposition, it is worth developing this contrast in some detail.

Ironically, in much contemporary scholarship, the *origins* of the modern American and Swedish welfare states, as a response to the consequences of the Great Depression, are seen to be remarkably similar. Thus Weir and Skocpol (1985) contrast the shared response of the US ('commercial Keynesianism') and Sweden ('social Keynesianism') to the traditionally deflationary policy of the British government. Gøsta Esping-Andersen has argued that 'at least in its early formulation, the New Deal was as social democratic as was contemporary Scandinavian social democracy' (1990, p. 28). In both countries, this period of welfare state enhancement also saw profound political realignment and the installation of the Democrats and the Social Democrats, respectively, as 'the natural party of government'. Yet the contexts in which these 'similar' institutions were to be developed (and indeed the intentions of those who initiated and developed them) were profoundly different.

It is one of the many myths of the American welfare state that there was little or no public provision of welfare before the 1930s. In fact, 'American welfare practice has a very old history', but it is a practice that 'has always been mediated by the complex structure of American federalism'. Similarly, 'public welfare always has supported more dependent people than private relief'. Yet, in the 'protean mix' of public and private provision which characterizes every welfare state, the private and especially the corporate provision of welfare has always had an unusually prominent role (Katz, 1986, pp. xiii, x, 291).

At the turn of the twentieth century, such limited public relief as there was in the US was largely locally administered according to local poor-law customs (Quadagno, 1984, p. 635; Axinn and Levin, 1975; Katz, 1986). At the local level, public welfare rolls fluctuated wildly in response to changing social and political regimes (Katz, 1986, pp. 3–109). Federal provision was substantially confined to pensions for (northern) veterans of the Civil War. However, by 1900 these federal veterans' pensions had come to constitute an extremely extensive system of surrogate social welfare. At this time, 'at least one of every two elderly, native-born, white Northern men and many of their widows received a pension from the federal government' and 'pensions were the largest expense in the federal budget after the national debt' (Katz, 1986, p. 200). In 1913, I. M. Rubinow, 'one of the nation's leading social insurance advocates', calculated that American pensions were costing three times as much as the supposedly advanced British system of old age pensions and covering 'several hundred thousand' more people (cited in Skocpol and Ikenberry, 1983, p. 97; Katz, 1986, p. 163). It is little wonder that Skocpol concludes that 'in terms of the proportional effort devoted to public pensions, the American federal government was hardly a "welfare laggard"; it was a precocious social-spending state' (Orloff and Skocpol, 1984, pp. 728–9; Skocpol, 1992). However, as the number of veteran claimants and their dependants declined in the early years of the twentieth century, and despite the mobilization of pensions advocates such as Rubinow, Seager and the American Association for Labor Legislation, there was no attempt to replace the veterans' programmes with a more universal system of old age pensions (see Orloff and Skocpol, 1984, p. 735; Skocpol and Ikenberry, 1983, pp. 95–100; Katz, 1986, p. 128). There was some advance in other areas of welfare provision by the individual states in the years immediately prior to the First World War. Between 1909 and 1920, forty-three states enacted legislation on workmen's compensation, and within two years of Illinois's 'Funds to Parents Act' of 1911, twenty states had provided similar cash relief programmes for widows and dependent children. Indeed, Skocpol argues that with the lapse of the veterans' pension programme 'the United States looked briefly as if it would fashion an internationally distinctive maternalist welfare state', and we now have an extensive historical record of the major part played by professional women in forging a distinctive welfare regime for mothers and children in the 1920s and into the 1930s (Skocpol, 1992, p. 526; Gordon, 1994). Yet the financial impact of these measures was severely limited and, although there was some programme enhancement in the 1920s, the prevalent welfare trend in the postwar New Era was away from the European model of social insurance towards a reliance on occupational welfare (employee representation, workers' shares, company welfare and pensions) under the rubric of welfare capitalism. However, this welfare capitalism was always largely confined to the 'progressive' corporate sector of American capital (to large companies such as Proctor and Gamble, Eastman Kodak and General Electric). It was more important as a legitimating ideology than as an effective social practice and certainly wholly unable to respond to the scale of social need generated by the Great Depression (Axinn and Levin, 1975, pp. 130–4; Brody, 1980; Skocpol and Ikenberry, 1983).

Opinions as to which social, economic and political forces shaped and were served by the expanded social policy of the New Deal are vigorously divided. So are judgements as to whether it was the 'social' or the 'economic' side of the New Deal that had the most lastingly influential impact. However, there is near universal agreement that the 'social' side of the New Deal, embodied in the 1935 Social Security Act, 'declared the birth of the [American] welfare state and established a basis for its growth and development' (Axinn and Levin, 1975, p. 195). It is also widely argued that this 'charter legislation for American social insurance and public assistance programs' set the parameters for virtually all further developments in America's 'Semi-Welfare State' (Skocpol, 1987, p. 35; Katz, 1986, pp. ix–xiv; Quadagno, 1988b).

The 1935 Act legislated for the following (Berkowitz and McQuaid, 1980, p. 103):

- A federal-state unemployment insurance programme.
- Federal grants-in-aid to the states for assistance to:
  - needy dependent children;
  - the blind;
  - the elderly.
- Matching federal funds for state spending on:
  - vocational rehabilitation;
  - infant and maternal health;
  - aid to crippled children.
- A federal old age insurance programme.

Although the 1935 Act brought the US in some measure into alignment with the welfare states of Western Europe, it was still a quite limited initiative. The provision of welfare was largely devolved to the individual states, funded from (regressive) payroll taxation rather than from general tax revenue, and allowed for very considerable state 'discretion' and for very substantial 'exceptions'. (Initially, half the employed workforce, notably black southern farm workers, was excluded from participation in Old Age Insurance.) There was an emphasis on actuarially sound insurance principles and 'earned benefits', the rhetoric of which long outlived its early compromise in practice. Generally, where entitlement was not earned through insurance payments, benefits were means tested and the 1935 legislation institutionalized the time-served distinction between social security entitlement and residual claims to 'welfare'. Traditional relief of destitution (among the able-bodied poor) remained a local responsibility. The legislation made no provision for either health insurance or a family allowance.

Sweden: 'Historic Compromise'

The 1930s was also a decade of major change in the Swedish welfare state and of a still more profound political realignment, the nature of which is no less fiercely debated than that surrounding the New Deal. In fact, the background of national public welfare was already more extensive in Sweden than in its North American counterpart. Sweden had a more developed national bureaucracy and a centralized state tradition dating back over several centuries. Schooling had been compulsory since 1842, state support of sickness and occupational injury insurance had been legislated around the turn of the twentieth century and Sweden had been the first state to introduce universal and compulsory (if minimal) old age pensions in 1913. At the start of the 1930s, its social expenditure as a proportion of GDP stood at 7 per cent, compared with 4.2 per cent in the US (Olsson, 1986, p. 5). However, Swedish provision compared with that of its near neighbour Denmark, for example, was very modest. As Esping-Andersen notes:

> the long era of conservative and liberal rule [prior to 1932] had produced remarkably few social reforms. There was no unemployment insurance, except for financially weak union funds, and insurance coverage for sickness was marginal . . . old age pension . . . benefits were meager at best. In addition, no system of public job creation was in effect when the economic depression led to explosive unemployment. (1985, p. 153)

It was under these circumstances, with unemployment rising rapidly, that the first Scandinavian Social Democratic government was elected in Sweden in 1932. In fact, the Social Democrats, with 42 per cent of the popular vote, were reliant on the coalition support of the peasant-based Agrarian Party, and were consequently obliged to compromise the interests of their own core working-class constituency (in welfare reform and full employment) with policies for agricultural price support (in the interests of the rural peasantry). While 'social reform was a top priority [and] the party actually developed a long-range strategy for full social and industrial citizenship . . . by and large, political energies were concentrated on the immediate problems of crisis management and economic relief' (Esping-Andersen and Korpi, 1987, pp. 46–7).[13]

A still more important accommodation was that struck by the newly empowered Social Democrats and organized capital. Rather than pursuing the traditional (maximalist) socialist policy of pressing for immediate socialization of the ownership of capital, the Social Democrats, recognizing the stalemate between organized labour and organized capital that their election occasioned, pressed for a formalization of the division of economic and political control and a division of the spoils of continued and agreed capitalist growth. This celebrated 'historic compromise' ensured that capital would maintain intact its managerial prerogatives within the workplace, subject only to guarantees on rights to unionization, and capitalist economic growth would be encouraged. At the same time,

---

[13] This 'labourist' reading of Scandinavian experience has been extensively criticized by Peter Baldwin in *The Politics of Social Solidarity*. He insists that 'decisions in favour of a solidaristic solution to social insurance were, in fact, taken at a time before the left had much say in the matter and often against its will' (1990, p. 93). This reading of experiences in Sweden and the US is also challenged in Peter Swenson's *Capitalism against Markets* (2002). For a further re-evaluation of the importance of employer interests in the development of the welfare state, this time in France and Germany, see Mares, 2003.

the Social Democratic government would pursue Keynesian economic policies to sustain full employment and use progressive taxation to reduce economic inequality and promote provision for collective needs, such as education, health and housing. When in the post-Second World War period the defence of welfare institutions and full employment threatened inflation and the loss of international competitiveness, the compromise was complemented by the adoption of the 'Rehn' model, which entailed (1) an 'active manpower policy' – facilitating the redistribution and real-location of labour and capital from less to more efficient enterprises; and (2) a 'solidaristic' wage policy, which would allow for the centralized nego-tiation of wages and the reduction of wage differentials, through a prin-ciple of equal pay for equal work, irrespective of a given company's capacity to pay. In this way, it was hoped that welfare provision and a rising standard of living for the working population could be reconciled with continuing non-inflationary economic growth.

Thus, in the 1930s and beyond, the Swedish welfare state was secured as much by *economic* policy – the support of an active labour market policy, public works, solidaristic wage bargaining, deficit budgeting – as by social policy. Indeed, the Swedish Social Democrats have always shown an awareness of the intimate relationship between economic policy and social policy on which the institutional or social democratic welfare state is dependent and which is recognized in the twin-termed 'Keynesian Welfare' State (KWS).[14] Thus job creation or full employment may be seen as a more desirable alternative to the payment of unemployment com-pensation. It may also be the indispensable basis of funding a 'generous' welfare system.

In Sweden in the 1930s, it was probably Keynesian *economic* policies, rather than innovations in *social* policy, that were the most important com-ponent in the nascent welfare state. Nonetheless, there were significant and complementary social policy initiatives. Perhaps the most important of these was the 1934 legislation that increased the state's involvement in what had previously been exclusively a union-managed system of unemploy-ment insurance (Esping-Andersen and Korpi, 1987). In addition, between 1933 and 1938, the Social Democratic government also legislated for further welfare provision (Olsson, 1986, p. 5):

- new employment creation programmes;
- a housing programme for families with many children, including sub-sidies and interest-subsidized construction loans;

---

[14] Ashford (1986a) stresses the general importance of the interrelationship between social and economic policy. He argues that historically this was recognized in France but not in Britain; this led to the French welfare state being the more effectively entrenched.

- the indexation of pensions to regional differences in the cost of living;
- maternity benefits to around 90 per cent of all mothers;
- free maternity and childbirth services;
- state loans to newly married couples;
- the introduction of two weeks' holiday for all private and public employees.

A number of other states saw major developments in their welfare states between the wars. Denmark's 'Great Social Reform' of 1933, if less radical than its advocates have claimed, 'nevertheless, remained the fundamental administrative framework of the Danish welfare state for a quarter century' (Johansen, 1986, pp. 299–300; Levine, 1983). New Zealand, which had introduced the first comprehensive pensions for the needy elderly in 1898 and had been among the first to introduce family allowances in 1926, created, through its 1938 Social Security Act, 'what could be argued to be, in late 1930s terms, the most comprehensive welfare state in the world' (Castles, 1985, p. 26). It was stated that this unusually comprehensive measure was

> to provide for the payment of superannuation benefits and of other bene-
> fits designed to safeguard the people of New Zealand from disabilities
> arising from age, sickness, widowhood, orphanhood, unemployment, or
> other exceptional conditions; to provide a system whereby medical and hos-
> pital treatment will be made available to persons requiring such treatment;
> and, further, to provide such other benefits as may be necessary to maintain
> and promote the health and general welfare of the community. (Cited in
> Castles, 1985, p. 27)

Elsewhere, there were substantial if less spectacular advances. In Canada, (means-tested) old age pensions were introduced in 1927, and the 1930s saw a succession of federal-provincial unemployment compensation schemes culminating in the 1940 Federal Unemployment Insurance Act (D.F. Bellamy and Irving, 1989; Leman, 1977). Britain, whose interwar social policy was dominated by the spectre of unemployment, saw modest legislation on the social provision of housing and health care, education, contributory old age pensions, provision for widows and orphans and the steady 'break-up' of the Poor Law (Gilbert, 1970; Fraser, 1973; Thane, 1982). Yet, writing of the UK experience, Parry concludes that 'the cre-ative impulse of the welfare state progressed little from the 1910s to the 1940s' (1986, p. 159).

Even where initiatives in this period were very modest, some have argued that the *underlying* changes which permitted the flowering of the welfare state after 1945 were secured in the interwar years. Such a view is sometimes taken in describing the Beveridge Report not as the found-ing charter of a radically new British welfare state after 1945, but as a rationalization of existing prewar legislation. Addison, for example, suggests that Beveridge's 'background assumptions' – 'full' employment and a national health service – were much more radical and innovative than his 'fundamentally conservative' proposals on social insurance (Addison, 1977, p. 213). Similarly, Ashford argues that in France, where advances in pensions, health and accident insurance were limited and painfully slow between the wars, this was the period in which the political compromises and coalitions on which the developed postwar welfare state was built were themselves fought over and secured. Indeed, he suggests that the very slow-

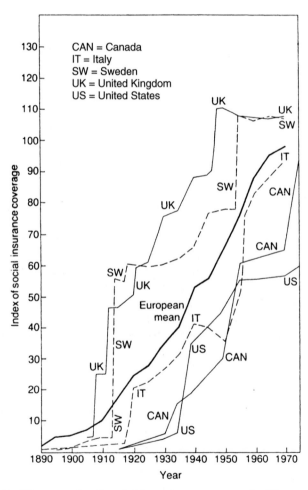

Figure 4.2   The growth of social insurance coverage in Western Europe
Source: Flora and Heidenheimer, 1981a.

ness and difficulty of achieving welfare advances in France compared with the UK made these victories and the welfare state thus constructed more secure and entrenched than its less contested British counterpart (Ashford, 1982, 1986a, 1986b). As we have seen, what remains the single most important innovation in the US welfare state dates from the 1930s.

Other significant developments of this period included the evolution in Germany and Italy of a pattern of social policy interwoven with the corporatist institutions of fascism. But everywhere, and particularly under the impact of the mass unemployment of the 1930s, the interwar years were marked by growing welfare expenditures. Indeed, between 1920 and 1940, Flora and Alber's index of social insurance coverage in Western Europe more than doubled (Flora and Heidenheimer, 1981a, p. 85).

1945–1975: 'The Golden Age of the Welfare State'?

Just as the interwar years have been seen as years of 'consolidation', so has the period after 1945 been widely characterized as ushering in a thirty years' 'Golden Age of the welfare state'. On such an account, the period between 1945 and the mid-1970s is seen as bringing (1) rapid initial reforms to create a much more comprehensive and universal welfare state based on the idea of shared citizenship; (2) a commitment to direct increasing resources towards the rapid expansion of benefits and coverage within this extended system; (3) a very broad-based political consensus in favour of a mixed economy and a system of extended social welfare; and (4) a (successful) commitment to economic growth and full employment.

In fact, this model of the postwar evolution of the welfare state has always been heavily dependent on the (unique) British experience, and indeed on a particular, broadly social democratic and 'optimistic' understanding of this experience. Great emphasis is placed on the consequences of the Second World War – its expansion of the powers and competence of government, the generation of new forms of collective provision and, above all, the broadly shared experience of austerity and mutual mortal danger generating a high degree of citizen solidarity in favour of radical reform. Also stressed is the 'messianic' quality of Beveridge and his proposed reforms, the radical break occasioned by the election of the postwar Labour government, and the subsequent development of a broad cross-party consensus ('Butskellism') in favour of a compromise between the interests of capital and labour, within which the welfare state was a crucial component.

Recently, this synoptic view of the postwar history of the (British) welfare state has itself come under increasing challenge. First, claims about the impact of the Second World War on the development of social policy have been questioned. It has been argued (1) that the experience of government planning and state intervention in the wartime period was not an especially promising one; (2) that sympathy for collective provision arose not from the bonds of mutual citizenship but from the perceived threat of a commonly uncertain future; and (3) that the pressure for social policy reform came less from a radicalized citizenry than from a trade union movement whose industrial muscle had been much strengthened by wartime full employment. Secondly, it is widely insisted that the social policy reforms proposed by Beveridge (and only partially enacted in the postwar period) represented not a radical charter for a new social order, but a tidying up and codification of prewar social legislation. Thirdly, it is argued that the consensus within which the postwar welfare state was said to have developed either never existed or else was much more limited than the traditional social democratic account has allowed (Barnett, 1986; Dryzek and Goodin, 1986; Addison, 1977; Taylor-Gooby, 1985; Deakin, 1987; H. L. Smith, 1986; Pimlott, 1988).

There are then serious doubts as to whether this model is fully applicable even to the British experience.[15] Yet it retains a significant (if varying) element of truth. In 1948, Article 40 of the newly founded United Nations's Declaration of Human Rights proclaimed that:

> Everyone has the right to a standard of living adequate for the health and well-being of himself and his family, including food, clothing, housing and medical care and the necessary social services, and the right to security in the event of unemployment, sickness, disability, widowhood, old age or other lack of livelihood in circumstances beyond his control. (United Nations, 1948)

Similarly, Article 38 of the constitution of newly independent India declared that 'the State shall strive to promote the welfare of the people by securing and protecting . . . a social order in which justice, social, economic and political shall inform all the institutions of national life' (cited in Brownlie, 1971, p. 43). Within the developed West, many countries other than Britain saw major social policy reforms immediately after 1945. In France and Ireland, for example, there was a period of rapid policy innovation in the late 1940s, and these policy changes had an immediate effect on the proportion of GNP devoted to social welfare (Ashford, 1986b, pp. 255–65; Hage et al. 1989; Maguire, 1986, pp. 246–7; Kennedy, 1975, p. 11). Indeed, throughout the developed capitalist world, the postwar period was one of unprecedented growth and prosperity, and of new and varied forms of government intervention in the economy.

---

[15] It has been very properly objected that 'intensive study of the British case' may not be 'the optimal way of starting to grasp the general characteristics of welfare state development' (Flora and Heidenheimer, 1981b, p. 21).

Table 4.5 Growth in social expenditure (seven major OECD countries), 1960–1975, as a percentage of GDP

	1960	1975
Canada	11.2	20.1
France	14.4	26.3
W. Germany	17.1	27.8
Italy	13.7	20.6
Japan	7.6	13.7
UK	12.4	19.6
USA	9.9	18.7
Weighted average	12.3	21.9

Source: OECD, 1988a, p. 10.

By almost any criteria, these were years of rapid expansion in welfare state provision. Thus, for example, in Western Europe in the early 1930s only about a half of the labour force was protected by accident, sickness, invalidity and old age insurance. Scarcely a fifth was insured against unemployment. However, by the mid-1970s more than 90 per cent of the labour force enjoyed insurance against income loss due to old age, invalidity and sickness; over 80 per cent were covered by accident insurance; and 60 per cent had coverage against unemployment. The average annual rate of growth in social security expenditure which stood at around 1 per cent in 1950–5 had accelerated to 3.4 per cent in the years 1970–4. Broadly defined, social expenditure which had in the early 1950s consumed something between 10 and 20 per cent of GNP had grown to between a quarter and something more than a third of a rapidly enhanced GNP by the mid-1970s (Flora, 1986, vol. 1, p. xxii). A further indication of this rapid growth after 1960 is given in table 4.5.

However we choose to explain this development, the sheer growth in social expenditure throughout this period is one of the more remarkable phenomena of postwar capitalist development.

For many commentators, these developments in social policy may only be properly understood in the much broader context of what in the US was styled the 'post–World War II capital labor accord' and is more familiarly described in Britain and Western Europe as the 'postwar consensus' (Bowles and Gintis, 1982). In this view, the new social, political and economic order of the postwar world was to be secured around (1) Keynesian economic policies to secure full employment and economic growth domestically within the agreed parameters of an essentially liberal capitalist international market; (2) a more or less 'institutional' welfare state to deal with the dysfunctions arising from this market economy; and (3) broad-based agreement between left and right, and between capital and labour, over these basic social institutions (a market economy and a welfare state) and the accommodation of their (legitimately) competing interests through elite-level negotiation (Bowles and Gintis, 1982; Taylor-Gooby, 1985; Kavanagh, 1987; Kavanagh and Morris, 1989). These liberal democratic or social democratic institutions were seen as the best guarantee of avoiding both the economic disasters and the concomitant political polarization of the interwar years.

This postwar consensus may be thought of in two ways, as a consensus between *classes* or as a consensus between political *parties*. At the *class* level, consensus involved the abandonment by labour of its traditional aspiration for socialization of the economy and of the ideology and practices of 'class war'. For capital, it meant an acceptance of the commitment to full employment, to the public ownership of strategic utilities and support for the welfare state. Both labour and capital were to share in the common objectives (and rewards) of sustained economic growth. This compromise was to be managed by the overarching presence of the government, which would coordinate relations between unions and employers, secure the background conditions for economic growth and administer the welfare state. In its *party* form, consensus indicated broad agreement on the constitutional rules of the political game, the marginalization of the extremes of both left and right (both within and outside 'mainstream' parties), a political style of compromise and bargaining, the broad acceptance of predecessors' legislation and the 'mobilization of bias' in favour of certain interests and ideas, including organized capital, organized labour and Keynesian economics (Kavanagh, 1987, pp. 6–7).

In both formulations, there were certain core public policy elements around which the compromise was built. Internationally, there was an endorsement of the open international market and commitment to 'the collective defence of the Western world' (both under American leadership). Domestically, it meant a commitment to (1) the maintenance of a comprehensive welfare state; (2) support of the 'mixed economy' of private and public enterprise; and (3) policies of full employment and sustained economic growth.[16]

For many commentators in the 1950s and 1960s, the coming of the postwar era of consensus politics seemed to herald 'an irreversible change'. Within the sphere of the welfare state, Tom Marshall argued in 1965 that there was now 'little difference of opinion as to the services that must be provided, and it is generally agreed that, whoever provides them, the

---

[16] On consensus, see Kavanagh and Morris, 1989, and Deakin, 1987; for a sceptical view see Pimlott, 1988.

overall responsibility for the welfare of the citizens must remain with the state' (Marshall, 1975, p. 97). Still more confidently, Charles Schottland (1969) proclaimed that 'whatever its beginnings, the welfare state is here to stay. Even its opponents argue only about its extension.' Much more recently, Mishra comments that 'state commitment to maintaining full employment, providing a range of basic services for all citizens, and preventing or relieving poverty seemed so integral to post-war society as to be almost irreversible' (1984, p. 1).

We have already noted that recent scholarship has cast doubt on the reality of the postwar consensus. Most sceptically, Ben Pimlott has written of 'the myth of consensus', while Deakin insists of the British experience that while 'real convergences in policy between the major political parties and individuals within them certainly took place . . . there was far less homogeneity than is usually believed' (Deakin, 1987; Pimlott, 1988; Taylor-Gooby, 1985). In Sweden, once identified by right-wing social democrats as the definitive terrain of the consensual 'middle way', there has been an attempt to redefine the historic accommodation of organized capital and organized labour as a temporary and strategic compromise of irreconcilable differences of interest which have become increasingly manifest over the past fifteen years (Childs, 1961; Crosland, 1964; Tingsten, 1973; Tomasson, 1969, 1970; Scase, 1977a, 1977b; Korpi, 1979; Stephens, 1979; Himmelstrand et al., 1981; Korpi, 1983; C. Pierson, 1986, 1991; Huber and Stephens, 2001).

Yet even for its most enthusiastic supporters, the politics of consensus was always recognized to be a *positive-sum* game. Agreement rested on the capacity to generate a growing economic surplus with which to satisfy simultaneously a multiplicity of disparate claims. In this way, it was reliant on the fourth element we have identified in the postwar period, that is the commitment to economic growth and full employment.

Economic growth was seemingly the irreplaceable foundation of the traditional welfare state. It was the basis of Keynesian policies to induce capital investment, the stimulus to support economic activity at levels securing full employment and the fount of resources for increased expenditure on health, education, welfare and social services. It was economic growth that made a reconciliation of the opposing interests of capital and labour viable and sustainable. Fittingly, what has been described as 'the Golden Age of the welfare state' was also a period of unprecedented and unparalleled growth in the international capitalist economy.

Table 4.6 gives some general indication of this growth. In the seven major OECD countries (which at the start of the 1950s accounted for 90 per cent of OECD output), annual growth in GNP stood at 4.4 per cent in the 1950s, rising to 5.5 per cent in the years between 1960 and 1973. There was substantial international variation in rates of growth. The UK struggled to achieve growth above 3 per cent even in the years of the most

Table 4.6 Annual growth in GNP (seven major OECD countries), 1950–1981, annual average percentage rates of increase

	1950–60	*1960–73*	*1973–81*
Canada	4.0	5.6	2.8
France	4.5	5.6	2.6
W. Germany	7.8	4.5	2.0
Italy	5.8	5.2	2.4
Japan	10.9	10.4	3.6
UK	2.3	3.1	0.5
USA	3.3	4.2	2.3
Weighted average	4.4	5.5	2.3

Sources: OECD, 1966, p. 20; Bruno and Sachs, 1985, p. 155.

rapid expansion, while Japan's remarkable growth exceeded 10 per cent per annum throughout the period. In the years after 1960, a number of previously 'underdeveloped' economies (for example, in Spain, Portugal, Greece and Turkey) achieved levels of growth in excess of 6 per cent per annum. Throughout the 1950s and 1960s average annual growth rates in the OECD economies as a whole stood close to 5 per cent, while inflation, though rising slowly, stayed below 4 per cent until the late 1960s. This contrasts sharply with experience after 1973 when the average rate of economic growth was more than halved (falling as low as 0.5 per cent in the UK). At the same time, inflation became a persistent problem, peaking at 14 per cent in 1974.

Table 4.7 reveals a parallel pattern in terms of employment. The years of sustained, low inflationary economic growth were also years of particularly low levels of unemployment. The period between 1959 and 1967 in which the average levels of unemployment in six major OECD countries stood at 2.8 per cent contrasts markedly with the experience in 1933 at the height of the depression, when unemployment reached 13 per cent. In fact, the figure for the 1960s is distorted by the persistently high levels of unemployment in Italy and the US, all the other countries showing averages significantly below 2 per cent. These figures from the 1960s also contrast sharply with the experience *after* 1970. Unemployment rose throughout the 1970s, peaking at about 8.5 per cent in 1983. This period also saw a particularly steep increase in youth unemployment and in long-term unemployment. In Britain, for example, youth unemployment reached 23.4 per cent in 1983, and the proportion of those unemployed for more than a year rose above 40 per cent in 1986, while overall unemployment rates in the early 1980s came close to the worst levels of the 1930s. Thus

Table 4.7 Unemployment rates (six major OECD countries), 1933–1983, percentage of total labour force

	1933	*1959–67*	*1975*	*1983*
France	–	0.7	4.1	8.0
W. Germany	14.8	1.2	3.6	8.0
Italy	5.9	6.2	5.8	9.7
Japan	–	1.4	1.9	2.6
UK	13.9	1.8	4.7	13.1
USA	20.5	5.3	8.3	9.5
weighted average	13.0	2.8	4.7	8.5

Source: Godfrey, 1986, p. 2.

the 1950s and 1960s defined a period of sustained economic growth and full employment which contrasted not only with the prewar years but also with experience after 1973.

Figure 4.3 illustrates the way in which this pattern of sustained economic growth was coordinated with an increase in the proportion of national product directed towards social expenditure.

'The Middle-Class Welfare State'

Two further social and political consequences of this rapid growth of the welfare state in the postwar period are worthy of particular attention. First, expansion of the social budget brought with it some 'universalization' of the constituency of the welfare state. Tomasson has written of three characteristic phases in the development of the welfare state:

> Social welfare before the First World War was a concern of the political Right for the poor. Between the World Wars social welfare was adopted as an issue by the political Left, still for the poor. After the Second World War social welfare became a concern of both right and left but . . . 'not for the poor alone'. (1983, p. ix)

Rarely has the postwar welfare state served simply the interests of society's poorest and most distressed. Almost everywhere, 'the non-poor play a crucial role of (variously) creating, expanding, sustaining, reforming and dismantling the welfare state' (Goodin and Le Grand, 1987, p. 3). Consequently, the nature of *middle-class* involvement has been one of the most important (if sometimes neglected) aspects of later welfare state evolution. In fact, the expansion of the welfare state in the postwar period has tended

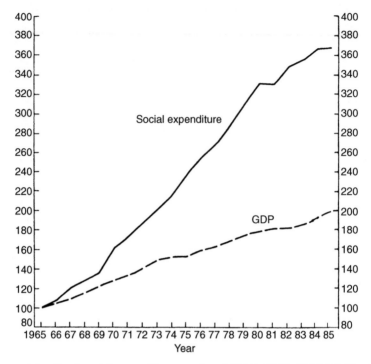

Figure 4.3   Real social expenditure and real GDP, 1965–1985 (1965 = 100)
Source: OECD, 1988a, p. 13.

to benefit members of the middle class both (1) as *consumers*, giving rights of access to facilities in health care, education, housing, transport and so on which 'actually benefited the middle classes . . . in many cases more than the poor', and (2) as *providers*, increasing professional employment opportunities within the public sector (Goodin and Le Grand, 1987, p. 91). As Le Grand's work on the British welfare state suggests (see table 4.8), perhaps counterintuitively, the principal beneficiaries of such redistribution as the broad welfare state allows have often been middle-class elements.

The Growth of Welfare State Employment

A second general consequence of the rapid expansion of the welfare state in the postwar period is to be found in the radical changes in the composition of the workforce that it has effected. The state, and more especially the welfare state, is now a major employer in all advanced societies. In the 1980s, the British National Health Service became the single largest employer in

Table 4.8 The distribution of public expenditure on the British social services

Service	Ratio of expenditure per person in top fifth to that per person in bottom fifth, 1980s
Pro-poor	
Council housing	0.3
Equal	
Primary education	0.9
Secondary education	0.9
Pro-rich	
National Health Service	1.4
Secondary education (16+)	1.8
Non-university higher education	3.5
Bus subsidies	3.7
Universities	5.4
Tax subsidies to owner-occupiers	6.8
Rail subsidies	9.8

Source: Goodin and Le Grand, 1987, p. 9.

Western Europe, with an annual wages bill in excess of £13 billion (Department of Health, 1989). Within the more general shift in employment from manufacturing to the service sector, state welfare has had a peculiarly prominent role. Studying changes in employment patterns in Germany, Sweden, the US and the UK, Martin Rein concludes that between the early 1960s and the 1980s, social welfare and 'services to business' have been the only two areas of the service sector of the economy to experience real growth. By the latter period, the 'social welfare industry' accounted for between 11 per cent (Germany) and 26 per cent (Sweden) of overall employment, and social welfare jobs accounted for between 20 and 40 per cent of all employment in the service sector (Rein, 1985, pp. 39–40).

OECD figures suggest that in Denmark by the mid-1980s, government employment (about two-thirds of which is in the social welfare sector) *exceeded* employment in manufacturing. In other countries (for example, Norway and Sweden) the two sectors were close to parity, while in *every* country reviewed, the gap between employment in manufacturing and government services had significantly narrowed since the early 1970s (OECD, 1989, pp. 120–2). Rein noted that the consequences of expanded welfare state employment were particularly pronounced for women, and especially for those women who had passed through higher education. In 1981, between 65 and 75 per cent of college-educated women in Germany,

Sweden and the US were employed in the 'social welfare industries'. The growth of the welfare state has clearly been a major area of growth in female labour force participation, especially for the growing number of professionally qualified women (Rein, 1985, pp. 43–5). In Sweden, for example, very high rates of female labour force participation combine with a strongly gender-segregated labour market, with a substantial proportion of this employment in the welfare sector (Daly and Rake, 2003, pp. 74–5).

A number of profound (political) consequences have been seen to follow from this pattern of middle-class involvement and expanded employment in the welfare state. Therborn, for example, takes it as evidence of the 'creeping universalism' of the welfare state, which rendered New Right attempts to dismantle it electorally impossible. For the New Right itself, the growth of a highly unionized, middle-class public sector workforce was a major source of economic and political crisis in the 1970s. Others have identified new lines of electoral cleavage developing around the welfare state (reliance on the public sector versus reliance on the private sector), displacing traditional cleavages along the lines of social class (Therborn, 1987; Dunleavy, 1980). Esping-Andersen has argued that middle-class participation is actually essential to the maintenance of a generous and 'solidaristic' welfare state (Esping-Andersen, 1990). In welfare states where all are beneficiaries, it is more likely that welfare will authentically be seen as part of citizenship and it is more likely that middle-class taxpayers will be willing to pay for good quality services through their taxes. (By the same token, universalistic welfare states in which the middle class participate fully are likely to be expensive). Meanwhile, Claus Offe has argued that the secure employment and comparative affluence which first attached the middle classes to the 'welfare state project' are now increasingly threatening their defection to neoliberalism and a consequent residualization of state welfare. Some of these themes are further developed in chapters 5 and 6. For now, we return to a more detailed assessment of social policy changes in the postwar period.

1945–1950: Reconstruction

Within the very broad parameters of 'the Golden Age', or more soberly the era of welfare state expansion between 1945 and 1975, it is both possible and useful to offer some further periodization. Thus we may think of the immediate postwar period down to 1951 as defining a period of *reconstruction* following the devastation of the Second World War. In this period, a number of countries created that broad and systematic platform on which the developed welfare state was based. In the UK, even before the end of the war, the coalition government had passed legislation to reform secondary education and to introduce family allowances. In the immediate postwar period, the Labour government (partially) implemented Beveridge's reform proposals with the setting up of the National Health Service, the final abolition of the Poor Law and the reconstruction of national insurance and national assistance. The essentials of the postwar British welfare state were in place by 1948.

In France, where social policy enhancement between the wars had been modest, there was a 'major commitment to social security in 1945 and 1946' (Ashford and Kelley, 1986, p. 257). This included a law providing sickness and disability insurance, pension legislation and a law providing for the elderly poor. There was also an enhancement of the 1932 Family Allowances legislation, providing prenatal payments, additional payments for the third child and a rising scale of benefits as families grew larger (Ashford, 1986b, pp. 183–4). In Finland, where prewar provision had been still more limited, the years between 1945 and 1950 saw a spectacular average growth rate in social expenditure of 22.2 per cent. Social expenditure as a proportion of central government spending rose from 3 per cent to 13 per cent in the same period. Most of this increased effort was directed towards children and families, health care, the organization of social services, benefits for war victims and state-supported housing construction (Alestalo and Uusitalo, 1986, pp. 202–3, 246). Similarly in Ireland, 'the period from 1945 to the early 1950s was a time of heightened interest and activity in the area of social policy.' During these years, the share of social expenditure in GDP rose by almost six percentage points. The reforms included the enhancement of public health provision, the expansion of social insurance coverage and improved state aid for housing in both the public and private sectors (Maguire, 1986, pp. 246–8, 252; Kennedy, 1975, p. 5).

Not every developed capitalist country participated in this rapid enhancement of social legislation after 1945. In Italy, for example, proposals for a systematic reform of social insurance were rejected following the election of a Christian Democrat-dominated coalition government in 1948, which opted instead to restore the prewar institutional framework (Ferrera, 1986, p. 390; 1989, p. 124). In New Zealand, the major period of welfare state expansion had *preceded* the Second World War, while it has been said that 'by the end of the Labour administration in 1949 Australia hardly possessed a welfare state' (Michael A. Jones, 1980, p. 36). However, the single most (strategic) nation in this period of international welfare state expansion was probably the 'laggardly' US. While Bowles and Gintis (1982) identify the emergence of a 'capital labor accord' in a number of legislative initiatives in the immediate postwar years, additions to America's own 'semi-welfare state' were quite limited. It was, however, American military and economic power which underwrote the postwar reconstruction of Europe and the new political and economic order of which the welfare state was an essential feature. America was the guarantor and sponsor of Western

Europe's 'embedded liberalism' (economic liberalism in a context of state intervention), and thus 'ironically, it was American hegemony that provided the basis for the development and expansion of the European welfare states' (Keohane, 1984, pp. 16–17).

1950–1960: Relative Stagnation

By contrast with the burst of legislative and executive action in the immediate postwar years, which for many commentators heralds the *real* coming of the welfare state, the 1950s was a decade of *relative stagnation*. In what was generally a period of sustained economic growth, the proportion of resources directed to social expenditure rose very slowly compared with both the years before 1950 and those after 1960. In Western Europe, the average growth in central government social expenditure as a percentage of GDP was something under 1 per cent for the whole decade (Flora, 1987b, vol. 1, pp. 345–449). Strong economic growth means that such figures often mask sustained growth in real social expenditure. Jens Alber writes of the period 1951–8 as the 'take-off' phase of the West German welfare state, but while average real growth in welfare expenditure rose over 10 per cent, its share in a rapidly growing GDP rose by just three percentage points in the same period. Social expenditure commanded a very similar proportion of national wealth at the end of the decade as it had at its beginning (Alber, 1986, pp. 15–16; Alber, 1988a; Maguire, 1986, pp. 321–30). However, there were some countries in which the proportion of social expenditure actually fell during the 1950s. In Ireland, for example, central government social expenditure as a proportion of GDP *fell* by 3.6 percentage points between 1951 and 1960. The share of social expenditure in GDP did not recover its 1951 level until 1964. In the period between 1952 and 1966, public social security expenditure in Australia rose by two percentage points, but this was from 6.1 per cent of GNP to a still modest 8.2 per cent. In New Zealand, growth in the same period was less than 1 per cent. (Kaim-Caudle, 1973, p. 53). Of course, these figures for proportionate social expenditure do not give an exhaustive description of welfare state developments. Political disputes over welfare policy – the Swedish pension reforms of 1957 or the introduction of health charges by the British Labour government in 1951, for example – are not captured by these statistics (Esping-Andersen, 1985; Sked and Cook, 1984, p. 96). Nonetheless, the contrast with the 1940s and the 1960s is quite clear.

A number of reasons have been advanced to explain this comparative decline in social expenditure growth. Some have suggested that need was adequately met by the levels of expenditure established in the late 1940s. Others point to the increased private affluence and low unemployment achieved in the sustained economic growth of the 1950s. For some, the element of mutual risk and austerity which wartime conditions generated had evaporated by the 1950s. Tom Marshall wrote 'that the welfare state reigned unchallenged while linked with the Austerity society and was attacked from all sides as soon as it became associated with the Affluent Society' (Marshall, 1963, p. 282). Others argued that the succession of defeats of left-wing governments marked a political realignment towards the right and the end of the zeal for reform which had characterized the immediate postwar years.

1960–1975: Major Expansion

From about 1960 onwards, we enter a third phase in the postwar development of the welfare state, one that lasts some fifteen years and which is best characterized as an era of *major expansion*. In terms of the resources devoted to social expenditure, this is perhaps the most remarkable period in the whole evolution of the international welfare states. Thus the proportion of GDP devoted to social expenditure rose from 12.3 per cent in 1960 to 21.9 per cent in 1975. Both absolute levels and rates of growth varied. By 1975, six countries – France, Germany, Belgium, Denmark, the Netherlands and Sweden – were devoting in excess of 25 per cent of their GDP to social expenditure. Among the seven major OECD economies, only Japan (13.7 per cent), the USA (18.7 per cent) and the UK (19.6 per cent) now devoted less than a fifth of GDP to social expenditure. In the 1960–75 period, average annual real growth in social expenditure was in excess of 8 per cent in Australia, Denmark, Japan and Norway. It fell below 4 per cent only in the UK and Austria. The overall average for the OECD countries throughout this period was 6.5 per cent per annum (OECD, 1988a, p. 11).

As figure 4.4 illustrates, the annual real growth rate of social expenditure ranged between 7 and 10 per cent throughout the period 1960–75. It experienced a sharp rise in the period immediately after 1973 but fell sharply after 1975. The average growth rate for the years 1975–81 is little more than half of what it had been in the period prior to 1975.

Again, while there was some international variation, three areas – education, health and pensions – commanded some four-fifths of resources throughout this period. There was some change in the distribution of effort between these three areas as expenditure on education first rose and then declined, while expenditure on health and pensions increased steadily. Of the three, pensions appeared to be least vulnerable to retrenchment following the economic reverses of the mid-1970s. Even with the rapidly rising levels of joblessness in the late 1970s, unemployment compensation remained a minor programme, commanding on average less than 5 per cent of social expenditure (OECD, 1985a).

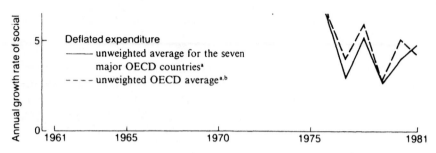

[a] Prior to 1975 there are no figures for expenditure on education in France. Therefore, only the growth rates for the years after 1975 reflect the growth in expenditure on education in France. The pattern of growth rates over these later years is unaffected by their inclusion.
[b] Average for 17 countries (excluding Denmark and Switzerland except for 1981, when Belgium and Greece are also excluded).

Figure 4.4   The rate of growth of social expenditure in the OECD area, 1961–1981
Source: OECD, 1985b, p. 19.

A number of reasons have been advanced to explain this remarkable growth. In part, these are demographic, reflecting not just the growing numbers of old age pensioners but also the rise in the ratio of elderly (who are also disproportionate users of health services) to the economically active. Some point to the central role of the growth of prosperity in this period as generating the necessary resources for the expansion of social programmes (Alber, 1988a). Others offer more political explanations of the growth of social spending, stressing, for example, the mobilization of labour movements, socialist parties and others (including the civil rights movement in the US) in favour of enhanced welfare; the essential role of social spending as a part of the 'capital–labour' accommodation of the postwar consensus; the growing density and capacity of interest groups to mobilize in favour of sectional interests within the welfare state; and the increase in urbanization and educational provision leading to greater social and political mobilization.

Many commentators link these explanations of the rapid growth of the welfare state down to 1975 with its problems or 'crisis' thereafter. Indeed, in more or less apocalyptic terms, 1975 is often seen to mark the end-point of nearly a hundred years of welfare state growth and to bring the threat or promise of its imminent dismemberment. It is to these developments 'after the Golden Age' that we turn our attention in chapter 5.

5
'Crisis' and 'Containment'

Most commentators on the historical evolution of the welfare state have been agreed in identifying a break with a longstanding pattern of growth and development in international social policy from the early or middle years of the 1970s. Some have done no more than draw attention to the slackening pace of welfare state growth in this period (Flora, 1986; Alber, 1988b). Others, particularly those writing from the perspective of the 1970s, drew a much more alarming picture of 'crisis' and 'contradiction' in the welfare state, an unstable condition which challenged its continuation or even the integrity of the democratic capitalist order itself. It was in this period of the early and mid-1970s that social democratic confidence in the competence of the mixed economy and the welfare state to deliver continuing economic growth allied to greater social equity came under increasing challenge. It was also, as we have seen, the period of the flowering of New Right and neo-Marxist accounts of the welfare state, both of which concentrated on the ubiquity of crisis arising from the inherently unstable and contradictory elements within the postwar welfare capitalist consensus. Thirty years later, these more apocalyptic visions of the 'end of the welfare state' seem misplaced. Yet contemporary social policy regimes do seem quite different from those that prevailed in the period down to the 1970s. In this chapter, we begin to make sense of this rather puzzling trajectory of the welfare state.

Even in the 1970s, the belief that welfare capitalism was beset by contradictions and vulnerable to crisis was not all that new. It is a view rooted in the work of the great classical political economists and it had continued to be voiced by a minority on both left and right throughout the postwar 'Golden Age' of welfare. What was new in the 1970s was not these arguments themselves but rather their remarkable authority. It seemed as if, in an instant, 'complacency about the momentum of the welfare state gave way to doom-mongering by many in the intellectual elite' (Heclo, 1981, p. 399). With astonishing speed, the warnings of a looming crisis (particularly those of the New Right) seemed to replace the benign assumptions of social democracy as a privileged discourse among governing and 'opinion-forming' elites.

Yet precisely what was intended by the newly authoritative discourse of 'crisis' and 'contradiction' has never been entirely clear. Alec Pemberton complains that the meaning of 'contradiction' in Marxist analyses of the welfare state has always been 'notoriously imprecise'. He identifies two main variants: (1) contradiction as *'paradox'* (as in the claim that 'the working class struggles for welfare rights but this inadvertently strengthens the position of capital'); and (2) contradiction as *'opposite effect'* (as in the argument that 'the welfare state is introduced to assist the needy and deprived but, in practice, it worsens their position'). The principal difficulty identified in both usages is that it is unclear in what sense the relationships specified are truly 'contradictory'. The outcomes described may be perverse or even establish 'real oppositions', but they do not entail a contradiction which, properly speaking, is a description of the relationship between two logically inconsistent statements (of the kind, 'This is the final crisis of capitalism'/'This is not the final crisis of capitalism') (Pemberton, 1983, pp. 289–308; Benton, 1977; Offe, 1984, pp. 130–46). Although Pemberton's strictures are addressed to the neo-Marxist literature, the New Right employs the idea of contradiction in much the same way and the criticism may be applied with similar effect to its usage.

Similar difficulties surround the still more widespread usage, by both right and left, of the idea of a *crisis* of the welfare state. We can identify four distinct senses in which 'crisis' is regularly employed in contemporary discussions. The first (deriving from its medical and dramaturgical origins) sees crisis as a decisive phase in a process in which a longstanding or deep-seated struggle must be resolved one way or another. By analogy, this has been extended to describe any particularly strategic or decisive episode in the historical or social process (Rader, 1979, p. 187). A second usage understands crisis as 'a catastrophe caused by an external blow' (Moran, 1988, p. 397). Offe describes this as a *sporadic crisis concept*, in which the crisis is confined to one event or brief series of events. Offe himself prefers a third contemporary notion, that of 'a *processual* concept of crisis'. Here, crises are 'developmental tendencies that can be confronted with "*counteracting tendencies*" making it possible to relate the crisis-prone developmental tendencies of a system to the characteristics of the system'. On this reading, crises 'need not be seen as catastrophic events having a contingent origin'; rather they relate directly to Offe's (neo-Marxist) sense of contradiction as 'the tendency inherent within a specific mode of production to destroy those very preconditions on which its survival depends' (Offe,

1984, pp. 36–7). These contradictions when seen within the capitalist mode of production may call forth 'counteracting tendencies' (this is, indeed, very largely what the welfare state is), but the structural and systemic limitations on such counteracting tendencies reveal a chronic likelihood 'that contradictions will finally result in a *crisis* of the capitalist mode of production' (Offe, 1984, p. 133). At the same time, all of these more or less technical uses of the term are overlain by the ubiquitous and devalued modern currency of 'crisis' used to describe any (and every) large-scale contemporary problem.

For all its advocates, the idea of a 'crisis of the welfare state' may thus have a wide range of meanings. We may isolate the most important of these:

- crisis as *turning point*;
- crisis as *external shock*;
- crisis as *'longstanding contradiction'*;
- crisis as *any large-scale or longstanding problem*.

The Crisis of the Postwar Welfare State

The idea of a crisis or of contradictions surrounding the welfare state is then neither entirely new, nor unproblematically clear. We can, however, isolate the early 1970s as the period in which (particularly in the Anglo-American context) the idea of a crisis of the welfare state achieved an unparalleled prominence. The late 1960s had seen the emergence of a growing discontent among both left and right libertarians about the enervating bureaucratic and statist aspects of social welfare (Illich, 1973, 1978; Lasch, 1978, p. 224). It had also been a period of growing political mobilization and renewed industrial action, notably within the public sector trade unions that had themselves been a by-product of welfare state expansion (M. P. Jackson, 1987; Hyman, 1989b; Giddens, 1981b). All of these contributed to a climate in which social conflict was of renewed interest. But it was above all the end to uninterrupted postwar economic growth that undermined the incremental confidence of the social democrats and set the stage for 'the new pessimism' (Heclo, 1981, p. 398).

The nature of 'the Golden Age' of postwar capitalism is now itself much debated. There has been some tendency to redraw (and shorten) the parameters of the period of sustained economic growth and comparative social peace – on which both the 'end of ideology' and the perspective of open-ended economic expansion were premised – to cover little more than the fifteen years between 1950 and the mid-1960s.[1] But, wherever one

---

[1] The earliest version of James O'Connor's fiscal crisis theory appeared in 1970 (see below). On the postwar period, see Deakin, 1987; Kavanagh and Morris, 1989.

places 'the beginning of the end' of this era, by the early 1970s the signs of economic difficulty were unmistakable and the five-fold increase in oil prices which OPEC (the Organization of Petroleum Exporting Countries) was able to impose in 1973 precipitated (rather than caused) a severe slump throughout the Western industrialized world.

A few figures will illustrate the scale of this economic 'crisis'. Between 1965 and 1973, the economies of the OECD countries showed an annual average growth rate of about 5 per cent. In 1974, this annual growth rate fell to 2 per cent and in 1975, nine OECD economies 'shrank', bringing the annual average growth rate below zero. Although there was some recovery from this low point, there was to be a second oil price 'shock' in 1979, and for the decade 1974 to 1984 annual average growth was little over 2 per cent (Alber, 1988b, p. 187). These economic difficulties were not confined to sluggish growth. By 1975, unemployment in the OECD area had risen to an unprecedented 15 million, a figure that had doubled within a decade (OECD, 1989). At the same time, inflation accelerated and there was a growing balance of trade deficit throughout the OECD. The 'misery index' (the rate of inflation plus the rate of unemployment) which, for the seven major OECD countries, had averaged 5.5 per cent through the 1960s had risen to 17 per cent by 1974–5. Levels of investment and levels of prof-itability fell, while the value of disposable incomes stagnated. Govern-ments throughout the developed West were simultaneously failing to achieve the four major economic policy objectives – growth, low inflation, full employment and balance of trade – on which the postwar order had been based (Gough, 1979, p. 132; Goldthorpe, 1984, p. 2).

One of the clearest manifestations of this economic crisis was growing public indebtedness. As the economic recession deepened, so demands on public, and especially social expenditure grew, in part through the inertia of incrementalism, but also through costs that rose directly from economic recession (the costs of increased unemployment and social benefits claims). At the same time as demand grew, the slump in tax-generating growth meant that revenue declined. This manifested itself in a 'yawning gap between expenditure and revenues' and a rapid growth in the public sector borrowing requirement (PSBR). Most acutely in the period 1973–5, as economic growth (and the capacity to fund state expenditure) declined, public expenditure increased (Gough, 1979, p. 132). About half of the 10 per cent growth in the share of GDP devoted to public expenditure in the OECD countries between 1960 and 1975 occurred in 1974 and 1975 (OECD, 1985b, p. 14). In the same period, specifically social spending (on education, health, income maintenance and other welfare services) had taken an increasing share of this enhanced public expenditure, rising from 47.5 per cent in 1960 to 58.5 per cent by 1981 (OECD, 1985b, p. 21). Con-sequently, a concern about state indebtedness and public expenditure was above all a concern about the costs of the welfare state.

Different governments responded to this challenge in different ways and there was not only the customary discrepancy between what these governments *said* and what they *did* but also a divide between what these governments *did* and what people *widely believed them to have done*. But we now have sufficient evidence to place in context the 'crisis' theories of the 1970s, theories which were themselves a response to these profound economic difficulties and to the short-term reaction of government agencies.

Welfare Capitalism: From 'Contingent Crisis' to 'Systemic Contradiction'?

The initial response of policy-makers to the economic crisis of the early 1970s was to understand it, in Offe's (1984, pp. 36–7) terms, as a 'sporadic crisis'. On this view, the essentially sound and well-ordered international capitalist system had been subjected to an 'external shock' or series of shocks which had temporarily thrown it out of equilibrium. Most prominent among these shocks was the oil price increase of 1973 which had precipitated the deep recession of 1974 and 1975. Other candidates for disruption were the consequences of the longstanding US involvement in Vietnam, the rapid rise of (non-oil) basic commodity costs (notably of basic foods) and the breakdown of international monetary exchange relations. What was crucial about all these 'shocks' was that they were essentially *exogenous* (from outside the system) and if not non-replicable (after all OPEC could, and did, impose a second oil price hike) then certainly *contingent*. Paul McKracken's 1977 report prepared for the OECD, probably the most celebrated statement of this position, concluded that the recession of the early 1970s arose from 'an unusual bunching of unfortunate disturbances unlikely to be repeated on the same scale, the impact of which was compounded by some considerable errors in economic policy' (OECD, 1977). On such an account, crisis was *external* to the welfare state in two senses. First, the source of (temporary) economic problems lay outside the prevailing international market order; and second, in so far as there was a knock-on problem of funding for the welfare state, this was one which was wholly attributable to the shortfall in economic product and not to the (damaging) interrelationship between social welfare and economic performance.

However, this essentially optimistic view – of a 'hiccup' in economic growth leading to a temporary pause in welfare state growth – was increasingly overtaken in the welfare state area by studies which stressed the contradictions *within* the mixed economy (or liberal representative democracy or welfare capitalism) as the *real* source of crisis. The fivefold increase in crude oil prices was simply the dramatic precipitating event which disclosed the deep-seated *structural* weaknesses of the postwar political economy which had been in the making for twenty-five years, and manifest to the discerning eye since at least the late 1960s. At the heart of this account was the claim that the end of the period of postwar economic growth was not externally caused but *inherent* in the social, political and economic order of the postwar consensus and especially in its ameliorating institutions for the management of economically based political conflict.

It will be recalled from chapter 2 that this was precisely the position adopted by both New Right and neo-Marxist commentators in response to the events of the early 1970s. For both schools, this crisis could not be understood as 'simply' economic. Rather it was a crisis of the social and political order established after 1945 under the rubric of the Keynesian Welfare State. For both, the problems of the early 1970s expressed the economic and political contradictions inherent in a democratic capitalist society. Such an analysis embraced two further senses of crisis. First, for all of these commentators the postwar order was threatened by the consequences of a *'longstanding contradiction'*. Also, typically in its earliest, boldest and most apocalyptic formulations, this perspective raised the spectre of a historical *turning point*. That is, the contradictions of the postwar order were now so acute that a *radical* change was no longer simply desirable, but had become unavoidable. Whatever the radical alternatives, the status quo was not an option.

The neo-Marxist variant of this view was first stated with some force at the turn of the 1970s in James O'Connor's *Fiscal Crisis of the State*. O'Connor's study centred on the claim that 'the capitalistic state must try to fulfil two basic and often mutually contradictory functions – *accumulation* and *legitimization*'. On the one hand, the state must try to maintain or create the conditions under which profitable capital accumulation is possible; on the other, it must also try to maintain or create the conditions for 'social harmony'. He expands the contradiction thus:

> A capitalist state that openly uses its coercive forces to help one class accumulate capital at the expense of other classes loses its legitimacy and hence undermines the basis of its loyalty and support. But a state that ignores the necessity of assisting the process of capital accumulation risks drying up the source of its own power, the economy's surplus production capacity and the taxes drawn from this surplus. (O'Connor, 1973, p. 6)

In essence, these twin imperatives of accumulation and legitimation are *contradictory*. Expenditure to secure legitimization is essential, to defray the otherwise potentially explosive social and political costs of capitalist development, yet these costs must themselves be met via state revenues derived from the profits of capital accumulation. In this way the costs of legitimization, which are to secure circumstances for successful capital accumulation, themselves tend to undermine the very process of profitable accumulation.

Correspondingly, 'The socialization of costs and the private appropriation of profits creates a fiscal crisis, or "structural gap", between expenditures and state revenues. The result is a tendency for state expenditures to increase more rapidly than the means of financing them' (1973, p. 9).

This fiscal crisis is intensified by the pluralistic structure and accessibility of liberal democratic politics, which privileges the servicing of organized interests, furnishing 'a great deal of waste, duplication and overlapping of state projects and services'. Thus 'the accumulation of social capital and social expenses is a highly irrational process from the standpoint of administrative coherence, fiscal stability and potentially profitable capital accumulation' (1973, p. 9). By the early 1970s in the US (which was the focus of O'Connor's study) these problems had become intense. Growing tax resistance, intensified hostility to the authority of government, growing mobilization by new social movements among welfare recipients, heightened politicization among a growingly unionized state workforce all intensified those pressures on government which generated fiscal crisis. O'Connor insisted that 'by the late 1960s, the local fiscal crisis was almost completely out of hand' and federal attempts to cope with this simply intensified the difficulties at national level (1973, p. 212). O'Connor doubted that the crisis could be resolved within the parameters of the existing order. For him, 'the only lasting solution to the crisis is socialism' (1973, p. 221).[2]

The New Right and the Crisis of Liberal Representative Democracy

Even more influential and dramatic as an account of the crisis of the welfare state in this period were the writings of the New Right. From the turn of the 1970s, the technical arguments of Hayek and the public choice theorists (discussed in chapter 2) were given an enhanced prominence by critics who insisted that the general contradictions underlying social democracy were now beginning to manifest themselves in an immediate and profound crisis of the existing political order. In a 1975 'Report on the governability of democracies', Michael Crozier argued that within Western Europe 'the operations of the democratic process . . . appear to have generated a breakdown of traditional means of social control, a delegitimation of political and other forms of authority, and an overload of demands on government, exceeding its capacity to respond' (Crozier et al., 1975, p. 8).

---

[2] It is worth recalling that there were other important neo-Marxist accounts of this process which were less functionalist in character and placed a greater stress on welfare politics as an aspect of class struggle (see, for example, Piven and Cloward, 1971; Navarro, 1978).

For the neoconservatives, the core of this 'democratic distemper' lay in the decline in respect for traditional sources of authority and in the break with traditional constraints on individual aspirations. At the same time as democratic publics made greatly increased demands of their governments, they were becoming less willing to accept the decisions taken by these public authorities. Indeed, the decline in respect for executive authority and the decline in support for mainstream political parties suggested a general decline in attachment to the traditional forms of representative democratic life. There was a growing mobilization of sectional demands with no recognition of a greater public interest, whether or not represented by the existing government. At the same time, sustained postwar economic growth, the institutionalization of the welfare state and the 'bidding up' process of adversarial democratic politics had generated a 'revolution of rising expectations' among democratic publics. They were increasingly disposed to claim as non-negotiable 'rights', goods and services to which they had no sound claim. Decline of authority and mutual responsibility within the family meant that social welfare functions traditionally met within the private and family sector generated new claims on the state – and a population increasingly dependent on state beneficence.

If for the neoconservatives, the major problem was one of declining social control and public authority, for the neoliberals, following the public choice theorists, the major difficulties lay in the relationship between representative liberal democracy and the market economy. Thus Samuel Brittan wrote in 1975 of the danger of the (self-)destruction of liberal representative democracy being precipitated by 'two endemic threats':

- the generation of excessive expectations; and
- the disruptive effects of the pursuit of group self-interest in the marketplace.

In essence, the 'growth of expectations imposes demands for different kinds of public spending and intervention which are incompatible both with each other and with the tax burden that people are willing to bear' (Brittan, 1975, pp. 129–31). Marrying Schumpeter's account of democracy as the process of elite competition for votes to the insights of the public choice theorists, Brittan argued that liberal representative democracy is imperilled by two underlying weaknesses.[3] First, the process of political competition generates unrealistic and excessive expectations about the possibilities afforded by government action among a largely (and rationally) uninformed voting public. Parties and politicians are systematically

[3] On Schumpeter's account of democracy as elite competition, see Schumpeter, 1976; Held, 1987, pp. 164–85.

disposed to promise 'more for less'. A party which reminds the electorate of the necessary relationship between income and expenditure is likely to prove unelectable. Secondly, the growth of well-organized sectional interests (most especially trade unions), and particularly their willingness to use this power to achieve sectional ends, intensifies the difficulties of reconciling liberal and democratic government with national economic solvency. In the short term, this contradiction is likely to manifest itself in rising inflation, but 'in the last analysis the authorities have to choose between accepting an indefinite increase in the rate of inflation and abandoning full employment to the extent necessary to break the collective wage-push power of the unions'. However, such governments may be forced 'to choose between very high rates of unemployment and very high rates of inflation, neither of which can be sustained in a liberal democracy' (Brittan, 1975, p. 143). Consequently, Brittan judged that 'on present indications', liberal representative democracy 'is likely to pass away within the lifetime of people now adult' (1975, p. 129).

There were other elements in these accounts of the 1970s. Some argued that the growth in resources and personnel directed towards the public sector as a consequence of the rise of the postwar welfare state had 'crowded out' the private sector investment on which continued economic growth was dependent. Bacon and Eltis argued of the British experience that there was 'a strong case' for maintaining that 'the great increase in public-sector employment that occurred in Britain in 1961–75 [largely within the welfare state sector] played a significant role in the deterioration of Britain's economic performance' (1978, p. 16). Some stressed the growing difficulties of government macro-management in a more open world economy. Others highlighted the particularly entrenched position of *public sector* trade unions (itself a by-product of expanded (welfare) state employment), whose wages were politically rather than market determined (Rose and Peters, 1978, p. 23; Brittan, 1975).

For many of these commentators, government overload was intimately related to the spectre of growing *ungovernability*. Rose and Peters, for example, argued that a number of Western governments faced the imminent prospect of 'political bankruptcy' should they fail to show 'the political will to limit growth' of public expenditure in times of declining economic growth and falling take-home pay. While such 'political bankruptcy' would not mean anarchy and fighting in the streets, it would lead to an increase in citizen hostility to the conventional political process, accelerate the process of citizen indifference to the conduct of government and, perhaps most seriously, aggravate the tendency towards tax resistance, with an accompanying growth in the black economy (Rose and Peters, 1978, pp. 31–7). Most apocalyptically, Peter Jay (1977) insisted that 'the very survival of democracy hangs by a gossamer thread' and that 'democracy has itself by the tail and is eating itself up fast'.

Not all these commentators were so iconoclastic (nor can they all be identified unproblematically with the New Right). Rose and Peters, for example, insisted that any 'attempt to dismantle the policies of the contemporary welfare state would be a response out of all proportion to the cause of the problem' (1978, pp. 38, 232). Yet all were convinced that the continuation of the welfare state status quo was not an option.

Crisis? What Crisis?

The neoliberal version of this argument attracted enormous attention through the 1970s (and beyond) and yet, by the end of that decade, it seemed clear that expectations of a system-threatening crisis – whether a legitimation crisis of welfare capitalism or a crisis of governability of liberal representative democracy – were ungrounded. Nowhere in the advanced capitalist world had the system of representative democracy broken down and certainly no one could argue that the crisis of welfare capitalism had been resolved by a rapid transition to socialism! Certainly, there had been considerable resistance to retrenchment of public expenditure and rising levels of unemployment. There was some (extremely approximate) evidence of growth in the black economy (a 1986 OECD report placed it at between 2 and 8 per cent of total hours worked in the developed economies) and limited evidence of tax resistance, notably in the meteoric rise of the anti-tax Progress Party in Denmark in 1973 and in the passage of Proposition 13 statutorily restricting state taxation in California (OECD, 1986a). Yet none of this represented a real challenge to the prevailing order which had seemingly been endorsed by the electoral success of right-wing parties in the late 1970s and early 1980s. How then, with hindsight, should we evaluate the 'crisis' theories of the 1970s?

Welfare state crisis as 'external shock'

With the rise to prominence of the more dramatic accounts of the New Right and the neo-Marxists, it became commonplace to dismiss the idea of a 'one-off' crisis arising from the quintupling of oil prices as a naive hankering for the 'good old days' of social peace and economic growth of the 1950s and 1960s. Certainly, it was a view with very real weaknesses. First, its confidence in the early re-establishment of the political and economic status quo ante was misplaced. Secondly, it lacked a sense of the interrelatedness of the political and economic problems of the advanced capitalist societies. Finally, it showed little awareness of the very real changes in the balance of economic and political forces that had been the consequence of twenty-five years of postwar economic growth. Yet it is an approach which, with the benefit of still more hindsight, can be seen to have had some substantial strengths. Certainly, the crisis presented itself to many contemporaries as a problem of inadequate economic resources (trying to pay for more welfare with a stagnating national product), and there is indeed good reason to think that the crisis of the early 1970s was, in some senses, much more 'purely economic' than later critics were to allow. Thus much of the perceived 'spiralling' of welfare costs was not due to 'democratic distemper' but to the logic of demographic pressure and statutory entitlement under circumstances of recession. Further, as the more spectacular predictions of neo-Marxists and New Right analysts have failed to materialize, it seems that the difficulties of the welfare state are indeed more substantially about the shortfall of resources available to fund further growth. Such a belief is buttressed by evidence that the best indicator of the capacity of national welfare states to weather the difficulties of the 1970s was not so much a reflection of their *political* complexion (the intensity of their democratic contradictions) as of a given nation's *economic* strength before the 1970s and of its capacity to absorb the oil shock of 1973 (Schmidt, 1983, pp. 1–26).

Even if we concentrate solely on economic developments, however, it is clear that the changes observed in the early 1970s were both more profound and longer lasting than the idea of a one-off 'shock to the system' suggests. This new economic context is not adequately defined by one or two hikes in the price of basic commodities, but rather by a whole series of changes in the international political economy which cumulatively shattered the stability of the postwar economic order. Such changes include the decline in stable exchange rates, the loss of the hegemonic role of the US, changing international terms of trade, the rise of newly industrialized countries, changing financial institutions and the sustained impact of new technologies.

The welfare state and the crisis of liberal democratic capitalism

The theoretical poverty of the perspective of 'external shock' has often been contrasted with New Right or neo-Marxist critics who are seen to have penetrated the 'depth structure' of contradictions in the welfare state. Certainly, there are considerable strengths in the shared features of these accounts of crisis. They were among the first to develop a 'political economy' approach, indicating that while the *symptoms* of the difficulties of the 1970s were economic, their *causes* lay in the interrelation of social, political and economic forces. They were also among the first to see that the recession of 1973–4 was not simply a 'blip' in the continuing process of unfettered postwar economic growth. They demonstrated that inflation had not just a political *consequence* but also, in part, a political *cause*. They

drew out the political consequences of the growing complexity and complicity of government, of greater bureaucratic and organizational density
and of the rise of organized and sectional interests, under circumstances
of representative democracy and full employment.

The glaring weakness in this analysis, however, was that its claims about
a challenge to advanced capitalism and/or liberal representative democracy went largely unfulfilled. In the UK, where the prognoses were often
the most gloomy, there was very little real threat to the political process.
There was some evidence of growing electoral volatility (sometimes
masked by the plurality voting system), of declining public deference to
government, of the intensified prosecution of sectional interests and of a
break with elements of consensus government. During the 1980s, there
was an erosion of local government democracy, the circumscription of
some civil liberties, the curtailment of trade union rights and quite substantial changes to the welfare state itself. All of these met with more or
less fierce resistance. But there was no breakdown of liberal democratic
government and, until the election of the Blair government in 1997, limited
interest in major constitutional reform. In the same period, a right-wing
government was returned to office four times, while welfare spending in
the major areas (pensions, health and education) remained largely intact
(Hills, 1997).

Why were analysts on both right and left so mistaken about the *consequences* of the welfare state structures they helped to reveal? First, there
is an element of misunderstanding the nature of the welfare state. For the
New Right, the welfare state was seen largely as an unproductive dead-
weight on the economy, imposed through the dynamics of irresponsible
(social) democracy. In the prevalent Marxist account, the welfare state was
the necessary legitimating trade-off for (the unacceptable social costs of)
capital accumulation. For both, the inevitable outcome was fiscal crisis.
But such a view is difficult to reconcile with the historical development of
the welfare state outlined in chapter 4. The welfare state was *not* generally
an imposition of organized labour through the pressure of electoral politics. It was as much (if not more) status preserving or market supporting
as it was decommodifying. In fact, evidence that, as both New Right and
neo-Marxists seem to assume, the welfare state dampens capitalist economic growth is limited at both 'micro' and 'macro' levels (Pfaller et al.,
1991). Similarly, the claims that public spending displaces private investment or that social benefits represent a real disincentive to labour are
thinly grounded. Certainly, under some circumstances and as part of a
broader constellation of forces, social spending might be complicit in poor
economic performance. But this is something very different from the claim
that social spending *causes* poor economic performance (Pen, 1987, pp.
346–7). Indeed, Nicholas Barr argues that the welfare state has a 'major
efficiency role' and that, in a context of market failures, 'we need a welfare

state for efficiency reasons, and would continue to do so even if all distributional problems had been solved' (Barr, 1987, p. 421; Blake and Ormerod, 1980; Block, 1987).

The British case is peculiarly instructive in this context. Britain was often portrayed in the literature of the 1970s as the country with the most pronounced problems of overload, ungovernability and welfare state malaise, so much so that this complex was often identified as 'the English disease' (see, for example, Jay, 1977). Yet we have seen that the UK was not an especially large welfare spender, nor were the terms of its social benefits either especially generous or particularly 'decommodifying'. There were consistently more extensive and generous welfare states with a far better economic record. The size and disposition of the UK public sector *might* have contributed to Britain's economic difficulties, but only in a context of much longer established problems of economic growth and capital formation (Gamble, 1981). Conversely, as Mishra points out, New Right critics at least tended to neglect those welfare states with a good economic record (Austria, Sweden) or else attribute their success to fortunate and extraneous circumstances (Mishra, 1984, p. 56). In general, this 'Anglocentric' bias (which has long been observed by continental analysts of the welfare state) is also a clue to the weakness of the more apocalyptic theses of contradiction and ungovernability (Flora and Heidenheimer, 1981b, p. 21). Thus Anthony Birch maintains that the New Right thesis is only sustainable for Britain at a very particular historical moment. Seeking to extrapolate from these very particular circumstances a general theory of the prospects for liberal representative democracy is quite unwarranted (Birch, 1984, pp. 158–9).

A number of more specific problems can also be identified in these accounts. New Right critics certainly overstated the power of trade unions in the 1970s. Even at the height of their ascendancy, unions were essentially the reactive and defensive organizations of labour (Clarke and Clements, 1977; Hyman, 1989a). All governments, and not only those who saw it as potentially therapeutic, found it difficult to control unemployment. This, in concert with growing international competition and greater capital mobility, radically curtailed even this limited power of trade unions. Similarly, there has been no inexorable rise of (social democratic) parties, irresponsibly promising 'more for less'. Indeed, the British Labour Party consummated its electoral rehabilitation by insisting on every possible occasion that it had ditched the commitment to 'tax and spend'. Despite the ubiquitous talk of governments 'buying' electoral victories through irresponsible manipulation of the economy, such empirical evidence as there is suggests that the impact of the 'political business cycle' has been greatly exaggerated (Alt and Chrystal, 1983).

Finally, it is worth drawing attention to the inadequacies of the accounts of legitimacy that underpin many of these accounts of crisis. Both left and right suggest that the difficulties surrounding the welfare state are likely finally to express themselves as a crisis of legitimacy of the democratic capitalist order (Habermas, 1976; Wolfe, 1979). But it seems clear that this is to operate with a conception of legitimacy which belongs to constitutional theory rather than to political sociology. The principle of legitimacy as the acknowledged right to rule is not one that has a prominent place in the day-to-day thinking of the democratic citizen. As Rose and Peters (1978) indicated, even 'political bankruptcy' does not mean fighting on the streets. Michael Mann has given definitive expression to the view that the 'social cohesion of liberal democracy' rests primarily on an *absence* of considerations of legitimacy, on the fact that the average citizen does not have a comprehensive view of the legitimate claims and limitations of governmental authority. It is a mistake to look to a legitimation crisis where legitimacy is not constituted in the way that analysts of its anticipated crisis suppose (Habermas, 1976; Wolfe, 1979; Mann, 1970).

Restructuring and Retrenchment: The Crisis Contained

Under these circumstances, attention gradually shifted away from 'crisis' and towards an assessment of the ways in which the end of the postwar growth society had been 'managed' from within the parameters of existing economic and political institutions. At the end of the 1970s, Ian Gough raised the perspective of crisis as a process of *restructuring*, in which a new basis could be established for the restored accumulation of capital. Gough argued that such a restoration of long-term profitability was only possible through a systematic weakening of the power of working-class organizations and a *retrenchment* of the political and social rights that had been institutionalized in the welfare arrangements of the postwar advanced capitalist world (1979, pp. 151–2).

This perspective came to set the agenda for a second and distinctive species of theories that dominated discussion in the 1980s. Following Taylor-Gooby (1985, p. 14), we may think of these as '*crisis containment*' theories. In such accounts, it was argued that the challenge which seemed in the 1970s to be addressed to democratic advanced capitalism itself had, in practice, been displaced on the social and economic policies that constituted the postwar welfare state. In practice, interventions in areas of social and economic policy had been successful in the limited though decisive sense that they managed to contain and control, if not actually to resolve, those tendencies which earlier theorists had thought would imperil the very continuation of liberal democracy. If it was any longer appropriate to speak of a crisis, this was now a crisis *within* the institutions of the welfare state itself.

Three sets of claims are characteristic of this 'crisis containment' theory. First, it was suggested that throughout the advanced capitalist world there was a break with the political consensus for a managed economy and state welfare that had characterized the postwar period. Secondly, this change was itself seen to have been made possible by a 'sea change' in public opinion, which had moved from support for collective solutions to problems of social need to a preference for market provision to satisfy individual welfare demands. Thirdly, and most importantly, these changes had in their turn opened the way for cuts in welfare entitlements and a 'restructuring' of public welfare provision. This indicated a move away from the model of a universalist, rights-based welfare state towards a more residualist, needs-governed system of public relief. We should specify each of these claims in a little more detail.

The 'end of consensus'

'Crisis containment' theorists argue that while critics were right to observe a severe challenge to the postwar consensus in the heightened social and political struggles of the early 1970s, they were wrong to identify this with an unmanageable threat to the prevailing democratic capitalist order. The perceived 'contradictions' of welfare capitalism have been, if not definitively resolved, then at least effectively managed. This has been achieved through a radical reconstruction of the social and political order of the advanced capitalist societies, a reconstruction in the interests of capital and parties of the right, achieved through an abandonment of the postwar consensus.

Although this process was seen to have taken different forms in differing countries, according to specifically local conditions, its definitive and most articulate expression was often identified with the rise of 'Thatcherism', both in the UK and, by extension, elsewhere. In the 1979 election campaign, the Conservatives presented themselves as a party that was breaking with the exhausted legacy of postwar politics. This break extended to each of the major policy elements of consensus. In terms of the 'mixed economy', there was a commitment to return publicly owned industries to the private sector and to limit government interventions in the day-to-day management of relations between employers and employees. There was a commitment to sustained or enhanced economic growth, but this was to be achieved by an *abandonment* of Keynesian economics and the commitment to full employment in favour of monetarism and supply-side reforms. On the welfare state, there was to be a drive to cut costs by concentrating resources on those in greatest need, to restrain the bureaucratic interventions of the 'nanny state' in the day-to-day life of citizens, to give a greater role for voluntary welfare institutions and to encourage individuals to make provision for their individual welfare through the private sector (encouraging private pensions, private health care and private education). These were initiatives that were seen to have an international impact. According to Dennis Kavanagh:

> economic recession and slow economic growth undermined popular support for the welfare consensus in a number of . . . states. The Thatcher governments' policies of tax cuts, privatization, 'prudent' finance, squeezing state expenditure and cutting loss-making activities . . . had echoes in other western states. (1987, p. 9)

It is not perhaps surprising that 'the Thatcher agenda' should have had an appeal for right-wing incumbents in the UK, the US and perhaps West Germany in the early 1980s. What was seen as still more decisive for the proponents of 'crisis containment' was the extent to which avowedly socialist or social democratic governments were forced to adopt 'austerity' measures which mimicked the policies of right-wing governments. This might be taken to describe the experience of the Labour government in the UK in the late 1970s (especially for those who see the decisive change in British government policy coming not in 1979 but in 1976). To an extent, it even spread into the heartland of the welfare state in Scandinavia (particularly in Denmark). But perhaps most instructive was the experience of Mitterrand's Socialists in France, who, though elected on a radical socialist manifesto in 1981, were abruptly forced to 'U-turn' and embrace the politics of austerity. What seemed to divide this 'Thatcherism with a human face' from the real thing was a lack of enthusiasm for the policies adopted.

The 'sea change' in popular opinion

This *political* abandonment of consensus could not have been effected, it is argued, had there not been a wholesale erosion of popular support for existing welfare state arrangements. There are some who argue that the working class never had a strong attachment to the idea of welfare rights and social citizenship (at least in the UK). They trace 'the long hostility of working people to what is perceived as dependency on public provision' (Selbourne, 1985, p. 117). Certainly, many commentators concede that public attitudes to welfare have always been ambivalent and that even where support for the welfare state has appeared to be strong, such strength has often been 'brittle'. According to John Alt, people's support for the welfare state was seen to be basically 'altruistic . . . supporting a benefit which will largely go to others'. In economic 'good times', when people's earnings are rising, they may be willing to afford such 'altruistic policies'. But times of 'economic stress', such as the 1970s, tend to be associated with 'less generosity' and a preference for 'spending cuts over taxation' (Alt, 1979, p. 258).

Perhaps the single clearest (and most widely challenged) statement of the case for a decline in public support for state welfare in this period came from the Institute of Economic Affairs. In a survey of British public opinion, Harris and Seldon claimed to have isolated 'a large, latent but suppressed desire for change in British education and medical care among high proportions of people of both sexes, all ages and incomes, whether officially at work or not, and of all political sympathies' (1987, p. 51; see also Harris and Seldon, 1979, p. 201).

Further evidence of decline in popular support for the welfare state was premised on the growing electoral difficulties of social democratic parties and the renaissance of the political right. Social Democrats have long been identified (rightly or wrongly) as 'the party of the welfare state'. Their rise in the 1960s was often associated with the incorporation of the welfare state in advanced capitalist societies. Correspondingly, the decline in their popularity in the 1970s was seen as evidence of a decline in support for the welfare state itself.

Here again, the most familiar examples are those of the UK, the US and West Germany. But perhaps more important were the examples of a shift to the right in the heartland of the welfare state. Of these, the most important examples were Denmark and, of course, Sweden where the return of a 'bourgeois' coalition in 1976 brought to an end forty-four years of continuous social democratic government. But evidence of the decline in support for socialist parties was Europe-wide. The proportion of votes going to all left parties (Social Democratic, Socialist and Communist) fell from 41.3 per cent in the 1960s to 40.1 per cent in the 1970s. In the same period, support for conservative parties crept up from 24.6 to 24.9 per cent. In the early 1980s, the share of the conservative vote advanced to 25.3 per cent. Between 1977 and 1982, incumbent socialists were defeated in Britain, West Germany, Belgium, Holland, Norway, Luxembourg and Denmark. In 1975, there were more than twice as many Socialist as Conservative cabinet ministers in European governments (54.1 per cent contrasted with 25.1 per cent). By 1982, the Conservative parties had established a one percentage point lead over the socialists (37.6 per cent Conservative, 36.4 per cent Socialist). Lane and Ersson concluded that the Socialist parties' position 'was reinforced during the 1950s and the 1960s; in the 1970s and early 1980s, however, a decline to a lower level set in'. For the parties of the right, by contrast, the data 'confirm the hypothesis of a conservative revival in the 1970s and early 1980s' (*Economist*, 1982a, pp. 35–6; Lane and Ersson, 1987, pp. 112–15).

'The cuts'

The third, and possibly the most important element in the 'crisis containment' perspective was the spectre of cuts and 'restructuring' in social expenditure. On the basis of a change in popular and electoral opinion, and given the successes of parties of the right and the breakdown of the politics of consensus, it seemed that the 1980s must be a decade of welfare retrenchment. Many commentators, both advocates and opponents, anticipated a retreat from a universal welfare state based on citizenship towards a more modest policy of the relief of destitution on the basis of demonstrated need in a context of declining resources for welfare.

Again, the Thatcher government was seen to have been in the vanguard of this development. The first Treasury White Paper of the newly elected UK Conservative government in 1979 maintained that 'public expenditure is at the heart of Britain's present economic difficulties' (HM Treasury, 1979). Accordingly, the welfare state looked particularly vulnerable to retrenchment and within a year of Thatcher's election Ian Gough was arguing that

> Britain is experiencing the most far-reaching experiment in 'new right' politics in the Western world. [A number of] policy shifts . . . contribute to this aim: legal sanctions against unions, mass unemployment by means of tight monetary controls, the cutting of social benefits for the families of strikers, a reduction in the social wage on several fronts, and a shift to more authoritarian practices in the welfare field. It represents one coherent strategy for managing the British crisis, a strategy aimed at the heart of the post-war Keynesian-welfare state settlement. (1983, pp. 162–3).

Much the same process was identified in the US. Here it was said in 1986 that 'the Reagan administration and its big business allies have declared a new class war' against the working class and those reliant on social assistance (Piven and Cloward, 1986, p. 47). Writing in the same year, Michael Katz insisted that:

> In the last several years, city governments have slashed services; state legislatures have attacked general assistance (outdoor relief to persons ineligible for benefits from other programs); and the Reagan administration has launched an offensive against social welfare and used tax policy to widen the income gap between rich and poor. (1986, p. 274)

But perhaps even more telling were the prospects for retrenchment in the continental European welfare state. In September 1982, *The Economist* argued that 'during the 1980s, all rich countries' governments . . . are likely to make . . . big cuts in social spending'. Within a month, it was reporting 'the withering of Europe's welfare states'. In Germany, there were to be delays in pension increases, the collection of sickness insurance contributions from pensioners and an end to student grants. Holland faced 'a savage cutback', while the one-time leading welfare state, Denmark, was to seek a 7 per cent cut in public spending through reducing levels of unemployment compensation and introducing new charges for children's day care. Most saliently, the newly elected socialist government in France was introducing new charges to meet non-medical hospital costs and increasing social security contributions in a quest to curb spending by $12 billion in a full year. Only the perverse Swedes were 'the exception that proved the rule', re-electing a socialist government on an anti-cuts programme (*The Economist*, 1982b, pp. 67–8).

Crisis Contained?

'Crisis containment' certainly offered clarity in its linked account of the breakdown of the postwar consensus, of a popular political shift to the right and of an unpicking of the fabric of the welfare state. It suggested that this change had successfully addressed the threat of systemic crisis that had been identified in the mid-1970s and had seen it displaced into a more modest and piecemeal, if squalid, crisis for those in society who were most reliant on the support of public services. Undoubtedly this approach captured *something* of the changes that took place in the 1980s. But by the end of that decade it looked as though welfare state experience was both much more varied and (for its supporters) much more positive than these critics supposed. As before in the welfare state story, it looked as though an account of the (quite unusual) experience of the US and the UK had been generalized to give a (quite inappropriate) account of welfare state experience elsewhere in the developed world.

The end of consensus?

We have seen that Britain under Margaret Thatcher is often identified with the most definitive end to the postwar consensus. Certainly, the polemical hostility to consensus was clear. In 1981, Margaret Thatcher dismissed consensus as 'the process of abandoning all beliefs, principles, values and policies' (cited in Kavanagh and Morris, 1989, p. 119), and the 1979 general election in the UK can certainly be described as a 'watershed'. Labour had been in office for eleven of the previous fifteen years. This election brought to power a Conservative government that remained in office for eighteen years and won four consecutive elections. The 1979 election also saw a major defection of skilled working-class voters from Labour to Conservative. Yet in judging the breach with consensus that it represented, one must be a little circumspect.

First, the break-up of consensus predates the election of the Conservatives in 1979. The first two years of the Heath government (1970–2) had been committed to the sort of neoliberalism that the 1979 Thatcher government promised. It was the Labour government of 1974–9 that presided

over the earliest retrenchment in welfare spending and a (then) unprecedented rise in postwar unemployment. In so far as there was a kind of
Keynesianism to be abandoned in Britain, the symbolic moment of change
is often identified with Prime Minister Jim Callaghan's speech to the 1976
Labour Party Conference. With the shift in Labour policy after 1976 (and
the imposition of cash limits) sentiment drifted away from the egalitarian
revisionism of the postwar period (in which welfare services were to be
part of a gradualist strategy of equality) towards the more residualist aspiration of 'protecting the weakest in hard times'. In the great public services (such as health and education) the watchword was affordability; in
terms of income maintenance and cash transfers, the ideology, at least,
was to concentrate resources where they were most needed.

Turning to the record of the Thatcher government after 1979, political
practice did not always match the radical party rhetoric. Certainly, unemployment was allowed to reach unheard of levels (officially in excess of 3
million), a string of major public corporations and utilities were returned
to the private sector (notably British Telecom, British Gas, British Airways
and water supply and sewerage services). There was a major (and popular)
drive to sell off public housing, and limited cuts in expenditure on education. Yet in the period of the first Thatcher administration total social
expenditure showed a significant growth of about 10 per cent, rising as a
proportion of GDP from 21.7 per cent to 23.6 per cent (though, of course,
much of this increase was the consequence of extremely high levels of
unemployment and low economic growth; Taylor-Gooby, 1985, p. 72). In
1985–6, social expenditure stood at £36 billion, a third higher than its 1979
level (Kavanagh, 1987, p. 217).

It was only under the third Thatcher Administration (after 1987) that
major reform of the welfare state (beyond the transformation of public
housing) was attempted. Indeed, this has been described as initiating 'the
most decisive break in British social policy since the period between 1944
and 1948' (Glennerster et al., 1991). As well as the implementation of
the government's Social Security Act of 1986, these years witnessed the
passage of the Education Reform Act 1988, the Housing Act 1988, the
National Health Service and Community Care Act 1990 and the wholesale reform of the NHS following the publication of the White Paper
Working for Patients in January 1989 (Department of Health, 1989).

These changes were certainly hugely consequential and, at the time of
their introduction, were vigorously contested both by the opposition
parties and by organized interests within the public sector as an assault
on the welfare state. Yet we should be clear that what was transformed by
this flurry of legislation was, above all, the accepted *modes of delivery* of
public services. There was certainly an aspiration to control costs, above
all by improving the 'efficiency' of the public sector, and this was often
presented in terms of the capacity of the market to extract a much

enhanced output from a more-or-less static input (or, rather less glam-
ourously, to increase workloads and squeeze the pay of public sector
workers). But this was not the classical New Right response to inefficiency
and illiberalism in state welfare (which is to transfer the provision of
welfare services from public administration to private markets). Although
there has been a significant privatization of welfare effort over the past
twenty years, this has more commonly been transferred to women in families rather than to markets and (again with the partial exception of
housing) there has been no wholesale transfer of state welfare provision
into the private sector.

Still more important than this, though, is the sense that experience in
the UK (and in other English-speaking countries) was atypical – or at least
that it represented just one form of response to the challenges of the 1970s,
one that was especially adapted to a particular form of advanced capitalist state, one in which 'market freedoms' were especially entrenched and
the institutions of consensus brittle and shallowly rooted. Elsewhere, and
especially in continental Europe, there was very limited evidence that a
more deep-seated societal consensus was in decline. The emergent literature on 'varieties of capitalism' (summarized in Hall and Soskice, 2001)
makes this especially clear. Observers of the differing 'varieties of capitalism' have identified two characteristic forms of advanced capitalist
economy: the liberal market economy (LME) – exemplified by Australia,
Canada, Ireland, New Zealand, the UK and the US – and the coordinated
market economy (CME) – typical of most of the countries of northern
Europe and Scandinavia plus Japan. LMEs are market focused and have
had social policy institutions which correspond to this – with a focus on
deregulated labour markets, external flexibility and means testing. In the
CMEs, welfare state institutions have been embedded in a coordinated
economy and much greater emphasis has been placed on training, more
regulated labour markets and less adversarial industrial relations negoti-
ated between the 'social partners' (Hall and Soskice, 2001, pp. 50–1). In
the CMEs, consensus has been societal and institutionalized rather than
'just political'. There have been examples of coordination breaking down
(for example, in centralized wage bargaining in Sweden) but this was more
a feature of the 1990s than the 1980s. In general, there was very limited
evidence to show that the social policy consensus had declined in
CMEs. Here, welfare state budgets proved remarkably resilient throughout the 1980s.

A changing public opinion

Evidence of a sea change in public opinion, measured either by changing
social attitudes or voting behaviour, is also rather poorly sustained.
Coughlin's comprehensive review of international public opinion on the

welfare state across a sample of eight rich nations at the end of the 1970s found that:

> public attitudes toward the principles of social policy have developed along similar lines both of acceptance and rejection. The idea of collective responsibility for assuring minimum standards of employment, health care, income, and other conditions of social and economic well-being has everywhere gained a foothold in popular values and beliefs. And yet the survey evidence suggests a simultaneous tendency supporting individual achievement, mobility, and responsibility for one's own lot, and rejecting the elimination of aspects of economic life associated with capitalism. (Coughlin, 1980, p. 31)

Levels of support have long varied between 'big spenders', such as Sweden and France, and 'low spenders', such as the US and Australia, but we can find broadly similar patterns across a wide range of countries. The same areas – pensions, public health insurance, family/child allowances – were the most popular (and expensive), and the same sort of provision – unemployment compensation and public assistance – the least popular. Not only between nations, but between social classes and across political sympathies, it seems that everyone likes pensions and no one likes 'scroungers' (Coughlin, 1980, p. 52).

Taylor-Gooby's (1989) review of the international evidence from six developed countries a decade later revealed lower absolute *levels* of popular support, but a similar *ranking* of both countries and programmes. The survey material recorded majorities everywhere for increased state spending on health care (88 per cent in the UK and 81 per cent in Italy), and a clear (unweighted) majority for increases in old age pensions (with support highest again in the UK and Italy, with positive responses of 75 per cent and 76 per cent respectively) (Taylor-Gooby, 1989, p. 41). Overall, Taylor-Gooby concluded that

> the attitudes of the citizens of the six nations correspond more closely to the traditional post-war settlement than they reveal any enthusiasm for change, although within this framework there are substantial national variations . . . Social welfare that provides for mass needs is warmly endorsed, but provision for minorities, whose interests challenge the work ethic, receives meagre approval. Direct social engineering to advance equality of outcomes is not endorsed. (1989, pp. 41, 49)

Projecting further forward, the International Social Survey Program (ISSP) undertook a survey of public opinion on the government's role in welfare in 1985, repeated in 1996. Both surveys reveal a wide diversity of support (with the Anglophone/LMEs generally registering the lowest levels of endorsement for government intervention). Across the decade, for those states for which the ISSP had data in both surveys (US, UK,

Germany, Australia and Italy), popular support for greater government action to redistribute income and to support public provision of health care, education and unemployment benefits actually rose. In the UK, levels of public support for greater public spending on health (92 per cent) and education (85 per cent) were high in absolute terms in 1996, and higher than they had been a decade previously (ISSP, 1985/1996).

Overall, the pattern of popular attitudes to state welfare is complex but surprisingly stable. There is public hostility to certain areas of state provision, probably some repressed demand masked by state compulsion, hostility to certain categories of beneficiary and some support for private/market provision of welfare services. These views are not new, however, and they coexist with widespread popular endorsement of the most expensive and extensive elements of state provision. There is little evidence here of a large-scale popular backlash against the welfare state.

The decline of the 'welfare state party'

Evidence of a decline in popular support for the welfare state expressed as a sustained and systematic fall in electoral support for parties of the left and centre-left is again very limited. It includes (1) a series of defeats of social democratic governments in Europe and North America between 1977 and 1982; (2) a long-term decline in left voting after 1960; and (3) a fall of more than a third in socialist participation in government between 1975 and 1982. It is clear that there was a movement (perhaps more properly a countermovement) against the left in the period between 1975 and 1982. However, with the benefit of greater hindsight, this reversal must be read as cyclical rather than structural. The combined electoral strength of the left in Western Europe, which had stood at 40.1 per cent through the 1970s, actually advanced to 42.5 per cent in the period 1980–3. In the 1980s, while the right captured or retained power in the UK, the US and West Germany, the left retained or reclaimed office in Sweden, Norway, France, Spain, Portugal, Greece, New Zealand and Australia (Mackie and Rose, 1991; *Electoral Studies*, 1989). If we go forward to the 1990s, the record continued to be a mixed one. The French Socialist Party rode a rollercoaster with its catastrophic defeat in the National Assembly elections of 1993, but its rejection was actually outstripped by the Canadian Conservatives, whose vote tumbled from 43 per cent in 1988 to just 16 per cent in 1993 (and their representation from 154 MPs to just 2!). In 1992 and 1996, the Republicans lost the US Presidential elections, while in 1997 the British Conservative Party, after eighteen years in office, went down to its worst defeat of the twentieth century. Meanwhile, in Australia, New Zealand and Spain, which had spent much of the 1980s under Labor or Socialist rule, electoral ascendancy passed to the right (though it has since swung back towards the left in both New Zealand and Spain). Lane,

McKay and Newton's long-term survey (1997) showed surprisingly little movement in overall levels of support for parties of the left (and the right) between the 1960s and the 1990s. Thus the view, sometimes expressed in the 1980s, that parties which called themselves Labour or Socialist or Social Democrat could never get elected, has proved to be quite unfounded (though parties have generally given up on the attempt to win office under the label 'Communist'). Much more salient is the issue of whether such parties can still pursue distinctively social democratic policy objectives and whether it is still appropriate to style them 'welfare state parties'.

'The cuts'

Overall, evidence that the 1980s was a decade of welfare state cuts of the kind anticipated in the literature of crisis containment is extremely thin. In the period between 1980 and the mid-1990s, social spending in most countries continued to grow faster than GDP. Certainly, there was a major slowdown in *rates of growth* of social expenditure. Between 1960 and 1975 real growth in social expenditure stood at about 8 per cent a year. Between 1975 and 1981 this rate of real growth was halved to just over 4 per cent, and during the 1980s growth in the proportion of GDP devoted to social expenditure fell again across the OECD to about 2 per cent, most of which growth had been achieved by 1983 (OECD, 1984; OECD, 1994, p. 69). But only three countries (Ireland, Belgium and West Germany) saw reduced social expenditure ratios in the 1980s, while these ratios continued to increase substantially in nine countries (Canada, Greece, France, Norway, Denmark, New Zealand, Spain, Italy and Finland). Overall, the pattern was similar to that experienced in the European Union:

> Between 1980 and 1983 social protection expenditure as a percentage of GDP continued the upward trend of the 1970s. The efforts of governments to reduce the burden of social protection were fairly successful between 1983 and 1989. After 1989, under the combined effect of increased demand on the social protection system and the economic recession, social protection expenditure as a percentage of GDP again began to grow rapidly. (Eurostat, 1996c, p. 133)

In the severe recession of the early 1990s, average expenditure on social protection throughout the European Union rose from 23.7 per cent of GDP to 26.5 per cent (Eurostat, 1996a, p. 168). In fact, average levels of social expenditure across the OECD were not to reach their peak (to date) until 1993 (OECD, 2005).

Yet this gross pattern of marginal long-term increases in social expenditure overlain by cyclical fluctuations relating to the state of the economy gives us a very partial picture of what was actually happening in this period. For we have to relate this incremental growth in social spending to a changing pattern of demand for social protection. The welfare state is quintessentially a form of provision for the elderly. Even in the depth of recession in the early 1990s, unemployment (and related job-creation measures) accounted for less than 10 per cent of social expenditure throughout the European Union. Expenditure on the elderly and health care (which is disproportionately concentrated on older people) accounts for some four-fifths of social spending. The world's population is ageing and with it comes a growing demand for effective forms of income maintenance (and health care and housing provision) for those who are no longer economically active. At the same time, other social changes – the growth in single parent families, the increase in part-time and 'non-standard' employment, persistent long-term unemployment and so on – place increasing pressure on social budgets. If we control for changing needs, the pattern of expenditures looks much more like stasis than incremental growth (for a discussion, see Castles, 2004, pp. 35–9). Interestingly, however, this general stasis conceals some significant changes in the performance of individual countries during this period – and the distinction between 'generous' and 'mean' providers persists.

There are also important changes in the distribution of the *costs* of this welfare provision. While governments' capacity to raise taxes has not collapsed (indeed the average tax take across the OECD rose from 34 per cent in 1980 to 37.4 per cent in 1996), there has been a change in the incidence of the tax burden (*Economist*, 1997). In general, governments have decreased their dependence on (progressive) income tax and taxes on corporations in favour of a greater reliance on indirect (sales) taxes and user charges. There is a widespread belief in governing opinion that we have reached the limits of what democratic publics are willing to pay in direct taxes (although these levels vary quite widely between states) and that, for example, more of the costs of employment-related benefits must be met by employees' social security contributions rather than by employers or general taxation. Similarly, across a range of jurisdictions, there have been moves to transfer part of the costs of the residential care of the infirm elderly towards these elderly people themselves or their families, and there is, as we shall see in chapter 6, an almost desperate search to find alternative forms of pension provision to relieve the state of part of its present burden. There are also historically deeply embedded differences in the way that welfare is paid for – principally by taxes (for example, in Australia) or primarily through charges on employers and employees (as, for example, in France).

In practice, what we see is that even the most committed neoliberal governments (under Reagan and Thatcher in the 1980s) found it extraordinarily difficult to 'roll back' welfare state expenditures. There have been some real cuts. The first Bolger administration in New Zealand implemented benefit cuts of unprecedented severity in its 1991 budget. But even this most committed of neoliberal governments was forced to back down on its plans to curtail (comparatively generous and expensive) state superannuation for the elderly, and social expenditure actually *rose* between 1989 and 1993 from 20.2 to 23.9 per cent of GDP (Kelsey, 1995, p. 276). This reflects a more general pattern. There have been real cuts in some forms of welfare provision (reduction in levels of benefit or the elimination of public services). More generally, the value of benefits has been allowed to fall (through a failure to upgrade in line with general inflation), access to services or benefits has been made more difficult (more means testing and tighter eligibility criteria) and recipients have had to pay for more of the services they receive (reducing government subsidies to service providers, more asset testing, a greater reliance on co-contributions). This pattern of retrenchment is reflected in table 5.1. But, given the overall increase in levels of expenditure through the 1980s, it is hard to see that even this amounts to an endorsement of the 'cuts' that many anticipated at the start of that decade.

Table 5.1   Retrenchment of benefits in OECD countries in the 1990s

Type of benefit	Change	Examples
Old age pensions	Raising retirement age	UK, New Zealand, Italy, Japan
	Increase in qualifying period for a full pension	France, Portugal, Ireland, Finland
	Lowered basis for upgrading of benefits in line with inflation	UK, France, Spain
	Income testing of pension	Austria, Denmark, Australia
Disability	Stricter test of incapacity	UK, US, Netherlands, Norway
	New time limits, reduced benefits	UK, US, Netherlands
Unemployment	Reduction in duration of benefits	Belgium, UK, Denmark, US
	Reduction in level of benefits	Germany, Ireland, New Zealand, Switzerland
	Reduced eligibility	Netherlands, UK, Belgium
Family allowances	Declining real value or decreasing eligibility	UK, Spain, Netherlands

Source: Ploug, 1995, pp. 65–7.

Conclusion

Talk of a 'crisis' of the welfare state remained ubiquitous throughout this period (indeed, it continues down to the present). Yet evidence of crisis in any of the principal senses in which it has been identified in this chapter is extremely thin. Claims about the destabilization of liberal democracy, the decimation of social expenditure or the withdrawal of public support for major welfare programmes have been poorly vindicated. By contrast, the experience of welfare states in the period after 1975 is perhaps captured in terms of a process of *structural adjustment* (see, for example, OECD, 1987b). Although often thought of as a process of retrenchment recommended by First World bankers to Third World governments, structural adjustment actually describes a much broader repertoire of strategies which have been pressed on governments across the globe. In the face of profound changes in the national and international economic environment, governments are seen to have 'adjusted' their social policy regimes. Echoing the arguments about post-Fordism, governments have sought to adapt their national economic regimes to a changed climate for investment and to promote movement in the direction of greater 'flexibility' and enhanced 'competitiveness'. In general, this has meant promoting microeconomic reform (more flexible labour markets, privatization, flatter tax regimes, greater openness to foreign investors), bearing down on public expenditure (by reducing the level and incidence of public services and introducing 'efficiency gains' in the public sector) and trying to move from a 'passive' (social transfers) to an 'active' (retraining and work placement) welfare state. Although the policy agenda is seen increasingly to be set by (global) markets, this is not quite the response that the New Right anticipated (and would have welcomed). For while the state may increasingly act through *regulating* rather than actually *delivering* services, at the same time it may actually become more active and intervene more intensively (and intrusively) in the day-to-day life of (at least its dependent) citizens. There has certainly been no straightforward 'withdrawal' of the state in favour of markets.

Yet the consequences of structural adjustment are still likely to be profound. Exposing national economies and national corporatist arrangements to a largely unregulated world economy has transformed the circumstances under which any government might seek, for example, to pursue a policy of full employment or to redistribute wealth through a progressive taxation system. Secondly, changes in the economy nationally and internationally (and the social policy reforms that follow from this) may transform the configuration of individuals' interests and the political articulation of those interests. The character of a welfare state cannot be adequately measured by levels of aggregate spending. Long-term high levels of unemployment amidst societies of generally rising affluence, increasingly segmented labour markets and new patterns of consumption may change the disposition of social expenditure. Rising levels of social spending and continuing public endorsement of the popular elements of the welfare state may well be consistent with an internal transformation from a solidary, universalistic, citizenship-based welfare state towards a system based on the more generous provision of insurance-style entitlement and a further deterioration in the position of the poor and stigmatized (Alber, 1988b, pp. 187–9; see also Parry, 1986, pp. 155–240). This is reflected in the concerns of those who have written of the emergence of a '40–30–30 society' in which the opportunities and circumstances of those in the bottom third of society increasingly diverge from those of the most affluent 40 per cent (Hutton, 1995).

We return to some of these issues in the concluding chapter. For now, we turn to a consideration of the ways in which this process of 'structural adjustment' has developed since the early 1990s.

6
Retrenchment and Recalibration

A Changing Agenda: 'Recalibration' under Diversity

As we trace the evidence of change and continuity in welfare states since the early 1990s, two analytical developments are of especial importance. These are first, and following Esping-Andersen's seminal texts, *The Three Worlds of Welfare Capitalism* (1990) and *Social Foundations of Postindustrial Economies* (1999), an increased emphasis on the importance of the *diversity* of experience among differing types of welfare state-regime; and, secondly, following Paul Pierson's work on 'the new politics of welfare' in *Dismantling the Welfare State?* (1994) and *The New Politics of the Welfare State* (2000), a greater emphasis on the historical embeddedness and robustness of existing welfare regimes and a reform agenda built around the idea of 'recalibration' rather than retrenchment. We need to give some attention to these two analytical developments before we can offer an account of what has happened to welfare in the last decade.

The Diversity of Welfare State Experience: The World of Welfare Regimes

The twin insights that underlie Esping-Andersen's work are, first, that not all welfare regimes are the same and, secondly, that the variation between them is not most effectively captured by a sole focus on social expenditure (in which the distribution between low and high spenders is assumed to correspond to the spectrum from mean/residual to generous/inclusive welfare states). In Esping-Andersen's view, if it is appropriate to think of all the states of developed capitalism as welfare states, then these are clearly welfare states of rather differing kinds. These differences are not however linearly distributed between low spenders and high spenders or between residual and institutional models. Indeed the *level* of social expenditure may not be a reliable indicator of the character of any given welfare state. More important is the extent to which welfare state measures are either market supporting or market usurping (*decommodifying*) for workers. Given this logic, welfare states are seen to cluster around three ideal-typical regime types (Esping-Andersen, 1990, pp. 26–33; see also Rein et al., 1987; Esping-Andersen, 1999):

1   The *liberal welfare state* is dominated by the logic of the market. Benefits are modest, often means tested and stigmatizing. The principle of 'less eligibility' requires that welfare should not undermine the propensity to work. The state encourages the private provision of market forms of welfare (private insurance/occupational welfare).
    Typical examples: US, UK, Canada, Australia, New Zealand.

2   In the *conservative/'corporatist' welfare state*, 'the liberal obsession with market efficiency and commodification was never pre-eminent' and correspondingly the granting of social rights was never so contested. Private insurance and occupational welfare are 'minimal'. However, the emphasis of social rights is on upholding existing class and status differentials and its redistributive effects are 'negligible'. Such welfare states often have their origins in pre-democratic or authoritarian regimes which sought to use social policy as a means of defusing the threat of working-class mobilization (Bismarck in Germany, Taafe in Austria). In many cases, corporatist regimes are shaped by the church (especially Catholic social thought), and this tends to determine their conservative attitude to the family (gender differential benefits to support the traditional form of the male-dominated family), and their support of the principle of *subsidiarity* (in which the state should support and deliver only those forms of welfare which other intermediary institutions, and notably the church, are unable to provide).
    Typical examples: Austria, France, Germany, Italy.

3   The *social democratic welfare state* is characterized by universalism and the usurpation of the market. It is envisaged as 'a welfare state that would promote an equality of the highest standards, rather than an equality of minimal needs'. Benefits are graduated in accordance with earnings, but this is a way of securing universal support for, and participation in, a universal insurance system. Unlike the other regimes, the state is not seen as a second or last resort, but as the principal means of realizing the social rights of all its citizens. It is, of necessity,

Table 6.1 Characteristics of regime types

	Liberal	Social democratic	Conservative
Role of			
Family	Marginal	Marginal	Central
Market	Central	Marginal	Marginal
State	Marginal	Central	Subsidiary
Welfare state			
Dominant mode of solidarity	Individual	Universal	Kinship, corporatism, etatism
Dominant locus of solidarity	Market	State	Family
Degree of decommodification	Minimal	Maximum	High (for breadwinner)
Modal examples	USA	Sweden	Germany, Italy

Source: Esping-Andersen, 1999, p. 85.

committed to the principle of full employment, since 'the enormous costs of maintaining a solidaristic, universalistic and decommodifying welfare state' can be best and perhaps only achieved 'with most people working, and the fewest possible living off social transfers'.
Typical examples: Sweden and Norway.

Conservative/corporatist welfare states may have spending levels that approach those of the social democratic states but their distributional consequences and the political interests and strategies that they articulate may be quite different.

One of the key criticisms of this first formulation of Esping-Andersen's regime types came from those feminists who saw his characterization of the welfare state as too focused on the labour market and employed workers, failing to capture the salience of differing policies towards families and informal care as a key indicator of regime type and strategic purpose. Responding to these criticisms, Esping-Andersen's later configuration of differing regime types took the slightly different form shown in table 6.1.

The Regimes Debate

Much of the burgeoning comparative welfare state literature of the 1990s and beyond can be seen as a 'settling of accounts' with Esping-Andersen.

Two of these developments have been of especial interest. First, there has been an attempt to identify additional or alternative 'regime types'. Secondly, there has been an insistence that Esping-Andersen's focus on *decommodification* (and thus, by implication, the world of waged work) needs supplementing with other classificatory criteria. (For an excellent survey, see Arts and Gelissen, 2006.)

In the first category is Castles and Mitchell's (1992) reinterpretation of Esping-Andersen's original classification. Castles and Mitchell insist that there is a fourth and 'radical' regime type lurking in Esping-Andersen's evidence. These states (Australia, New Zealand and the UK) appear as 'liberal' in Esping-Andersen's classification, but Castles and Mitchell insist that their distinctive combination of low expenditure *plus* high levels of redistribution merit consideration as a distinctive *radical* regime type. Of course, this 'radicalism' may now be a part of history, since taxation regimes in all these states (especially New Zealand and the UK) are much less progressive now than when the relevant data was collected (in the 1980s). But their analysis contains a more general and extremely salient point, which is especially well illustrated by the Australian experience. It is that quite conventional welfare state goals may be delivered through quite unconventional (and sometimes consequently unreported) channels. Thus a quite central aspect of 'decommodification' in the Australian context was the industrial 'award' system of judicial wage-setting which dates back to the 1920s (and which has been incrementally legislated away over the past twenty years). Similarly (internationally quite variable) levels of home ownership may have a decisive impact on the (in)equality of welfare outcomes which standard redistributive indices do not fully capture. Even means testing has a quite different resonance in Australia from that which European commentators might anticipate (and perhaps incorporate in their welfare models). Interest in these welfare state alternatives (which their supporters, at least, would classify as broadly social democratic in intent) has intensified as the social democratic welfare state and, above all, 'the Swedish model' have been seen to be in serious difficulties (Lane, 1995; C. Pierson, 2001).

A second area of particular interest for those seeking to build on Esping-Andersen's typology has been the emergent welfare states of southern Europe. Stephan Leibfried (1993) has identified a distinctive type of welfare state in what he characterizes as the 'Latin Rim' countries of the European Union (Portugal, Spain, Greece and, in some limited respects, Italy and France). He described these as 'rudimentary welfare states', playing 'catch up' with their more developed northern neighbours. Typically, these welfare states promised much but had quite underdeveloped delivery systems and relied, in practice, on much older systems of social support from the family and the Catholic church. More recently, Mario Ferrera (1996) has outlined a number of distinctive features which serve to define the 'southern' model of welfare. These include a highly fragmented and distorted system of income maintenance (with pensions ranging from the hugely generous to the negligible), a (partially realized) commitment to national healthcare systems and the delivery of services through a mixture of underdeveloped state institutions and clientelistic party political networks. There is an indication that in some of these states the combination of substantial policy commitments, clientelistic party politics and a weak state capacity (to raise taxation and deliver well-regulated services) may trigger 'fiscal crises' more severe than those so far weathered (with some difficulty) in northern Europe. There has also been an ongoing debate about whether Esping-Andersen has slotted the nations of Europe into the right classificatory category. There is, for example, keen disagreement about whether the Netherlands can properly be described as 'social democratic', with Esping-Andersen (1999) himself seeming now to see it as a social democratic–conservative hybrid. More recently, Martin Seeleib-Kaiser (2002) has mounted a fairly frontal assault on the idea that Germany can be described as an exemplar of the continental conservative-corporatist welfare model.

So far, the comparative study of welfare states and the attempt to construct sophisticated typologies has tended to be focused on those countries with the most developed economies. These are the states with the richest statistical bases and in which most of the researchers live! There has, however, been increasing interest in welfare arrangements outside these areas. The political economy of Japan and its employment-related welfare have long been part of the ageing industry of 'explaining' the Japanese 'economic miracle'. In more recent years, this interest has spread into the neighbouring 'Asian tigers' although, thus far, attempts to construct a Japanese or 'Confucian' model of welfare have met with qualified success (C. Jones, 1993; Goodman and Peng, 1996; Esping-Andersen, 1997; Gough, 2001). Another area of heightened interest has been the 'transition' welfare states of the former Soviet Union, particularly those in eastern Europe (see Deacon, 1992, 1997; Manning, 2004). Of course, welfare was deeply embedded in the 'full employment' regimes of the old Soviet-style economies. A crucial aspect of processes of marketization and privatization in these states has been the transformation of public welfare provision. There is evidence of substantial variation in post-communist experience, related to both the general state of the economy and the administrative capacity of the new states. Finally, there has been a growing interest in welfare arrangements in Latin America. Object of the greatest attention here has been the Chilean pension system, which has been exhaustively surveyed and reviewed ever since the World Bank (1994) recommended it as a model to be followed throughout the Western world and 'the answer' to the problems of ageing societies. (For a fuller discussion of development in Latin America and East Asia, see C. Pierson, 2005a).

A third set of responses to Esping-Andersen has come from those who insist that the almost exclusive focus on labour market indicators to classify welfare states is misplaced. *Decommodification* is an inappropriate measure of welfare entitlement for those whose welfare opportunities are not (or are not predominantly) defined by their relationship to the formal labour market. Critics insist that Esping-Andersen is still too beholden to a traditional social democratic model of what a welfare state should be (a full employment society with extensive universalist rights) and unaware of the limitations of such an account as an ideal of social citizenship. The most important source of these criticisms has been a number of feminist writers. Thus Jane Lewis (1992) constructs an alternative typology comparing a number of European welfare states in terms of their varying correspondence to a 'male-breadwinner model' in which social policy is built around the gendered division of 'breadwinning for men and caring/homemaking for women'. Within this typification, Lewis identifies Britain as a 'strong male-breadwinner' state which, despite the removal of many explicit forms of discrimination against women, still underwrites a gendered welfare state (through, for example, its failure to make adequate childcare provision): 'while no effort is now made to stop women working, the assumption is that women will be secondary wage earners and, despite the large numbers of women in paid employment, they tend to be in short-term, part-time, low status work' (Lewis, 1992, p. 165). In Lewis's classification, France is characterized as a 'modified' male breadwinner state (with much of the modification being routed through family policy), with Sweden as the weakest male breadwinner state. In a similar contribution, Orloff (1993) seeks to reconcile mainstream and feminist accounts in proffering an account of regimes which is much more sensitive to the gendered impact of existing social policy provision (and omissions). She draws attention to family as a dimension of welfare delivery, to the gendered impact of the state's treatment of paid and unpaid labour and to the gender-blindness of prevailing conceptions of welfare citizenship and decommodification. She adds two further elements to regime classification: differential access to paid work and 'the capacity to form and maintain an autonomous household' (Orloff, 1993, pp. 318–20).

Finally, in this context, there has been a growing concern that Esping-Andersen's classification applies best to more traditional 'employment societies', that is to societies which, even if they did not support full employment, built their welfare apparatus around lifelong (male) involvement in waged work. Increasingly, developed economies have deviated from this model. Apart from the obvious rise in unemployment, there has been a transformation in the gender composition of the workforce, in the balance between full-time and part-time employment, in (perceived) levels of job security and so on. Increasing numbers of people enter the workforce late or leave it early or participate on an intermittent basis. Low wages, short hours and activity in the informal economy mean that a declining proportion of the adult population of working age are developing an entitlement to 'earned' or contributory benefits (see, for example, Commission on Social Justice, 1994). This relates closely to the idea of 'new social risks' to which I return in the next chapter.

The debate over welfare regimes is far from exhausted and it continues to provide the overarching framework within which much comparative work on the welfare state is discussed. Though many of the key issues remain contested, what emerges clearly from all this discussion is that welfare states are not all the same and that their variation is not just one of size or expenditure but also one of institutional organization, political purpose and social effect. As we shall see in the next chapter, the crucial lesson is that, even under 'the pressures of globalization' (whatever these are), welfare states continue to be different.

'Crisis, What Crisis?', Again

A second framing contribution to welfare state debate over the past decade has come from the innovative work of Paul Pierson (especially P. Pierson, 1994, 2000). Pierson's contribution is indicative of a generally much enhanced interest in welfare states among the US political science community. Although some American political scientists have long taken an interest in welfare politics (Frances Fox Piven and Richard Cloward provide an excellent example; see Piven and Cloward, 1971, 1977, 1985), the level of interest is something new. A leader in this field was Theda Skocpol whose work on the historical origins and development of social policy in the US focused heavily on the active role of the state, following her own programmatic call to 'bring the state back in' (on the former, see Skocpol, 1980, 1987; Weir et al., 1988b; on the latter, see Skocpol, 1985). The field became heavily, though far from exclusively, populated by advocates of a new 'historical institutionalism', who stressed the independent importance of states and state actors in accounting for social policy development, and who emphasized 'path dependency', the idea that prior accumulations of programmes and institutions are a core determinant of the range of options open to current policy-makers.

Working within this paradigm, Paul Pierson was not the first to question whether the welfare state was really being actively dismantled in the 1980s (among other sources, see the first edition of this book published in 1991). He was, however, perhaps the first to develop a comprehensive account of why welfare states proved to be (as we have seen) so robust in the face of a sustained and frontal ideological assault through most of that decade (though, for an anticipation of some of these arguments, see Therborn, 1986, 1987). The paradox from which Pierson began was this. As we have seen, there was a widespread view among many commentators that the 1980s would prove to be a decade of welfare state retrenchment. Indeed, even at the decade's end, some supposed that it had been. But Pierson's case was that, even in those countries where the assault on the welfare state had been most committed and where the political climate for change seemed most favourable, welfare state retrenchment had been very limited.

In the US and the UK in the 1980s, politics had been dominated by the political agenda of Reagan and Thatcher – a new breed of avowedly ideological, New Right politicians dedicated to 'rolling back the state' and cutting public (and hence social) expenditure. But despite their formidable political resources and extended periods in office, in the end their ambitions for welfare reform were largely frustrated. There were significant changes – particularly in relation to social housing and unemployment insurance – and in the wider economy this was a decade of rapidly growing income inequality in both countries. A creeping decrementalism left Britain, for example, with a significantly changed pensions regime by the end of the decade. But the spectacular changes that were promised – and which, in other policy areas such as privatization and trade union reform were, to some considerable extent, achieved – failed to emerge. In both the US and the UK, the percentage of GDP devoted to social expenditure was higher at the end than at the beginning of the 1980s. Just why did these most committed of welfare state reformers operating in the most advantageous political circumstances fall so far short of their expectations?

For Pierson, the explanation lay in the institutional character of the welfare states themselves and in the fact that the logic of the 'politics of retrenchment' was very different from the logic of welfare state expansion. Welfare states are large. They have broad constituencies of support in those who deliver and receive services and among the millions who rely on state transfers to maintain their incomes. They are also deeply embedded in the daily social and economic life of ordinary citizens. This institutional embeddedness of existing welfare institutions makes rapid and radical change hard to effect. And this resistance to change is amplified by the ways in which democratic procedures – especially those which build in a large number of institutional and constitutional *veto points* – tend to favour maintenance of the status quo. The politics of retrenchment is not simply an inversion of the politics of welfare state expansion. In the latter, democratic politicians were keen to secure the credit for new programmes and expanded expenditure. The politics of retrenchment, by contrast, is largely a politics of *blame avoidance*. Given that the pain is concentrated and the pay-off diffuse, programme-cutting is not good politics in a democracy. Politicians are therefore encouraged to seek decremental changes and cuts by stealth, rather than taking the credit/blame for major retrenchment in welfare programmes. Voters don't like taxes but in the end they are reluctant to support parties that will really and openly take the axe to widely valued public services. Of course, this does not mean that nothing has changed or will change. Pierson himself addresses a series of long-run challenges (ageing, permanently lower economic growth, the changing employment structure of the economy) which are bound to drive an ongoing reform process. But his overall conclusion is clear:

> The broad scale of public support, the intensity of preferences among pro-gramme recipients, the extent to which a variety of actors (including employ-ers) have adapted to the existing contours of the social market economy, and the institutional arrangements which favour defenders of the status quo, make *a frontal assault on the welfare state politically suicidal in most coun-tries.* (P. Pierson, 2000, p. 416, emphasis added)

The new politics of welfare then promises not so much retrenchment as *recalibration*: 'reforms which seek to make contemporary welfare states more consistent with contemporary goals and demands for social provi-sion' (2000, p. 425).

In their differing ways, the work of Esping-Andersen and Pierson has helped to define the principal approaches to welfare state study over the past decade. From Esping-Andersen has come an emphasis on diversity read through the prism of regime types; from Pierson has come an empha-sis on welfare state resilience – a focus on 'recalibration' rather than 'retrenchment' – mediated by the logic of path dependency. These will prove to be recurrent themes throughout this chapter.

'Recalibration' and the New Public Management

The 'frontal assault on the welfare state' may have failed to emerge but this does not mean that nothing has changed. Indeed, the defeat of neolib-eral ideas was never quite so comprehensive as a cursory reading of Paul Pierson's work would suggest. The aspiration to reduce the absolute size of the (social) state may have been frustrated but there were other elements in the New Right approach. These included the introduction of market like mechanisms into the area of welfare provision and the reform of trans-fers (and their funding) to make these more market conforming or, in Esping-Andersen's terms, less decommodifying. Indeed, in so far as there is an emergent agreement across a broad swathe of international social policy-makers about the imperatives of welfare reform, it is not so much a libertarian commitment to the smallest possible state but rather an endorsement of the welfare elements of the 'Washington Consensus' (see Williamson, 1994). The 'Washington Consensus' is a shorthand for the shared views of those very senior policy-makers in international organizations such as the International Monetary Fund, the World Bank and the OECD who 'advise' governments throughout the world on the best (or as it may seem only) means of securing the great desideratum of long-term economic growth. Of especial importance in relation to social policy are the following key priorities:

- *fiscal discipline*: government budget deficits should be small or preferably non-existent;
- *tax reform*: tax regimes should be broadened and redesigned to reduce marginal rates and spur economic participation;
- *public expenditure*: government spending should be concentrated on those areas which are economically productive (giving priority to 'investment' in health and education rather than 'redistribution' through social transfers);
- *deregulation*: governments should reduce regulation to promote economic activity (including the deregulation of labour markets and a reduction of social costs for employers).

To these can be added the following:

- *an active social policy*: this embraces the view that within any area of social policy (and not just the regulation of labour markets) there should be a prejudice in favour of measures which encourage economic activity (whether as employment or investment);
- *markets and quasi-markets*: there is a widespread assumption that, irrespective of questions of private or public ownership, markets or market-like mechanisms ('quasi-markets') are generally the best way of securing maximally efficient outcomes (in traditional welfare areas, as in almost all others).

As we would expect, these ideas have a differential impact in different welfare regimes. Although they have had some impact almost everywhere, they have certainly been most warmly welcomed (and most influential) in liberal or English-speaking welfare states. One of the clearest institutional expressions of this newer consensus has been the widespread dissemination (first and foremost in Anglophone nations) of what has been called the *new public management*. The new public management has its intellectual roots in the public choice theory which we saw in chapter 2 to be one of the key underpinnings of the New Right's critique of the state as an agent of welfare. At its core lies the belief that where the state is a monopoly supplier of (welfare) goods, provision will tend to be inefficient, unresponsive to consumers, and producer dominated. The belief of reformers was that introducing private sector management, organization and labour market practices into the public sector would deliver the sorts of service and efficiency that it is supposed the private sector (and its competitive environment) has already realized. It can be summarized around the following eight points:

- a belief in the superiority of the market and therefore an attempt to introduce markets and quasi-markets into the public sector;
- the notion that organization should be flexible and responsive rather than hierarchical;
- decentralization and the de-layering of decision-making, with the disaggregation of government into agencies;
- the use of performance indicators and output targets as mechanisms for the creation of incentives for more effective work practices;
- a focus on efficiency;
- management by results and a much greater emphasis on the role of managers and their freedom to make decisions;
- the use of new technology;
- an increased role for audit.

The reformers' aspiration is neatly caught in this characteristic statement of intent from the UK Treasury:

> The Government's public service reforms aim to deliver efficient, responsive public services, with high standards achieved across the country, through:
>
> - clear, long-term, outcome-focused goals, set by the Government;
> - devolution of responsibility to public service providers themselves, with maximum local flexibility and discretion to innovate and incentives to ensure that the needs of local communities are met;
> - independent and effective arrangements for audit and inspection to improve accountability; and transparency about what is being achieved, with better information about performance both locally and nationally. (HM Treasury, at www.official-documents.co.uk/document/deps/hc)

In part, this reform agenda is about the introduction of 'internal markets' within the domain of public provision. Under such reforms, public funding is retained but steps are taken to increase the powers of the consumers of public services over against their providers. The intention is that individual units (schools, colleges or healthcare trusts) should compete for consumers of their services. The purchasers of these services (parents, students, patients or their surrogates) should be able to transfer their custom between providers with relative ease – and public resources should follow these choices. Greater information (examination results, waiting list times, proportion of successful procedures, prices) should make it possible for consumers to make effective choices. At the same time, providers can be held to account for the level and standard of service delivered. Although this is primarily a system for delivering greater accountability and efficiency within the public sector (or so it is hoped), the reform agenda does involve the transfer of some activities outside the state sector, in some cases to voluntary or not-for-profit concerns but in others to fully commercial operators, as in the case of the UK's Private Finance Initiative or PFI (see below, p. 187; Regan, 2003; Flinders, 2005).

Clearly the 'internal market' has rather less purchase in the field of income maintenance. But, even here, there is scope for change. Thus support for the unemployed can be made conditional on job-seeking activity or even involve working for benefits ('workfare'). Those previously excluded from the workforce (single parents with young children, the disabled) could be assisted into the labour market with a series of incentives (tax credits) and/or penalties (reduced benefits, more stringent medical tests for incapacity). And the state's employment searching function could be contracted out to private providers (as in Australia; see Halligan, 2004). Above all, this reorientation requires that we move from a *passive* welfare state focused on the payment of benefits to maintain the incomes of the economically inactive to an *active* welfare state which privileges work as 'the royal road from welfare'. In the US, this reorientation was a part of the celebrated agenda for Reinventing Government which the Clinton administration took up with such enthusiasm (Osborne and Gaebler, 1992). In the UK, it has been seen as a definitive part of the otherwise rather elusive politics of 'the Third Way' (see Giddens, 1998).

Towards the Third Way

In Britain, this approach has been quite central to the claim of (New) Labour to have forged a new politics of the Third Way. Despite the rhetoric of the Conservatives after 1979 (which identified public expenditure as Britain's number one problem), we have seen that there was quite limited reform of the welfare state in the first half of the 1980s. There was a much more extensive programme of reforms after 1987. Yet, whatever the aspirations to cut expenditure, this was, above all, about the *reorganization* of services and the *respecification* of benefit entitlements in a context of cost containment. Indeed, there were many ways in which the new regime increased the powers of the central state (removing the influence of local democracy and for the first time introducing a national curriculum determined by the Secretary of State for Education). In the key service areas of health and education, public funding was retained but steps were taken to divide the *purchasers* from the *providers* of services. Resources were supposed to follow the choices of consumers – students and patients or, more normally, their surrogates, parents and doctors. Steps were taken to increase the surveillance and auditing of welfare professionals, most notably with the introduction of the Office for Standards in Education (OFSTED), and to publicize the outcomes of these surveys. The reorganization of GP's practices as purchasers of services was intended to make hospitals compete to deliver secondary medical care. The introduction of 'real' budgets – and of a stratum of managers to manage them – was designed to bring financial discipline into an area which had been seen to be vulnerable to chronic cost-inflation throughout its history. Under John Major's Conservative government (and under the impact of a pronounced recession) social expenditures climbed in the early 1990s, reaching a peak in 1993 (OECD, 2005). Meanwhile health expenditure continued its decades long rise (from 6 per cent to 7.6 per cent through the 1990s) and state education spending flat-lined at just below 5 per cent (OECD, 2005).

In turning to the period after 1997, there is considerable continuity with the foregoing reforms. The 'New Labour' government elected in that year had kept its pre-election commitments to a minimum. Although the Social Justice Commission, established by the former Labour leader John Smith before his untimely death in 1993, had given Labour a potential blueprint for updating its traditional welfare aspirations, the party came to power without a clear agenda for reform (Commission on Social Justice, 1994). It entered the election with a series of five key pledges. Three of these commitments related to improved performance in the public services: cutting waiting lists for hospital treatment, reducing class sizes in primary schools and reducing youth unemployment. The fourth commitment related to increasing the speed with which young offenders would be pushed through the legal system. The final commitment was not to increase the basic rate of income tax. Far from committing itself to spend more public money, Labour pledged to maintain Conservative plans for public expenditure through the first two years of a Labour administration. After the election, the free-thinking Labour backbencher Frank Field, who had always shown an especial interest in social policy, was appointed as Minister for Welfare Reform. His commission lasted little more than a year. Beyond that point, Labour settled down to an incremental welfare reform agenda which owed much to the international policy ideas associated with the Washington Consensus and to the domestic welfare reforms of the Major government of 1992–7. The 'newness' of New Labour's agenda was promoted through the idea that it represented part of the new governing logic of the 'Third Way'.

At its simplest, the Third Way represented an attempt to give some coherence (and justification) to the general policy reorientation which informed the New Labour project. The Third Way lay between but more importantly 'beyond' two alternatives that were seen to have failed – not just the market-led neoliberalism of Margaret Thatcher but also the state-led, producer-driven, paternalistic management of the old-style social democracy, including its commitment to a 'passive' welfare state. Under radically changed circumstances, progressives had to shift their aspirations from the defence of the 'welfare state' and demand management to the active promotion of the 'competition state' and reform of the supply-side of the economy. In a globalized economy, it is no longer possible for the state itself to guarantee the economic security and social protection of its citizens. Its new challenge is to legislate for flexibility and the enhancement of human capital in a symbiotic relationship with domestic civil society and an increasingly global business and financial community. A social democratic government can still use the resources generated by a success-ful internationalized economy to help to fund high-quality public services. And this is an important part of its continuing commitment to the *social inclusion* of all citizens. But it will increasingly rely on market-mimicking mechanisms at arm's length from government to deliver these services and will look to them to improve overall levels of social capital among a pop-ulation now seen increasingly as a pool of flexible and skilled labour. (On the typification of the Third Way, see Blair 1998; Blair and Schröder, 1999; Giddens, 1998, 2000, 2001.)

The welfare state that emerges from these changes is enabling or facil-itating rather than providing. Globalization requires that states should focus on the 'competitiveness' of their increasingly exposed economies – above all, raising the productivity of their domestic labour supply (justi-fying expenditure on education and training). If standards of living are to be protected in an increasingly competitive global marketplace, developed economies have to secure a productivity premium. They have to be able to develop a workforce which is multiskilled, flexible, adaptable and 'clever' – or they will find themselves engaged in a battle to provide cheap labour which they cannot win. Demographic changes (above all the ageing of the population) reinforce this imperative for greater productivity and require that states seek to displace social costs (such as the income maintenance of the elderly) on citizens themselves. Increasingly there is an attempt to redefine the role of the welfare state for the elderly in terms of the guar-antee of incomes (and thus selective intervention) rather than universal provision on the basis of a shared citizenship. Overall this suggests a future in which welfare states focus on social investment rather than social costs. Welfare states should be enabling rather than providing, customized rather than generic, smaller but smarter.

New Labour, New Welfare State?

In essence, the New Labour case for welfare reform was this. The original New Right agenda which had called for a radical reduction in the size of the public sector and the reallocation of public services to the private sector was wrong. There were and are things that should be delivered in the public sector either because this is (potentially) more efficient, or because these services should be available on the same basis to all citizens, or equity requires that outcomes are not simply left to the (radically unequal and unfair) outcomes of markets. But the old ways of delivering public service (through a highly bureaucratic and inflexible state, delivering standardized services to a passive population who have very little say over the nature and standard of the services that they receive), are outdated. In a much more affluent society in which citizens are used to high levels of service and responsiveness among commercial providers of goods and services, the public sector has to be radically rethought. Public services must become consumer focused, outcomes focused, responsive to clients' needs, accountable, reflexive and entrepreneurial. They need to be tested by audit, public measures of performance and (where appropriate) competition. The ambition is not to minimize the public sector (the aspiration of the New Right) but to optimize the level and quality of services that the citizenry pays for through its taxes. Here is a characteristic formulation from Tony Blair (2004):

> In simple terms, we are completing the re-casting of the 1945 welfare state to end entirely the 'one size fits all' services and put in their place modern services which maintain at their core the values of equality of access and opportunity for all; base the service round the user, a personalised service with real choice, greater individual responsibility and high standards; and ensure in so doing that we keep our public services universal, for the middle class as well as those on lower incomes, both of whom expect and demand services of quality.

Blair defined the 'four principles of public service reform' as:

- guaranteed national standards of service;
- devolution of power and innovation to the front line;
- a new deal for public service staff, combining better rewards for increased professionalism;
- greater choice for the consumer. (2002, p. 20)

In its first two years in office Labour made modest progress in terms of its aspiration to improve the public services (largely because it had committed itself to stay within the limits of growth in public expenditure projected by the previous Conservative administration). Indeed, public expenditure on services as a proportion of GDP did not return to its 1996–7 level until 2003–4. But expenditure on key public services – especially health and education – rose significantly after 2000. Expenditure on health rose by a half in the first eight years of Labour government. In the same period, expenditure on education rose by nearly a third (HM Treasury, 2005).

This substantial growth in expenditure is reflected in a recent expansion of employment in the public services – particularly in health and education. Total public sector employment fell throughout the years of Conservative administration, from a high of 7.5 million in 1979 to just under 5 million in 1997 (though much of this decline can be attributed to the transfer of 'privatized' jobs into the private sector). Since 1998 public sector employment has risen sharply, especially in health and education – with half a million new jobs, representing growth of more than 10 per cent in six years. Together, education and health now account for just under 60 per cent of total public sector employment compared with around 40 per cent twenty years ago.

There is considerable continuity between New Labour and the immediately preceding administrations in their treatment of the public services. This was, after all, a reform agenda that could be seen very widely across the Anglo-Saxon world – especially where the principal governing institutions were parliamentary (as in Australia and New Zealand; though, of course, the home of *reinventing government* was the US). This even extends into the area of privatization (in prison management and air traffic control, for example, where Labour had been fiercest in its opposition to the Conservatives). If anything, New Labour has placed more weight than its predecessors on audit, leadership and managerialism (rather than competition) as the mechanisms for delivering change and achieving high standards. In health care, the White Paper *The New NHS: Modern, Dependable* (Department of Health, 1997) established a new framework for primary health care built around Primary Care Groups (PCGs) and Primary Care Trusts (PCTs). This effectively replaced the Conservatives' model of an internal market in primary health care. It incorporated the government's commitments to localism, devolution and focusing on local services tailored to local needs. At the same time, it embraced the new culture of managerialism and accountability with performance benchmarks and national targets, clinical audit, performance related rewards and league tables (on waiting times and even clinical outcomes). In the field of education, Labour retained the inspections framework provided by OFSTED and tightened the proscriptions of the National Curriculum, introducing a standardized 'literacy hour' and 'numeracy hour' across the primary school system. The government pinned its hopes of an improvement in overall standards around a series of targets for literacy and numeracy to be met by students taking nationally administered tests at key stages in their primary school education. The government also sought to diversify the nature of secondary state school provision. The powers of Local Education Authorities were further marginalized and the power of school management (especially of head teachers) increased. Numbers in higher education were substantially increased (towards a target of 50 per cent participation among 18–30 year olds by 2010), though it was not clear that this has had a real impact on the limited access to university of children from less privileged backgrounds. The culture of management, auditing, testing, performance-related rewards, standardization and choice featured across the breadth of New Labour educational reforms.

Although health and education are by some way the biggest spending areas in the public services, the category also embraces government delivery in the areas of transport, housing, employment and, crucially, law and order. Although the delivery of law and order has not historically been regarded as part of the welfare state in the same sense as other services, it has become an increasingly controversial and contested area in recent years. Labour has attempted to refocus attention in the law and order area away from security as a defining feature of the state's activities towards its reconstitution as a service delivered (by the police and the courts) to the public. The same apparatus of reforms – focusing on targets, outputs and performance – has been used to deliver the message that, in the area of law and order, the consumer is king. Labour has repeated the message that the provision of a safe environment – free from the threat of crimes against person and property, including low-level crimes of 'yobbishness' – is a service to which voter-taxpayer-citizens are entitled.

At the same time, Labour has intensified the Conservatives' drive to find new sources of funding for welfare services. It has, for example, extended the principle of students making a contribution to the costs of funding higher education (through the introduction of tuition fees and a retention of the system of student loans rather than maintenance grants). One of the most controversial areas has been the government's commitment to the Private Finance Initiative (PFI) – through which public sector infrastructure is provided by the private sector and then loaned to public authorities. Most new schools and hospitals in Britain are now built on this basis. In 2004, the government entered into twenty-eight PFI deals in the NHS (worth around £3 billion) and twenty deals in education (worth around £700 million) (www.hm-treasury.gov.uk). PFI places much smaller costs on public expenditure (in the short term) but critics have insisted that it represents very poor long-term value for the public at large. In some circumstances, the mixture of public and private financing has been especially controversial. This is true of plans partially to privatize or privately fund renovation of the London Underground system – given the poor record of private sector companies responsible for railway infrastructure maintenance and involved in a series of fatal railway crashes on the national rail network. The government has also sought to extend the 'user pays' principle in new ways – for example, discharging the additional costs of late night city-centre policing on those clubs and pubs that are deemed responsible for generating a problem of drunken and loutish behaviour.

New Labour, New Deal

At least as important as the delivery of public services in New Labour's reform agenda were changes in the labour market and in the rewards for (especially low-paid) work. 'Welfare to work' – the commitment to maximize workforce participation (and minimize 'welfare dependency') through a series of active labour market measures – was a 'flagship' policy of the New Labour administration after 1997. Its principal vehicle was the multifaceted 'New Deal'. This programme was designed to deliver on the first half of New Labour's new welfare mantra: 'work for those who can, security for those who cannot' (Blair in DSS, 1998a, p. iii). The policy identified a series of categories of groups who might need assistance to acquire work – starting with the young unemployed, moving on through the long-term unemployed to lone parents and those with a disability. To these were added distinctive branches of the New Deal to offer assistance to partners of the unemployed and to those over fifty. Characteristically, the programmes involve an element of job subsidy with a private sector employer, work placement in the voluntary sector or with an environmental task force (and with appropriate training) or full-time education. The system is built around a network of personal advisers and more or less intensive case management. For the young and long-term unemployed, participation is mandatory (with the sanction of a potential withdrawal of benefits). (For a useful summary, see Finn, 2003.)

Alongside the New Deal went a range of other measures designed to 'make work pay'. These included the early introduction by Labour of a minimum wage and 'opting back in' to the European Union's Social Charter. Also crucial was the introduction of the Working Families tax credit (mimicking a similar measure introduced in the US under Clinton), a Disabled Person's tax credit and a childcare tax credit. By the end of 2001, 1.25 million families were receiving the Working Families tax credit and expenditure on tax credits far outstripped the monies allocated to the New Deal (Finn, 2003, pp. 116–17). In addition, the government took various measures to make working conditions more 'family friendly' – facilitating the growth of dual-earner households in a context in which childcare and childcare costs were seen to be a real disincentive to maximum economic participation. Critics suspected that these were not so much family-friendly employment policies as work-friendly family policies, but their intention to maximize participation of the largest possible number of able-bodied adults was clear. As with other work activation measures around the world, the impact of the New Deal on unemployment levels is contested (with many supposing that it is the general strength of the economy rather than active labour market measures which have led to raised levels of economic participation). Dan Finn's measured judgement is that 'the balance of the evidence supports the conclusion that the approach accelerates the return to work, especially of the long-term ployed, and that the programmes contribute at least to some si increase in employment' (2003, p. 125).

How 'New' was New Labour?

In the light of all this evidence, it would be wrong to think of welfare reform under New Labour as just 'Thatcherism with a new label'. Labour has certainly emphasized the priority of welfare through work, it has increased the role of means testing and de-emphasized the idea of welfare as citizenship. In contrast to what Esping-Andersen supposes to be the defining mark of a social democratic regime, it has done much to *recommodify* welfare. Nonetheless, the distributional outcomes of its new policy regime, especially since 2000, differ quite substantially from what went before. After the standstill occasioned by its pre-election commitment in 1997 to maintain the Conservative government's spending plans for the first two years of a Labour government, Labour has made significant (if discreet) efforts to redistribute wealth. Since 2000, levels of inequality have fallen slightly, though this had not by 2002–3 fully compensated for the growth in inequality since 1996–7. In fact, in the period since 1996–7, between the 15th percentile point and the 85th percentile point, income inequality has fallen – so that within this comparatively large group, it is the poorer individuals who have gained most. Much of the work of increasing inequality lies with the populations *below* and *above* this threshold. It is the income status of the very richest and the poorest 15 per cent that explains much of the recent growth in income inequality, with incomes accelerating rapidly at the very top of the profile and falling substantially at the bottom of the profile. We have to remember that some growth in income inequality is consistent with the government's undertaking (quite substantial) work of redistribution. Brewer et al. (2004) estimate that budget changes from 2000 onwards – including large increases in some means-tested benefits and tax credits, particularly those aimed at families with children and at pensioners – lowered the implicit growth in the Gini index (the leading international indicator of income inequality) by about 1.5 percentage points. This contrasts markedly with the record of the Thatcher governments through the 1980s, when the index rose by ten points – though it leaves absolute levels of inequality that are high by the standards of most comparably developed economies elsewhere.

Labour has made a particular commitment to address child poverty. Its target is to halve childhood poverty by 2010 and to eliminate it by 2020. Between 1998–9 and 2002–3, according to government figures, just over 1 million children were moved out of poverty, bringing the figure from 4.2 million to 3.1 million (after housing costs) (Brewer et al., 2004, p. 39).

Much of this work was done by tax credits for working families with children. This contrasts markedly with the record of the preceding Conservative governments. Nonetheless, Labour showed an extraordinary commitment to the 'work first' welfare state and an almost religious faith in the capacity of targets and auditing to produce positive change.

Diversity: Other Ways of Welfare

In some ways, the UK's policy was typical of at least the centre-left parties in liberal welfare regimes in the 1990s and beyond. 'Work first' welfare measures were introduced in the period not only in the UK but also in the US and Canada, in Australia and New Zealand (see Kelsey, 1995; C. Pierson, 2002). And this was a reorientation that went beyond the traditional heartlands of the 'liberal' welfare state. The OECD (1989) and the World Bank (1994) were among those key international players which called for a change of emphasis in social policy. Perhaps most instructive (within Europe at least) was the shift of emphasis in thinking within the European Union represented by Council meetings at Amsterdam (in 1997) and Lisbon (in 2000). The EU has often been seen as the key exponent and defender of the European 'social model'. Yet, at Lisbon, the Council declared that the ambition of the EU over the following decade was 'to become the most competitive and dynamic knowledge-based economy in the world capable of sustainable economic growth with more and better jobs and greater social cohesion'. Crucial to this was the development of 'an active and dynamic welfare state'. The Commission's subsequent Social Policy Agenda established that the 'guiding principle [was] to strengthen the role of *social policy as a productive factor*' (cited in Geyer, 2003, p. 291; more generally, see Geyer, 2000). This initiative suggested that continental European governments were also concerned with reforming the welfare state in ways that were more 'active' and 'work friendly' (especially given the much higher rates of unemployment that persisted on the continent compared to the UK). To date the impact has been rather variable.

Welfare Regimes in Europe: Frozen or Fluid?

As the 1990s progressed, the view emerged that the welfare states of continental Europe were resistant not just to retrenchment but indeed to fundamental change of any kind. Esping-Andersen (1996) wrote of the continental welfare states as being part of a 'frozen landscape' – in which the easy expansion of the 1960s and 1970s was no longer possible but in which at the same time it was extremely difficult to change the institutional arrangements that had been put in place during those decades. One of the key problems of the contemporary welfare state was that it was designed to address the risks of the political economy of the postwar world but was quite unsuited to the changed circumstances of a post-industrial economy (Esping-Andersen, 1999, pp. 32–3). France and Germany were seen to be exemplary cases of the resistance to change that Paul Pierson had identified in *Dismantling the Welfare State?* (1994).

For Germany, this case is well made by Leibfried and Obinger (2003). The social market economy established after the Second World War was increasingly challenged from the mid-1970s onwards by rising unemployment, an ageing population profile, adverse changes in economic and family structures and rising income inequality. West German federal governments (principally those of Chancellor Kohl) had some success in restraining the social budget through the 1980s but they were much less successful in achieving institutional reform of the traditional high wage–high social cost economy, increasingly addressing labour market rigidities with a rather indiscriminate policy of early retirement. The process of national reunification after 1989 placed enormous stress on the existing institutional and budgetary structure. The rapid assimilation of the eastern half of Germany and its much less efficient economy into the social welfare apparatus of the western half of the country triggered a rapid rise in unemployment and with it a rapid growth in social expenditure. 'As large-scale eastern unemployment was absorbed through welfare state means, spending skyrocketed to an extent never observed in a western democracy. In 1992, expenditures in East Germany peaked at 55.5 per cent of the GDP, topping Sweden by far' (Leibfried and Obinger, 1993, p. 205).

Under both Christian Democrat and then Social Democrat regimes, Leibfried and Obinger observe budget constraint and a creeping decrementalism, which they label 'retrenchment by stealth'. But in neither case do they identify the passage of those fundamental reforms – above all to Germany's 'rigid' labour market institutions – that would enable the country to address the twin problems of high unemployment and overstretched welfare budgets. They conclude that 'while the numerous measures aimed at cost containment have made the German welfare state more viable, neither the Kohl nor the Schröder government have been able to overcome the fundamental structural weakness of Germany's welfare state' (Leibfried and Obinger, 2003, p. 214).

Manow and Seils (2000) offer a comparably gloomy account of the incapacity of the German welfare regime to achieve necessary change. Germany has become caught in a vicious employment-reducing, social cost-raising circle:

Economic slumps since the early 1970s – including the unification crisis after 1992 – have regularly triggered a pathological response pattern of the

> German economic and political system leading to ever higher levels of
> unemployment, to a low level of total employment, and to steadily increas-
> ing non-wage labour costs, in particular continuously rising social insurance
> contributions. In turn, high non-wage labour costs have adverse effects on
> job growth in the low wage (service) sector and on the competitiveness of
> German industry in world markets. (Manow and Seils, 2000, p. 138)

This sets up a malign 'welfare-without-work' equilibrium which political
elites have struggled to overcome. Manow and Seils conclude, 'in our view,
the current turmoil in German politics indicates that while the traditional
strategies of economic adjustment have become disadvantageous for the
key actors responsible, the search for alternatives remains costly and
conflict-ridden' (2000, p. 157).

Many of the same arguments are deployed in the debate over the
'frozen' character of the French welfare system. The French social security system has often been seen as notoriously 'unreformable'. Attempts to
reform pension policy in France in the 1990s (under the Juppe Plan) led
to demonstrations on the streets and defeat for the government (Bonoli,
2000, p. 260; Pitruzzello, 1997). Because so much social security activity
in France is in the hands of the social partners and non-state agencies, it
has often proved difficult for the government to exercise the sorts of con-
trols over expenditure (and its terms and conditions) that have been possible elsewhere. France is also seen to suffer from a pathology of high
unemployment–high social costs–high labour market entry costs. Overall
social costs have remained stubbornly high, close to those of the largest
spending social democratic states such as Denmark and Sweden (OECD,
2005).

These views have not gone unchallenged. Martin Seeleib-Kaiser (2002)
argues that over the past twenty-five years we have in fact seen a 'dual
transformation' of the German welfare state. The state has reduced its
longstanding commitment to maintain the previous living standard of
former wage-earners – which had been 'the key normative principle of the
German welfare state in the post-war era'. This has been replaced (in a
series of changes culminating in the Labour Promotion Reform Law of
1997) by more conditional support and an active labour market policy
designed to get workers back into employment. At the same time, costs
have been trimmed (by the reduction of replacement rates) and entitlements reduced (Seeleib-Kaiser, 2002, pp. 31–2). The other branch of
Germany's 'dual transformation' has been an expansion of family support
through limited provision of childcare, parental leave and some upgrading of child allowances (Seeleib-Kaiser, 2002, pp. 32–3). Overall, 'there
is clear evidence of change along the dimensions of retrenchment, recommodification, and recalibration leading to a new paradigm . . . The
institutional logic of the German welfare state today clearly differs from

the logic during the golden era of welfare state capitalism' (Seeleib-Kaiser, 2002, p. 42).

Mark Vail (2004) draws broadly similar conclusions. The idea of the frozen welfare state in Germany and France is 'a myth'. The illusion of 'no change' is achieved by a limited focus on social expenditures (which have indeed continued to grow through the 1990s and into the new century). This fails to capture the *institutional* changes that lie behind continuing high levels of expenditure. Vail notes that in recent years German governments have sought to curtail their traditional recourse to early retirement as a 'solution' to the problem of high unemployment. They have encouraged the emergence of a low-wage labour market and introduced into the western half of Germany active labour market measures that were originally developed in the east. More recently, the Schröder government pressed ahead with the process of labour market reforms recommended by the Hartz Commission, including, most controversially, 'Hartz IV', which aims both to reduce unemployment benefits and to curtail the period during which these will be paid to most displaced workers. The federal government has also introduced significant cuts and a recalibration of pension entitlements and new charges in the public health care system (Vail, 2004, pp. 171–3).

Assessing the French experience, Bruno Palier (2000) detects a series of reforms which, while operating within the parameters of existing social welfare politics, have achieved real change. These reforms would include the new unemployment benefit, AUD (Allocation Unique Degressive), the introduction of a politics of economic *reinsertion* (including the RMI or Revenu Mimimum d'Insertion), reform of the regime for minimum incomes of old age pensioners and limited reforms in the public health-care sector. Palier concludes:

> These structural reforms all contribute to changing the original Bismarckian nature of the French social security system, and a move toward a state-run, tax-financed logic and practices, at least in the area of health care, family benefits and poverty alleviation, which were alien to the French post-war tradition of welfare . . . these reforms are not marginal, but concern a significant proportion of the population, an important share of the financing and have given the state more possibilities to intervene within the system. (2000, p. 133)

Vail's conclusions are similar: 'During the past decade, France has witnessed major reforms in its system of social protection . . . Although such reforms have clearly not resolved the financing crisis of the French welfare state, they show a capacity for dynamic adjustment that belies prevailing accounts of the French welfare-capitalist system as "frozen"' (Vail, 2004, p. 165).

The Dutch 'Miracle'

Different again is the experience of the Netherlands in which changes to the established welfare regime have been seen to be so substantial as to merit the label 'the Dutch miracle'.[1] In the early 1980s, the Netherlands was often depicted as the classical case of an overloaded continental European welfare state, trapped in a costly cycle of 'welfare without work'. In the severe recession of 1981–3, unemployment rose well above 10 per cent, government deficits amounted to 10 per cent of GDP, investment collapsed and 6 per cent of all jobs in the economy were lost in just two years. Within a decade, the situation was seemingly transformed. The economy added 1 million new jobs in ten years. Indeed, in this period the Netherlands outperformed the US 'jobs machine' (without a matching increase in income inequality). Labour market participation rates increased from 52 to 64 per cent (between 1983 and 1994), including a transformation in levels of participation by women (female labour force participation in this period rose from 35 per cent to 55 per cent). In 2001, the unemployment rate fell to 2.5 per cent (OECD, 2004). At the same time, the budget deficit was brought below 3 per cent and the GDP share of taxes and social charges fell consistently year on year. In the first half of the 1990s, the Dutch economy consistently outperformed the EU average in job creation, investment, private consumption and GDP growth. (All data from Hemerijck and Visser, 2001.)

How was this transformation achieved? Characteristically, there are seen to be three components to the Dutch miracle. First was the restoration of Dutch corporatism under the terms of the Wassenaar Accord, agreed between Dutch employers and unions on 24 November 1982. In the first instance, this was an agreement (by the unions) to accept wage moderation and to improve the profitability of investment as the price to be paid for renewed job creation. There was to be some compensation through modest reductions in working hours. This was to blossom into a major shift in the Dutch economy towards part-time work, which was a major source of the radically increased participation of women. The second policy shift involved major restructuring of the social security system. The Netherlands had come to use two devices to mask unemployment and to ease the move out of the workforce – disability insurance and sickness leave. These had helped to lower the rate of labour force participation among older males (aged 60 to 65) from 70 per cent in 1973 to just 22 per cent by 1991. In the early 1990s (initially unpopular) steps were taken to reduce eligibility for disability and sickness benefits (by this time,

---

[1] The account here relies heavily on Hemerijck and Visser, 2001.

one-sixth of the labour force was in receipt of disability benefit) and there were more general reductions in the value of social security benefits. The third element in the Dutch reform package was the commitment to active labour market measures designed to create more jobs. This represented 'a U-turn in attitudes to the labour market: the overarching policy objective is no longer to keep overt unemployment down by channelling people into social security programmes, but rather to maximize the rate of labour force participation' (Hemerijck and Visser, 2001, p. 233). This was assisted by the enormous growth in part-time employment. The share of part-time work in the economy rose from 15 per cent in 1975 to 35 per cent in 1994. Of all part-time jobs 75 per cent were held by women, and 63 per cent of all women were employed part-time. The comparable figure for men was 16 per cent. All these figures substantially exceeded the average across the fifteen members of the European Union (Hemerijck and Visser, 2001, pp. 222–7).

Not everyone is convinced that all of this adds up to a 'miraculous' transformation. As Hans Keman points out, much of the appearance of success in terms of employment in the Netherlands is explained by the transition towards a part-time economy (Keman, 2003, p. 131). The Netherlands has virtually the lowest annual work hours of any member of the EU (EIRO, 2004). The part-time economy is in part about sharing out the work, rather than growing the economy. And even at the end of its growth spurt, the Netherlands still has levels of female labour market participation that are in the middle of the OECD range and well behind both leading social democratic (Sweden, Denmark) and liberal (US, UK) states (Hemerijck and Visser, 2001, p. 226). Long-term unemployment still remains persistently high (again in comparison to the record of the leading social democratic and liberal states). Nonetheless, the Dutch case does remain exemplary for those who believe that the problems of the seemingly immovable continental welfare states can be addressed without simply abandoning social concertation or opting for a huge growth in income inequality.

Conclusion: Sceptical about the Sceptics?

Our brief survey of developments in social policy in the more advanced industrial countries over the past fifteen years reveals a complex and sometimes confusing picture. We began this chapter by looking at the agenda-setting work of Esping-Andersen and Paul Pierson. The three key themes that this literature established were, first, a pattern of diversity (so that not all welfare states are the same, nor do they all react to the same set of challenges in precisely the same way); secondly, that we should be sceptical about the prevailing claims that welfare states have generally been caught in the grip of an inevitable process of 'retrenchment'; and, thirdly, that in an era of welfare state restraint, while institutions and their histories were important, political parties and partisanship were rather less so.

In some ways, all three claims are supported by the empirical evidence we have (however briefly) considered. As we move further into the second century of the welfare state, the differences between Sweden and the US remain enormous and we have seen that, even when states come under the same sorts of duress – from rising unemployment or heightened international trade, for example – their institutional *and* political responses may be quite different. We have seen, too, that through the 'golden decade' of the New Right, the 1980s, when many predicted the imminent demise of 'welfare as we knew it', social expenditure budgets continued to grow. At the end of Mrs Thatcher's reign in Britain, the social expenditure take from the nation's GDP had grown by about ten percentage points since 1979. When Clinton assumed the US Presidency in 1992, he inherited (from Reagan and George Bush senior) a social expenditure budget larger than that which had been left by Jimmy Carter, the last Democratic incumbent. Lastly, we have seen how parties of the left or centre-left have adjusted their own traditional programmes on welfare to take account not only of the repositioning of parties of the right but also of a changing international economy (often brought under the shorthand of 'the forces of globalization').

But the most recent empirical evidence also gives us some reason to be sceptical about each of these claims. Welfare states remain quite different. Indeed, given their differing points of departure in the period under review, it is hard to see how this could fail to be true in anything other than the very long term. But they have often reached for the same policy instruments to address the challenges of cost containment. Thus replacement rates for unemployment benefit were cut in the US and the UK during the 1980s, but they were also cut (albeit from and to much more generous levels) in Sweden and Finland in the early 1990s. A broad range of widely differing welfare state regimes have deployed the rubric of active labour market programmes and an *active* welfare state to underpin reforms over the past fifteen years.

At the same time, there is some reason to believe that the retrenchers have not been quite so unsuccessful as Paul Pierson believes. Ironically, social expenditure budgets in most countries peaked around the time that *Dismantling the Welfare State?* was published (1994). In both the UK and the US, the proportion of GDP devoted to social expenditure has been falling slowly but fairly consistently since 1993. In fact, average social expenditure peaked across the OECD in 1993 (at 23 per cent). It has since fallen by around 1.5 percentage points (OECD, 2005). Taking a slightly different indicator, Allan and Scruggs (2004) model real declines in levels of welfare state support across the period from 1975 to 2000. They argue that if we measure not aggregate levels of social expenditure but rather net replacement rates for the average benefit recipient (a measure of the adequacy of individual support) we find a general and pronounced pattern of retrenchment over the past two decades. In sixteen out of eighteen OECD countries surveyed, replacement rates for the unemployed are no longer at their historically highest rate (the exceptions are Italy and Japan). In most cases, the last year of the maximum replacement rate is to be found in the 1980s. In some cases, the rate of collapse has been precipitous, led by the UK, where the rate fell from 62.5 per cent in 1975 to 35 per cent ten years later (in a context where levels of unemployment went from below 1 million to in excess of 3 million).

Meanwhile in the US – often identified as a classically initiative-averse polity given its separation of powers, its federal structures and its abundance of veto points – 1996 saw the passage of the Personal Responsibility and Work Opportunity Reconciliation Act (PRWORA), probably the single most important and dramatic piece of welfare legislation since the New Deal of the 1930s. (For a detailed treatment, see Blank, 2002.) The law abolished Aid to Families with Dependent Children (AFDC), the key income maintenance programme of the American welfare system, replacing it with Temporary Assistance to Needy Families (TANF) and transferred all responsibilities (and budgets) for the new programme to the individual states. PRWORA instituted new work requirements and introduced lifetime limits for welfare support. In its wake, welfare rolls were slashed from over 5 million to around 2 million families (although the steep decline in clients actually dates from 1994). Unemployment rates for single mothers fell steeply. *The Economist* (25 August 2001) declared the reform 'a triumph' and claimed that it had redeemed Bill Clinton's pledge to 'end welfare as we know it'. Others were more critical:

> The bottom line is that there have been three outcomes for welfare leavers: first, there have been some functional individuals who were jolted out of their complacency or laziness and got normal employment; second, there is another larger slice who have been able to obtain low-paying, low-skill jobs and temporarily leave welfare, often at great cost to their children's development; and third, there is a group that has not been able to find and maintain jobs, and with time limits on cash assistance having come into play, they now are deeper in poverty than ever. (Caraley, 2001–2, p. 532)

There is some evidence that the poverty of single parent families was moderated in the late 1990s by the combination of TANF with earned income tax credits and an increased minimum wage. But since the accession of George W. Bush in 2000, poverty in the US has expanded to embrace 12.5 per cent of the population, a total of 36 million people, including 13 million children (US Bureau of the Census, 2003). Strangely, the passage of PRWORA had a limited impact on welfare expenditures –

the really steep decline in expenditures in the late 1990s was on the Food Stamp Programme; really rapid growth came in the costs of Medicaid (Caraley, 2001–2, p. 539). But there can be little doubt that PRWORA constitutes a major reform and has been used by the state governors (who now exercise substantial control over budgets) to constrain expenditure.

Allan and Scruggs (2004) also insist that their methodology reveals that there are still ongoing partisan variations in the severity of welfare state retrenchment. Overall budgets grew almost everywhere through the 1980s. At the same time, the generosity of replacement rates declined or stagnated everywhere. But the *severity* of cost containment varied substantially – with one of Pierson's surprising non-retrenchers, the UK, emerging as an almost uniquely severe budget-cutter through the 1980s. It is worth recording that this took place in the context of a decade in which income inequality in the UK rose steeply (with a Gini coefficient that grew by around 10 points in ten years; Brewer et al., 2004).

As we move on to consider the prospects for the future of the welfare state, we are left with a picture that combines diversity and commonality and a measure of uncertainty about the prevailing direction of welfare state reform. The two things about which it seems we can be certain are that welfare states are not about to disappear but that they will undergo continuing and quite profound change. In the next chapter, I look at three areas where the challenge and the pressure to change are particularly acute: first, the processes of 'globalization', second, the demographic challenges of ageing combined with low levels of fertility; and thirdly, the multifaceted challenge of what have been called the 'new social risks' of welfare.

PART III
Beyond the Welfare State?

7
Three Challenges

The Challenge of Globalization

I begin this assessment of the trends that may be carrying us to circumstances that are truly 'beyond the welfare state' with an evaluation of the contested impact on states' social policy of the processes of *globalization*. The idea of globalization has been called on to do an extraordinary amount of explanatory work in recent accounts of social and political change and, as such, it has generated a vast literature and a great deal of disagreement. At one extreme are those who believe that nation-states are increasingly losing their powers as ever more perfectly integrated international markets articulate the sovereignty of the global consumer across what is rapidly becoming a 'borderless world' (Ohmae, 1990). Sceptics, by contrast, doubt that there really is a new phenomenon of 'globalization', insisting that nation-states have always faced powerful transnational forces and that, in spite of these, they retain significant governing capacities and policy discretion (Hirst and Thompson, 1996). Unremarkably, the truth probably lies somewhere in between, although in the welfare state literature the sceptics have probably been more prominent in recent years. (Perraton et al., 1997).

Globalization is clearly a multifaceted phenomenon – an 'open-ended process' rather than a given 'end state' in Perraton et al.'s (1997) treatment – but its most significant impact on the welfare state is seen to arise from two sources. First, at least since the 1960s, there has been the emergence of a 'new international division of labour' which has seen the transfer of manufacturing activity and now increasingly tradable services (as well as the range of jobs that go with them) from the developed economies of the North to newly industrialized economies (NIEs), especially those on the

Pacific Rim. With new developments in transportation and communication technologies, NIEs are able to offer a low-wage, low-tax environment which draws investment away from traditional developed economies, presenting these economies with the twin problems of rising unemployment and a fiscal shortfall (see Martin, 1997). A second difficulty lies in the consequences of a seemingly exponential growth in transnational economic activity: increasing trade, rising foreign direct investment (FDI) and, perhaps above all, a rapid intensification of international financial movements. In Robert Cox's account:

> The two principal aspects of [economic] globalisation are (1) global organisations of production (complex transnational networks of production which source the various components of the product in places offering the most advantage on costs, markets, taxes, and access to suitable labour, and also the advantages of political security and predictability); and (2) global finance (a very largely unregulated system of transactions in money, credit, and equities). These developments together constitute a *global economy*, i.e. an economic space transcending all country borders, which co-exists still with an *international economy* based on transactions across country borders and which is regulated by inter-state agreements and practices. (1993, pp. 259–60)

This process affects different states in differing ways but generally, 'economic globalisation has placed constraints upon the autonomy of states' and, increasingly, 'states must become the instruments for adjusting national economic activities to the exigencies of the global economy' (Cox, 1993, pp. 262, 260). In a context in which it makes less and less sense to talk of distinct 'national economies', it is less and less possible for individual states to regulate the economic activity that goes on within and across their borders.

This loss of governing capacity is seen to be peculiarly consequential for traditional welfare states. Facing the heightened international mobility of capital, governments find themselves exposed to a 'permanent referendum' on their capacity to pursue what 'the markets' judge to be 'sound economic policy', and competition to attract capital encourages governments to establish a favourable climate for investment – which includes flexible labour markets, low social costs and low taxation (on capital, at least). Governments which defy international market opinion and seek to pursue expansionary economic policies (to increase levels of employment and/or to raise standards of social provision) face the prospect of catastrophic disinvestment (and an unsustainable accompanying rise in their welfare budget). NIEs, with much more rudimentary welfare states and much lower wages, are at a considerable advantage in the competition for job-creating employment (though behind the NIEs trail a series of still less developed states with still lower wages and worse employment conditions). If more developed states (such as Britain) are not able to compete by offering technically more proficient workers (and their advantages in this area are vulnerable to rapid advances in the transmissibility of information and in computer literacy), they face the danger of a competitive 'race to the bottom' in terms of social protection and/or the creation of a permanent 'underclass' of unskilled unemployables.

There are a number of ways in which established welfare states might respond to the challenge presented by globalization. They may, for example, modify their funding arrangements so that more of the costs of social provision fall on the users of services or on employees (rather than employers), with a consequent reduction in social costs for capital. Secondly, they may tighten eligibility for benefits (raising the retirement age or increasing qualification periods) or increase targeting (by, for example, means testing income maintenance). Thirdly, they can make their social provision more 'market supporting', by tying benefits to training or sponsoring more vocational education. The twin focus of such reforms is on reducing costs (particularly those costs levied on capital) and increasing the flexibility and productivity of labour (without raising its cost to employers). We have already seen (in chapter 6) how this perspective has become a part of the justificatory apparatus of the 'new' social democracy (especially in its 'Third Way' manifestation). On these accounts, it is not the welfare state itself but rather the welfare state status quo that is no longer an option.

Globalization: the evidence

There is seemingly plenty of empirical evidence to back these claims about the spectacular advance of globalization. World trade in goods has grown almost twice as fast as GDP since 1950. The trade in services also appears to have doubled in the period since figures were first reported in 1980, so that total world trade may now amount to as much as 45 per cent of world GDP. Although much of this trade takes place *within* the developed world or, even more narrowly, within its three key regional economies, there is some evidence of rising trade between developed and developing economies (although much of this growth has been focused on South East Asia). At the same time, the technologies of transportation and, above all, communication have been transformed and the associated costs have fallen substantially. Containerization significantly reduced the costs of long-distance sea transport in the postwar world (by up to two-thirds). International telephone traffic is rising by about 20 per cent per year (from around 67.5 billion minutes in 1996). The costs of computing technology have similarly continued to fall and, in the course of a decade, the internet has emerged as a form of 'mass' communication (if still for only a proportion of the population) throughout the developed world. The number of international tourists has risen from about 25 million with an expenditure of about $2 billion in 1950 to over half a billion in 1995 with an annual spend of $255 billion, taking unprecedented numbers of human beings (and their credit cards) around the globe. (See Held et al., 1999; Garrett, 1999.)

Also crucial is the growth in the numbers and influence of multinational corporations (MNCs) and rising foreign direct investment (FDI). In 1998, 53,000 MNCs had global sales of $9.5 trillion, accounting for about a quarter of world output and up to 70 per cent of world trade. The hundred largest MNCs had 6 million employees worldwide and accounted for about 20 per cent of global foreign assets. Though still disproportionately based in the US, MNCs can now be found across much of the world economy and, while once focused largely on primary goods and manufacturing, there is now a very significant level of multinational activity in the service sector. Alongside this growth in MNCs has gone a rapid rise in FDI, which grew fivefold between 1980 and 1994 to stand at around $250 billion. In the 1980s and 1990s, most developed states have seen an increase in both inward *and* outward FDI and this has contributed to a growing engagement of national economies with the global order. (Held et al., 1999, pp. 259–82.)

Still more dramatic are those figures that disclose a transformation in patterns of financial activity around the globe. In the context of twenty-four-hour trading and more or less instantaneous electronic transmission of data, turnover in foreign exchange markets had risen from $17.5 trillion in 1979 to over $300 trillion by the late 1990s. Only a small part of this increase is devoted to servicing the rapid growth in world trade (with the ratio of foreign exchange turnover to trade now standing at around 60:1). A good deal of this trading represents speculative activity, and with the combined reserves of all the world's central banks representing no more than a single day's trading volume, sustained movements against particular currencies triggered a succession of spectacular devaluation crises through the 1990s. The period since the mid-1980s has also seen the dramatic rise of trading in various financial derivatives (futures, options, swaps), and growth in international bank lending and in the issuing of international bonds. Governments now find that an increasing proportion of their debt is held by foreign investors and domestic stock exchanges have seen a near tripling in the foreign ownership of equities. Government restrictions on international capital flows have fallen steadily (generating a corresponding rise in capital mobility) since 1973 and, while there is no evidence of the emergence of a single 'world' interest rate (implying the frictionless mobility of capital), there are signs of convergence in long-term rates and that, at the very least, 'national interest rates are determined in the context of global financial markets and conditions' (Garrett, 1998, p. 56; Held et al., 1999, pp. 206–9, 216, 219).

A third crucial element in this story is the transformation in the international (and often consequently the domestic) division of labour. In its classical form, this account holds that there has (at least since the 1960s) been a tendency for manufacturing production (and, now, increasingly the production of services) to relocate away from 'the North' or the most advanced industrial states towards a succession of NIEs or 'the South' (Froebel et al., 1980). A number of changes have driven this move: (1) a flow of migrants into cities in less developed countries, producing a large pool of cheap labour, in a context where either (2) production processes rely on unskilled labour, or (3) existing levels of educational attainment are quite high, and (4) collapsing transportation and communication costs make production at sites remote from the point of consumption economically viable. Typically starting with textiles and steel manufacture (and now increasingly encompassing tradable services), a number of industries have migrated from developed to developing economies, creating a situation in which the less developed countries no longer simply export raw materials but also increasingly export manufactured goods (and services) which can now compete on world markets. The share of world exports of manufactured goods taken by developing countries (excluding China) doubled between 1980 and 1995 (Held et al., 1999, p. 173).

These changes in the location of production are seen to have an impact on patterns of employment in the developed economies (with the most extensive welfare states). In particular, there is a decline in the demand for unskilled labour and a growing premium for marketable skills. This is seen to feed a tendency for both growing unemployment among the unskilled and/or a greater dispersion in wages between the skilled and the unskilled. There is also a suggestion that, without some form of institutional intermediation, this will tend to generate a greater diversity in the dynamics through which wages are set in the traded and non-traded sectors of the economy.

The real impact of globalization on the welfare state

Despite the apparent weight of this evidence, there is still some uncertainty about whether this all really adds up to a qualitatively new era of economic 'globalization'. A number of sceptical voices (Hirst and Thompson, 1996; Rieger and Leibfried, 2003) point to the cyclical nature of phases of economic internationalization (and periods of countermovement). There are also those who argue that liberalizing global markets has advantaged not less developed states in the South but rather predatory businesses in the most developed (welfare) states in the West which have taken this opportunity further to depress the prices of raw materials drawn from the developing world and to smother less well established manufacturers in these less developed regions (see Ellison, 2005, p. 31). Similar reservations are voiced about the impact of the rise in FDI and greater capital mobility. Much of the growth in FDI is between already developed states in

Europe, North America and Japan, or even within the free-trading bloc represented by the European Union, and ever since the publication of Feldstein and Horoika's (1980) influential paper there has been an unresolved argument about the extent to which investment is really (newly) internationally mobile. Similar reservations surround the question of the (growing) international convergence of interest rates. (On all these, see the excellent and detailed discussion in Ellison, 2005, pp. 23–47.)

Of course, what really interests us here is the impact of these (contested) processes on the dynamics of the welfare state. In particular, we want to know whether globalization is inimical to welfare states or, indeed, whether globalization makes some welfare state regimes more sustainable than others. In the first instance, we want to establish whether the most developed welfare states are really engaged in a 'race to the bottom'.

Surveying recent historical data from across the OECD, Frank Castles's unambiguous answer to the last of these questions is that the idea of a welfare 'race to the bottom' is a 'myth' (2004, p. 45) . In the crucial period between 1980 and 1998 (across which we should be able to observe the consequences of a race to the bottom, however incomplete), only two countries in the OECD21 (Ireland and the Netherlands) saw a fall in the proportion of their social expenditure as a percentage of GDP. On average, resources committed to social expenditure grew by 4 per cent – less than half the rate of growth in the preceding twenty years, but still enough to carry average social expenditure to 22.7 per cent of GDP. In fact, the story of a general halt in expenditure growth in this period holds much more convincingly for overall public expenditure than it does for social expenditure (meaning that social expenditure grew as a proportion of overall public expenditure throughout this period). Public expenditure growth almost ceased after 1980 and in almost half the countries assessed overall public expenditure fell in the period 1980–8. But even this falls some way short of the anticipated race to the bottom, and in any case it coincided with considerable variation in individual states' experiences (with a number of southern European states and Finland seeing overall growth in excess of 10 per cent of GDP). Finally, Castles sought to measure changes in social expenditure against changes in social need or dependency. Adjusting for increased need, the level of welfare generosity represented by an average 4 per cent growth in social expenditure over the period from 1980 to 1998 is virtually unchanging. There is some variation in the patterning of generosity (with most of the erosion coming among those welfare states that were most generous at the start of the period) and some overall convergence in standards of provision across the OECD. But Castles concludes that this can be more compellingly explained in terms of a general welfare state 'growth to limits', rather than as a 'race to the bottom'. Nor was 'the bottom' static. At much the same time, social expenditure was growing (quite rapidly, though from a very low base) precisely in those countries (the newly industrializing economies of South East Asia) which were supposed to constitute 'the bottom' towards which the more developed states of the OECD were racing! (See C. Pierson, 2005a.)

Other elements in the globalization story have also come under sustained challenge. Certainly I think we have to reject any straightforward claim that trade openness in and of itself is inimical to existing welfare state practices – the view that states or, at least, successful states in an open trading environment will tend to be low in taxation and low in social provision. Katzenstein (1985) was one of the first to draw attention to the fact that several of the smaller and most open economies of northern Europe were also those with the largest public budgets and the most extensive social democratic institutions (in both welfare state and labour markets). A few years earlier, Cameron's (1978) survey had found that those countries with the most open trading economies had the largest public sectors and often the most strongly coordinated labour market institutions. These were societies which were generally successful in terms of a range of economic indicators (growth, employment and, though to a lesser degree, inflation). A widely canvassed explanation is that it was precisely the greater vulnerability to external shocks that led political forces in these states to construct an elaborate network of compensations (in welfare or public sector employment) for those who were disadvantaged by the open trading regime. From the general gains that trade afforded came the means to compensate those individuals and communities who were disadvantaged by it.

It might be argued that this association is time limited by (what was then) the lower mobility of capital. Rodrik (1997), for example, argues that while openness may once have put upward pressure on public expenditure, as trade expands alongside heightened capital mobility this pressure may have been reversed. By contrast, Garrett (1998) maintains that even with the intensification of globalization there are still good reasons to think that an extensive public economy can be maintained. In part, this is because much of government spending is an investment, enhancing productivity and securing collective goods that are undersupplied by the market (including education, training and the development of physical and communications infrastructure). But Garrett wishes to extend this argument to apply to what are generally seen as 'non-productive' elements in social expenditure – including moderately generous transfers for the old, the sick and the disabled. In essence, his case is that these forms of provision, and the containment of income inequalities, will be attractive to even the most footloose of mobile capital because they underpin the 'intangible' but real benefits of social security, social cohesion and trust which, in turn, make for high productivity. The counterfactual here is a state with low wages and levels of social expenditure but high levels of criminality, insecure property rights and heightened levels of social disorder.

Businesses, particularly in capital-intensive manufacturing, will not seek out the lowest (social) cost environment but those locations which will best guarantee their medium-term profitability. At the same time, globalization does increase the numbers of citizens who are economically insecure or vulnerable and, in this context, Garrett, in the face of most orthodox opinion, sees a potentially *growing* constituency for big government, welfare states and left-of-centre parties (1998, pp. 10–11).

The evidence that would give weight to Garrett's argument is a little ambiguous, especially for the period after 1990. Indeed, Garrett himself finds that in the most recent period those countries in which trade has expanded most rapidly have seen lower than average increases in the growth of government expenditure. In the same period, trade seems to have constrained budgets everywhere and there has been some convergence in expenditure trends (though from very different starting points, so that differences across states remain very substantial). But this does not furnish unqualified support for that story which sees jobs in the developed world being transferred to less developed economies. Despite some changes in the global distribution of trade, it remains the case that most of this increase lies *between* the developed economies, rather than between these economies and those in the developing world (Rodrik, 1997, p. 26; Held et al., 1999, pp. 171–2). This may still, of course, place pressure on domestic governments (and increase insecurity among workers) but that is not quite the same as saying that it is competition with the low-wage, low social protection sectors of the world economy that is undermining the integrity of welfare states in the advanced capitalist economies. At the same time, it just is not clear that those developed societies with the most extensive welfare states have actually fared any worse economically than comparable societies with a much smaller apparatus of social protection (Pfaller et al., 1991).

Similar reservations can be entered about the impact of growing capital mobility on the integrity of existing welfare state regimes. Thus, in a survey of seventeen developed states, Swank (1998b, p. 679) finds little evidence of changes in the levels of corporate taxation (as a percentage of operating income) between the 1970s and the 1990s. Any reductions in levels of taxation he finds to have been offset by the elimination of special incentives and allowances which governments had previously allowed to corporations. This is in line, so Swank argues, with a significant change in government policies, which have switched from being market regulating or market shaping towards being more market conforming. Indeed, one of the aspirations of reforming administrations has been to prevent their revenue-raising from 'distorting' economic behaviour. Certainly tax reform can be seen to have been one element in a widespread growth in income inequality in the 1980s and 1990s as states sought to 'flatten' their tax regimes. But governments have not for the most part been willing to see a significant decline in their overall tax take, and tax reforms of the 1980s and 1990s tended to be revenue-neutral and more about broadening the base or redistributing the burden than cutting the overall level of taxes.

Generally, it is the larger welfare states that have been seen to be peculiarly vulnerable to a tightening of financial disciplines because it is they who are perceived to be the most likely to run substantial budget deficits and/or to permit higher levels of inflation. These are the policy dispositions which it is thought international asset-holders are most likely to want to punish. This may not express itself directly as capital flight but rather as a bidding down of the value of the deficit country's currency (in the expectation of future inflation) and the imposition of a premium on the interest rates of the offending government. Swank's conclusions on this issue are interesting:

> Exposure to international capital markets . . . does not necessitate significant retrenchment of the welfare state at moderate levels of budget imbalance; when budget deficits don't exist, some expansion of social protection is possible even in the context of international capital mobility. *However, when budget deficits become high, capital mobility engenders cuts in social welfare effort.* (Swank, 1998b, emphasis in the original)

All of this lends weight to the judgement of Perraton and his collaborators (1997): 'rather than global financial markets imposing particular policies on national governments, they have significantly changed the costs associated with particular policies and instruments through their effects on interest rate risk premia and exchange rate movements.' At times, this may constitute an effective veto, with some economic options rendered 'prohibitively expensive', and it will certainly push governments 'to pursue national macroeconomic strategies which seek low and stable rates of inflation, through fiscal discipline and a tight monetary policy'. This may, in its turn, encourage us to modify the view that governments are increasingly 'powerless' in the face of global market forces. That the range of options open to particular (welfare) states are constrained and that the extent of those constraints varies from one (welfare) state to another in line with its geopolitical and economic strength is nothing new. The processes of globalization and even, to some extent, global 'talk' may shift opportunities and costs for policy-makers (among others). But they do not reduce the range of policy options to one, nor can they relieve policy-makers of other pressures, including those that come from organized interests, public opinion, entrenched institutions and the weight of accumulated entitlements and expectations. Even if the pressures of globalization were the same on all welfare states and were to drive them all in the same direction, they would be starting from very different positions and would still be likely to look quite different once the globalization 'shift' had been effected. We now have plenty of evidence that politics and institutions still matter, even, perhaps especially, in the politics of welfare retrenchment (P. Pierson, 1994, 1996). To put it simply, if we imagine that the United States and Sweden were to come under just the same pressure to retrench their welfare states and that both responded with substantively similar measures (in themselves, two rather implausible premises), they would both still look quite different at the end of that process.

This may point us towards a further qualification of the globalization story. In some circumstances, it may be that it is politicians or policy-makers who *choose* globalization. Of course, this is not a 'free' choice and may be made only because all the alternatives are so unattractive. Nonetheless, it may persuade us to reject the image of state actors rendered 'powerless' by globalization. Fligstein, for example, argues that the shift from countercyclical measures to the prioritization of price stability over the past twenty years originated not with the markets but with policy-makers convinced that their previous policies were contributing to uncontrollable domestic price inflation (1998, pp. 30–1). Fear of the reaction of international currency holders was only a part of this story. Indeed, the detailed consideration of any globalization 'episode' reveals complex interplay and feedback as politicians seek to anticipate markets and market actors seek to second-guess the politicians. Both have certain key resources at their disposal, but both also face severe external constraints. It is wrong, then, to insist that politicians had no choice, that globalization pressed on them an irresistible policy formulation. But, at the same time, globalization was much more than politicians being frightened by their own words and shadows. The room for policy manoeuvre is strictly limited and the room for preference-shaping policy, of the kind that Colin Hay (1997, 1999) recommends, is quite small.

Finally, we turn to the impact of those recent changes in the international and domestic division of labour that seem to have come in the wake of globalization. Most economists accept that the shift in unskilled labour from developed to developing worlds has had a real impact on unemployment and/or wage inequality in developed societies, and some have argued that the greater competition *between* the developed economies may also have contributed to greater job insecurity and a weakening of terms and conditions of employment (Cline, 1997; Rodrik, 1997). Certainly, the return of mass unemployment and growing wage disparities are widely regarded as a key challenge for welfare state policy-makers. Still, it remains the case that most economists attribute much the greater part of this decline in unskilled employment (and its consequent effect on wages and employment) to technological change. Schwartz insists that, even if the growth within newly industrialized countries may have displaced some workers in OECD economies, this actually 'created growth in the OECD that in turn could have provided a window for redistribution towards these [displaced] workers' (2000, pp. 20–1) . He cites evidence from Denmark (among others) that 'exogenously driven prosperity in the 1990s translated into increased rather than decreased transfers'. Iversen draws a similar conclusion (2000, pp. 74–5) . Deindustrialization 'is largely explained by a combination of rapid productivity growth in agriculture and manufacturing combined with a shift in demand away from manufactured goods towards services . . . There is no evidence that either trade . . . or capital market openness cause de-industrialization.' Deindustrialization may be a problem for welfare states – but not primarily as a consequence of heightened globalization.

An even more frontal challenge to the established orthodoxy on globalization and the welfare state can be found in the most recent work of Elmar Rieger and Stephan Leibfried. Their study of the *Limits to Globalization* (2003) reverses the usual direction of causality between welfare states and globalization. According to Rieger and Leibfried, it is the building of developed welfare states in the postwar period that made possible the more open trading regime which we associate with the coming of globalization. Postwar welfare states were a surrogate for protectionism. In providing, by other means, the forms of domestic defence to which the advocates of protectionism had (however mistakenly) aspired, welfare states made possible the international trading order of the postwar world:

> In the period after World War II the welfare state was able to assume the special functions of protectionism – the defence of employment and incomes via tariffs, import quotas, licensing and restrictions on capital flows – and thereby paved the way for trade policy to take advantage of an international division of labour . . . The welfare states themselves, by virtue of their domestic policies, are the major providers of order in the world economy. (Rieger and Leibfried, 2003, p. 13)

In the most recent period (and in the face of the orthodox view of globalization), 'the significance of government and politics has increased, not decreased, as a result of international economic integration' (Rieger and Leibfried, 2003, p. 21). The processes of deregulation that we most strongly associate with the latest wave of globalization were themselves the product of domestic democratic welfare state politics. They were a political response to the failure of existing regulated economies to deliver on the promise of prosperity: 'Globalization is not so much market driven as state driven. For this reason, the important thing about globalization is not its alleged autonomy-reducing form, but its democratic scope and above all its welfare-enhancing effects.' Welfare states are now so well entrenched and so widely supported (if not by the entire population then at least by 'relevant majorities') that 'the problem today consists not in the welfare state being too weak to defend its socio-political benefit standards, but in its inflexibility precisely because of its strength' (Rieger and Leibfried, 2003, p. 30). If globalization can precipitate a crisis of the welfare state, it is not a crisis of benefits and their provision but of the allocation of costs that is, primarily, of taxation (the one area in which Rieger and Leibfried seem willing to concede that capital is newly powerful under contemporary conditions). In the end, 'the fate of globalization was and is determined domestically' (Rieger and Leibfried, 2003, p. 51).

I have given so much weight to the *opponents* of the welfare globalization thesis precisely because the latter has become so much the assumed wisdom of our times. There are, though, still plenty of commentators who are sceptical about the sceptics. Korpi and Palme (2003), for example, insist that the process of retrenchment of welfare in Europe under the duress of globalization is real enough. Their counterargument is built around two features. First, they insist that the return of mass unemployment in Western Europe must itself be understood as a form of retrenchment of the implicit right to paid work (at least for men) which was a part of the postwar welfare settlement across the developed world. They also develop an index of social citizenship rights (SCIP, the Social Citizenship Indicator Program) which measures changes in individual entitlements and levels of benefits for claimants across a range of states. Measuring the level of these entitlements (rather than aggregate expenditures) shows a significant retrenchment almost everywhere, though one which is especially pronounced in 'liberal' states, above all in the UK under Margaret Thatcher (Korpi and Palme, 2003, pp. 432–9).

In a similar vein, Philipp Genschel identifies a real impact of global tax competition on the discretion of national governments:

> The conventional wisdom is correct: tax competition is a constraint on national tax policy. But this constraint makes itself felt differently than the conventional wisdom assumes. It does not force the welfare state into a race to the bottom but traps it in between external pressures to reduce the tax burden on capital and internal pressures to maintain revenue levels and relieve the tax burden on labor. The result is more austerity, more deficit finance, and a less employment-friendly tax mix than would have prevailed in a world without tax competition. (2002, p. 246)

The Challenge of Demographic Change

A second set of strategic challenges for contemporary welfare states arises from the dynamics of demographic change. Contemporary societies are subject to a whole range of these changes – fewer and later marriages, more divorces, smaller families, more single person households, changing female labour force participation – and the nature and scale of these challenges is subject to considerable international variation. They can also be seen to interact in potentially volatile ways with the 'imperatives' of globalization. In this section I deal with what has probably been the most prominent of these challenges – the consequences of rapid societal ageing, including the impact of rapidly declining fertility rates. I defer consideration of some of the other issues to our assessment of 'new social risks'.

Ageing societies

We live in societies that are rapidly ageing and, given that welfare states are, above all, systems of provision for the old, this represents a real challenge for social policy. According to World Bank (1994) statistics, in 1990 almost half a billion people in the world's population (about 9 per cent) were aged sixty or over. By 2030, this number is projected to nearly triple to 1.4 billion (16 per cent). In the developed states, the proportion of elderly people in the population averages around 15 per cent. By 2030 it will be close to 25 per cent (CSIS, 2002, p. 3). Despite the attention paid to ageing in the developed world, it is actually in less developed states (where resources are most limited) that the change will be most rapid. By 2030, for example, one-quarter of the world's old people will be living in China, and the doubling of the elderly population, which took 140 years in France, will occur in just thirty-four years in China (World Bank, 1994, pp. 33, 1).

Increasing life expectancies mean that in the future there will be a growing number of 'older elderly' people (conventionally defined as those over seventy-five or eighty), among whom many of the health and nursing care costs of ageing are concentrated. (Across a range of OECD countries, healthcare expenditures are on average two and half times as high for those over sixty-five as for the younger population.) Much higher ratios (up to five times the spend on the more youthful populations) are reported for those over seventy-five. In the OECD area, the population over seventy-five is set to double between 1990 and 2030, and this older section of the aged population is made up disproportionately of women, whose economic status tends to be worse than that of older men (OECD, 1996, p. 103; World Bank, 1994, pp. 28–30). At the same time, fertility rates in the more developed world have declined significantly, in some cases precipitously, over the past forty years. In the period between 1960 and 1980, fertility rates among women in the age group 15–44 fell across the OECD from 2.88 to 1.87 (Castles, 2004, pp. 142–3). In some states, fertility rates had 'collapsed' by the end of 1990s (standing at 1.3 in Greece, 1.2 in Italy and 1.16 in Spain). Were fertility rates to continue at 1.3 over a period of a century, the national population would be reduced to a quarter of its present size!

A crucial consequence of these several changes is a significant worsening of the elderly dependency ratio, that is the ratio between the growing aged population and the numbers of those of working age (defined as those between fifteen and sixty-four) out of whose productive activity the consumption needs of the elderly must be met. In the OECD as a whole, the elderly dependency ratio is set to rise from 19 per cent to 37 per cent between 1990 and 2030 – a near doubling in just forty years. For some states, the transformation is still more dramatic, with Japan's dependency ratio tripling by 2030 and increasing to more than 40 per cent in both Germany and Italy (OECD, 1996, p. 103). Lowered fertility rates will clearly accentuate this trend and may make the elderly dependency ratio still less favourable in the states of lowered reproduction. The CSIS report *The Global Retirement Crisis* estimates that by 2050 in Italy the elderly dependency ratio may exceed 100 per cent (CSIS, 2002, p. 14). Although projections across a range of states vary quite significantly, simply to maintain existing patterns of entitlement would require pension expenditures in the most severely affected OECD states (Japan, Italy and Germany) to rise above 15 per cent of GDP at some time in the next fifty years (OECD, 1996, p. 33).

For a number of influential international organizations (and increasingly for national governments), these trends are enough to precipitate a demographic crisis of the welfare state. Especially influential has been the authoritative and proselytizing work of international agencies such as the OECD (1988a, 1988b, 1992, 1998, 1999) and, above all, the World Bank whose revealingly titled 1994 report *Averting the Old Age Crisis* became required reading in social security ministries (and treasuries) around the globe. On the World Bank's account existing social security programmes are 'beset by escalating costs that require high taxes and deter private sector growth – while failing to protect the old' (1994, p. 1). These programmes have 'spun out of control' and require urgent reform. At its simplest (and most extreme), the argument is that the ageing profile of the world's national populations means that at some point in this century existing welfare state systems (and their patterns of income transfers) will become unsustainable. The mature welfare states were created in societies where pensions were small and the years spent in retirement comparatively few. We now have much more generous pension provision (and much more extensive public health care, a good which is disproportionately consumed by the elderly) and periods in retirement which may stretch into decades. The view is that, as the aged dependency ratio rises into the next century, the tax demand on a smaller working age population will become so excessive that the implicit 'intergenerational' pact on which welfare state funding depends will collapse.

Pension reform

On the World Bank's account, the problem we face is not just one of unfavourable demographic change. Indeed, rather more it is that most existing old age pension regimes will end up making the situation worse not better. This is because most systems of old age security are based on mandatory public schemes financed by payroll taxes and provided on a pay-as-you-go (PAYG) basis (James, 2000, pp. 271–2). Under such a regime, today's workers pay today's pensions in what has, up until now, been the confident expectation that the next generation of workers will pay for the pensions of the current working population once retired. This system may work reasonably well, so it is argued, while the pensioner population is relatively small and growth in earnings both makes worker contributions affordable and enables retired people to share in the general benefits of economic growth. However, when the demographic profile becomes less favourable, or wage growth falters, it sets in train a vicious circle. The increasing demand for resources to fund the pensions of a growing retired population must be met either out of the incomes of existing workers or their employers or by a growth in public debt. None of these solutions is satisfactory. Increasing the burden on the present generation of workers is unfair and may, indeed, prove regressive if costs borne by the comparatively low paid in the present generation are used to pay the pensions of even quite affluent older people. Such impositions are likely to be resisted either politically or by decreased economic participation in the formal economy (the level of payroll taxes acting as a disincentive to enter the labour market). Workers who exclude themselves from the formal economy will, of course, fail to build up their own entitlement to social insurance benefits and increase the pressure on those who do contribute. If it were possible to transfer these payroll costs entirely to employers (though most economists seem to believe that, in the end, it is workers who fund these payments) this would result in lower employment (especially in an environment where capital could be invested elsewhere), less investment and lowered economic growth. Personal savings would be depressed and other and more productive forms of public expenditure (for example, investment in infrastructure or education) would be crowded out. Countries that sought to fund their growing pension commitment through increasing public indebtedness would find their behaviour punished by international financial markets and end up with an increasing amount of GDP devoted to the entirely unproductive business of servicing the public debt. In the end, only economic growth can 'square the circle' of raising living standards for both retired and economically active populations but the dynamics of PAYG regimes are such as to distort economic incentives and further restrict economic growth.

The World Bank 'solution'

The World Bank's 'solution' combines a reduction in the public commitment to pension provision with reforms designed to raise levels of economic activity and, with it, the overall pool of resources out of which the needs of future generations of workers and retirees must be met. The Bank's recommendation involves moving to a three-pillared system of old age social security. The public pillar should provide a flat or means-tested pension or a minimum pension guarantee. Its principal aim should be to provide a 'social safety net' and prevent the incidence of poverty. It would be mandatory, tax-funded and index-linked to either wages or prices (or some combination thereof). Especially if it were combined with a raising of the retirement age, the reformed public pillar should prove much less costly than existing PAYG systems. The second pillar would also be mandatory but it would be fully funded and privately managed. Workers would contribute either to occupational plans provided by their employers or else to their own private pension schemes. The Bank's preference is for a Defined Contribution (DC) scheme in which the sum out of which a pension would be funded at maturity would reflect the cumulative value of sums invested in the fund, rather than, as in a Defined Benefit (DB) scheme, a formula based on final salary. The expectation is that access to equity markets would allow workers to participate more fully in the benefits of economic growth. Indeed their increased savings would provide the capital that would help to fuel such economic growth. In contrast to public schemes, 'competitively managed, funded pension plans . . . are more likely to enjoy the benefits of investment diversification, that protects them against inflation and other risks, and to spur financial market development, thereby enhancing economic growth' (James, 2000, p. 277). There would be a further fully funded voluntary pillar (which might or might not receive favourable tax treatment) for those who wished to increase their investment for retirement beyond that mandated in the second compulsory-but-private pillar.

The OECD's turn-of-the-millennium policy statement covers much of the same ground as the World Bank's 1994 report but its style – in keeping with its title, *A Caring World* – is a little gentler. In line with the OECD's own promotion of a more 'active' society (and a more 'active' welfare state to match), the key ambition of its 'new' social policy is 'to achieve social solidarity through enabling individuals and families to support themselves' and this is to be achieved, above all, by promoting 'employment-oriented welfare policies' (OECD, 1999, p. 4).

On ageing, it endorses the view that the status quo is not an option and supports calls for reductions in public pension benefits, increases in contributions and a move towards more advance-funded pension schemes. In line with its employment-oriented remit, it also pays particular attention to the secular decline in economic participation rates among older workers (particularly men in the age group 55–64). Participation rates for the 55–64 age group and effective retirement ages fell significantly between 1950 and 1980, while life expectancies rose and, in a number of countries, early retirement or a transfer of older workers from unemployment benefits to disability allowances was more or less consciously employed as an instrument of government policy (as we saw above, pp. 191–5; OECD, 1996, pp. 65–80). The OECD presses for a reversal of this trend, encouraging the fuller participation of older workers by removing existing financial incentives for early retirement. This fuller participation of older workers is seen as a way of significantly reducing the burden of pension (and associated social security) costs.

The OECD recommends three further measures to address the pensions challenge: (1) incrementally *raising the age of retirement* and encouraging those who wish to work beyond this age to do so, perhaps on a part-time basis; (2) promoting *general cost containment* by reducing replacement rates, moderating the effects of benefits indexing, requiring longer contribution periods for full benefits etc.; and (3) *targeting* benefits either explicitly through a means test or by increasing the liability of benefits to taxation. At the same time, contributions could be increased by raising levels or increasing the proportion of earnings which are liable for payroll taxation, though the OECD is clearly conscious of the threat that higher non-wage labour costs (or the 'labour tax wedge') present to a social policy based on maximum involvement in paid employment (OECD, 1996; OECD 1999).

Ageing societies and the welfare state: an assessment

How convincing is the rather alarming case set out by the World Bank and the OECD? In fact, there are plenty of dissenting voices from *within* the relevant policy community (see Beattie and McGillivray, 2000; James, 2000). In terms of the World Bank's proposals, a number of commentators point to the considerable downside involved in opting for fully funded Defined Contribution pensions. The argument here is that risks which were quite properly pooled through the state and the apparatus of social insurance would be displaced on to individual worker-savers. The responsibility for making very complex and hugely consequential decisions are thus devolved to individuals who, with even the most expert (and perhaps costly) of advice, will find it extraordinarily difficult to make rational choices. It is an area where an asymmetry of information and knowledge seems unavoidable. At the same time, pensioners with identical contributions records may find themselves with widely differing pension entitlements and standards of living (depending on the performance of those funds with which they have invested). This element of 'luck' may be acceptable for people's discretionary income. It is not clear that it will be seen as acceptable in securing their basic retirement income. Annuitization of savings also presents problems, especially if pensioners are obliged to purchase annuities at the point of retirement (when again values will be determined by immediate market conditions). Given their longer life expectancies, women ought to receive a lower annuity than men investing the same sum. Some states have legislated to equalize this anomaly (as in the US) but it is not clear why this equalizing principle should not be applied to iron out other 'anomalies' in the retirement system. There is also a possibility that within a system of mandatory private savings 'too much' capital will be saved or that the regulatory structure surrounding pension investments will mean that funds are managed too conservatively (thus failing to realize in full the anticipated bonus in terms of accelerated economic growth). Nor is it clear, despite the protestations of the World Bank report, that pensioners will be better protected against renewed inflation under a fully privatized scheme.

It appears that the merits of PAYG and fully funded systems are, at least in part, related to the respective growth in returns to either capital or labour (Aaron, 1966). Recent years have seen a shift in favour of investment income, favouring a fully funded regime, but a declining working age population plus a wealth of mandated investment funds might change this relationship again in the future. Nor is the management of private pensions regimes without its problems. The UK has a mature financial system and a longstanding tradition of occupational pensions in the private sector. Yet British experience of the drive to extend private pension coverage was marked by wholesale mis-selling and high charges, and proved peculiarly inappropriate for those on lower (but not the very lowest) wages (Waine, 1995). In practice, states will have to provide extensive income support to those with a history of no wages or low wages, and they will require an extensive and sophisticated regulatory apparatus (which will need to be funded) and a regulatory structure (determining the kinds of investments pension funds may make) which will reduce the likely profitability of the funds themselves. Mandating private individuals to commit a certain proportion of their income to saving instruments within a particular (and perhaps conservative) regulatory apparatus may actually dampen potential capital accumulation. There are potentially problems of legitimacy and authority, too, for states that require citizens to hand over a (significant) part of their income to a private investor but provide no guarantee of the returns that the citizen may expect from such a fund.

All of this is before we consider the difficult question of transition and the double burden (of paying present and future pensions) which must, in howsoever mediated a form, be placed on one or more transitional generations. (There is a natural and reasonable disposition to seek to spread the pain of systemic change, but the more the costs are dispersed, the less effective the reform will be.) As Paul Pierson points out (1998), pension reform generally makes for poor politics. Proposed reforms mean a large-scale reallocation of future resources and entitlements. In a democratic polity, the promise to increase costs and reduce benefits for a broad swathe of the population is likely to be resisted, as popular protests in France and Italy in the mid-1990s seem to suggest (Pitruzzello, 1997).

At the same time, there is a reasonable suspicion that the prospects of an unreformed future are made to look as frightening as possible at least in part to add imagined value to the trade-off between a little unpleasantness now and the prospect of catastrophic breakdown in the future. Thus, while future projections of the aged population may be quite accurate and future dependency ratios only a little less so, the economic consequences of these changes are rather less certain. For example, future projections are sensitive to the compounding of quite small variations in rates of economic growth and to changes in levels of labour force participation. (Thus, for example, the consequences of an aged dependency ratio of 3 : 1 will be quite different where the effective labour force participation of the 15–64 age group is at 80 per cent rather than 60 per cent.) Again, quite incremental changes in effective retirement ages make a potentially substantial difference to effective dependency rates and ageing may in any case change patterns of economic behaviour in ways that counteract the increasing number of elderly persons. Fougere and Merette, for example, insist that 'population ageing could create more opportunities for future generations to invest in human capital formation, which would stimulate economic growth and reduce significantly the apprehended impact of ageing on output per capita' (1999, p. 411). The scale of these changes could be very substantial (see, for example, the projected changes in Italy; Fougere and Merette, 1999, p. 425). The modelling of projected demographic change also indicates that adjustments to savings rates (generally, it is assumed that pensioners dissave) may not be so perverse as is often assumed and that anticipated increases in taxation may also be much more modest than projections of the 'aged burden' have suggested.

Other changes may not be just as the World Bank and OECD have assumed. Some have argued that the impact of improving health among the elderly may do more to offset the impact of ageing (though the growth in health expenditures arising from ageing are projected to be quite modest). Societal ageing, for example, is not just a reflection of the growing number of older people. It is as much, perhaps in industrialized countries rather more, an aspect of fertility (i.e. population replacement rates.) We know that in general fertility rates have fallen quite steeply in developed societies in recent decades and that this is part of the problem of societal ageing (especially in countries such as Italy, Spain and Germany). But we also know (Castles, 2004, pp. 141–66) that the relationship between fertility and female labour force participation has been changing and that those societies with a more generous system of family support have generally seen a lesser decline in fertility. Of course, there is no straightforward relationship between expenditure on childcare provision and fertility. (The history of states 'endowing' motherhood in the hope that it would persuade women to produce more babies is long but largely unsuccessful.) There is, however, enough of a relationship to believe that policy *may* have an effect on the decision to have children and, through this, on the overall demographic profile of the population. Also contentious but consequential is the impact of migration. Politicians, particularly those who have earned a little electoral credit by being 'tough' on immigration, may not regard this as an attractive option. In the years of welfare austerity, it has been much more common for politicians to argue that immigration is a luxury that cannot be afforded (see Golding and Middleton, 1982). But most if not all economists tend to follow the line taken by Razin and Sadka (1999) that, with a dynamic model of the economy, immigration is likely to represent a net benefit to all citizens – certainly in terms of the affordability of pensions.

Finally, we need to remind ourselves that, whether public or private, the consumption needs of future generations of pensioners (and other net beneficiaries) will have to be met from current economic output. Fully funded pensions *may* have the twin virtues of encouraging faster economic growth (so that the pie out of which the pensioners' slice must come will be larger) and/or of persuading current savers to commit more resources because of a confidence that their future entitlement is more secure (since the promise comes from a stockbroker and not a politician!). As with Australia's compulsory superannuation, mandatory contributions to private pension funds may avoid the stigma attached to personal taxation and may help to buffer politicians (at least a little) from popular demands for increasing pension income (see C. Pierson, 1998). But, in the end, affordability will strongly reflect economic performance and, in practice, all pension regimes will involve a mix of private and public provision. There may well be a feedback between social policy and economic performance, but levels of growth will also be effected by contingencies entirely outside the scope of social policy.

With all these qualifications in place, the 'unanswerable' case for immediate and radical reform looks a little less compelling. This is just as well, since experience suggests that, however strong the political will to reform may be, change in the social policy area is resolutely incremental and path dependency is strong (P. Pierson, 1998). As ever, it is the largest, most costly programmes (with the most beneficiaries) that are hardest to cut. The one 'virtue' of gradual pension reform as a political practice is that many of its costs may be concealed and postponed into a future which electors may discount even more strongly than politicians. Nonetheless, many states have moved to retrench their provision: raising the retirement age (UK, New Zealand, Italy, Japan), increasing the qualifying period for a full pension (France, Portugal, Ireland, Finland), lowering the basis for upgrading benefits (UK, France, Spain) and income testing the pension (Austria, Denmark, Australia). Parallel changes have been introduced in respect of disability benefits, unemployment protection and family allowances (see above. p. 168). But overall the impact of the reform agenda has been rather variable.

At first sight rather strangely, it is one of the states best placed to face the challenge of ageing, the UK (with its modestly ageing profile and its established system of funded pensions), that has embraced the reform agenda with particular enthusiasm. Thus New Labour's 1998 Green Paper *Partnership in Pensions* projected a *fall* of 1 per cent in the proportion of GDP devoted to public spending on pensions by 2050 (from 5.5 to 4.5 per cent), with 60 per cent of pensioner income expected to come from private pensions (DSS, 1998b). In fact what we see, rather less surprisingly, is that it is those states in which change is easiest to effect (because of existing private provision, a more favourable ageing profile and a governing system that facilitates change) rather than those where it is most urgent that have been the most active reformers. In Europe, it is probably the continental/corporatist regimes that stand most in need of reform; yet it is here that (so far) progress has been most limited (compared with some dynamism in both liberal and social democratic states) (Ellison, 2005, pp. 182–5). At the same time, we need to remember that there are plenty of reasons other than demography for states to be pursuing these reforms. In much of the European Union, for example, it was the desire to meet the public debt reduction criteria for membership of the single European currency that drove the pension reform agenda in the mid and late 1990s (Pitruzzello, 1997). Again, while the demographic imperative is one source of motivation for labour market reforms and 'lifelong learning', this is probably subordinate to a persistent concern with long-term joblessness and the call for greater 'competitiveness'. In the face of these qualifications, reform of social security was put at the top of the domestic political agenda of the second George W. Bush presidency, though it remains to be seen how effective the reform agenda is in practice.

The Challenge of 'New Social Risks'

In this final section, I address a disparate range of social changes and (consequent) social policy challenges that are frequently brought under the collective label of 'new social risks'. Of course, dealing with individual risk by collective means has always been a crucial part of what welfare states do. It is of the essence of the idea of social insurance. But a number of commentators have sought to isolate a range of 'new' social risks which have emerged in what they frequently characterize as increasingly 'post-industrial' societies over the past twenty years. These are typically the circumstances of the most economically developed countries (with the largest welfare states). They reflect important social changes (especially in the form and role of the family), as well as changes in economic organization (especially the development of economies in which service provision in both private and public sectors are newly important). The precise character of these new risks and the ways in which governments respond to them are also shaped by (the diversity of) pre-existing welfare arrangements. Given this, and as we might expect, the nature of and response to new social risks varies between (and, in practice, within) differing welfare regimes.[1]

Huber and Stephens (2006) neatly capture the generic contrast between 'old' and 'new' welfare states in the following terms:

> The 'old' welfare state is conceptualized as transfer-heavy, oriented towards covering risks from loss of earnings capacity due to old age, unemployment, sickness, and invalidity. The model (and modal) client of the old welfare state is seen as a male blue-collar production worker who is the breadwinner for the family. The family is protected through the entitlements of the main breadwinner. The 'new' welfare state is conceptualized as more service-heavy, oriented towards increasing the earnings capacity of individuals through support for continuing education, training and retraining, and socialization of care work to facilitate combining paid work with raising a family. There is no real modal client of the new welfare state, and it certainly is not the male family breadwinner. Individuals can be clients of the new welfare state at different stages of the life cycle, be it as children of working parents, as adolescents in training, as adults in retraining, as working parents with small children, or as elderly in need of care.

As Huber and Stephens point out, this contrast is an oversimplification. In fact, many of the 'old' risks persist and some of the 'older' welfare states (particularly those classified as 'social democratic') have long (and, at least in part, successfully) embraced policies which seek to address the supposedly 'new' types of risks. We seek to reflect this greater complexity in the account that follows.

We can assess the new social risks in terms of four key categories. First, and probably most important, are those risks which arise from changes in gender roles (especially changed patterns of participation in the formal economy) and greater diversity of family formation. Of particular significance in relation to the first of these are the problems of securing a work–life balance (and the provision of adequate and affordable childcare), and in relation to the second, the growth of single parenthood (in which problems of securing adequate income and economic participation

---

[1] For an excellent introduction to these issues see the contributions in Peter Taylor-Gooby (ed.), *New Risks, New Welfare* (2005). I draw extensively on the data in this edited collection in this section.

are particularly acute). Also important under this head is the issue of providing and funding adequate support for the elderly, especially the frail elderly. A second series of risks arises from changes in the nature of the labour market: the increasing skills premium, the decline of 'lifelong' employment, the inadequacy of earned incomes (and the re-emergence of 'the working poor'). Two further 'new' problems concern insufficiency of social security coverage (especially in those Bismarckian systems where adequate pensions or benefit payments rely on an adequate contributions record) and the problems of regulation and consumer vulnerability (in systems which have been reformed to allow for greater private provision, in pensions or childcare, for example). I shall explore each of these areas in turn.

Changes in family and gender roles

Typically, 'old' welfare states (at least those outside the Scandinavian/ social democratic model) were built around an expectation that most of the work of caring for children and the elderly would be undertaken, informally and unpaid, by women, who would either withdraw from the formal workforce, or indeed never enter it, in order to fulfil this task. Although this may never quite have conformed to women's lived experience, it is clear that over the last thirty years the nature of women's labour force participation (especially when compared to that of men) has been transformed. Despite substantial international variations, since 1970 women have become increasingly active in formal labour markets, while men's participation has fallen. Since 1970, across the EU, men's labour force participation has fallen from 89 per cent to 78 per cent, while the corresponding figure for women has risen from 45 to 61 per cent. Increasingly, women *with young children* have been active in the labour force. In 2000, participation rates for women with one child were in excess of 80 per cent in the Scandinavian countries; elsewhere in the European Union, this rate was generally above 60 per cent. Although it was lower in southern Europe (and Ireland), only in Spain was the rate still below 50 per cent. There is an enormous variation in the numbers of these women with young children working part-time (and often juggling work and childcare responsibilities), ranging from as low as 6 per cent in Denmark to 66 per cent in the UK; but everywhere there has been an increase in women's participation in full-time employment. There has also been a clear move away from that pattern in which women would withdraw from the workforce for extended periods while they had children of school age. At the same time, women tend to marry later (if at all), to be older at first childbirth and to have lower completed fertility rates.

This growing involvement of women in paid labour has also helped to contribute to a characteristic division in contemporary labour markets between work-rich and work-poor households, that is between those family households in which both parents are working and those in which no member of the household has paid employment (OECD, 1997, pp. 46–7; 1999, p. 23; 2001; 2002). Increasingly, a single household income is often seen to be inadequate to meet typical family needs. At the same time, it is clear that a disproportionate amount of informal care (for both children and elders) is still provided by women (see Eurostat 2002, tables A.17 and A.19).

At its simplest, the increasing participation of women in paid work has generated an acute need for additional childcare and, if to a lesser extent, elder care. In the Scandinavian welfare regimes, generous state support has long enabled fairly high full-time participation for mothers (including lone mothers). Traditionally, mothers' labour force participation in southern European states has been lower but with a substantial proportion working full time (and often relying on informal/family childcare). Liberal states (like the UK) have seen high levels of part-time work for mothers who have sought to reconcile their joint commitment to work and childcare without much state support (and through a mixture of informal and market-provided childcare). Where state support is low and informal/family provision less than it once was (as in southern Europe), the reconciliation of work and childrearing has tended to be manifest in much reduced levels of fertility (discussed above, p. 213).

The new challenges associated with women's increased participation in the formal economy are intensified by other changes in family formation. At its most traditional, the 'old' welfare state assumed stable nuclear families in which earned income (and often benefit entitlements too) derived from the lifetime work commitment (and social insurance contributions) of a male breadwinner. Although this always corresponded rather imperfectly to social reality, this pattern of family formation is increasingly *atypical* in developed welfare states. Increased divorce rates, rising levels of cohabitation, growing numbers of lone parent families and never-married mothers mean that the pattern of family formation is both complex and fluid. Greater family instability means that individuals are subject to much greater (and unanticipated) welfare 'shocks' at different points in their life. Divorce can be a major source of unanticipated loss of income, especially for women. It can also unseat anticipated patterns of welfare entitlement for separated couples (for example, lost pension credits). The challenge of reconciling work and childcare is especially acute for lone parents, particularly for those with low marketable skills and limited earning power (for whom market-provided childcare is likely to be prohibitively expensive). The numbers of such lone parent households has risen steeply in the past twenty years, especially in the Anglo-Saxon countries. By the 1990s, a quarter of all households with dependent children in the US and around a fifth of those in New Zealand and the

UK had a single head (Kilkey and Bradshaw, 1999). The number of children born to unmarried mothers has also risen sharply though unevenly (to over a third in the UK). Over 90 per cent of lone parent families where the parent is not widowed are headed by mothers and there is a disproportionate likelihood that these families (and the children within them) will be living in poverty (Saraceno, 1997, pp. 84–5).

Historically, the treatment of single parents (and the generosity shown towards them) has varied a great deal and there has always been a tension between seeing sole parents as breadwinners or as carers. Many welfare regimes have sanctioned single mothers' non-participation in the formal labour market while they have responsibility for their children but not generally in ways which have given households headed by a lone parent economic parity with other household types. Those who have wished to enter the workforce have often been discouraged by a mixture of low pay and expensive childcare. Increasingly, given the context of an 'employment-oriented social policy' and economic 'activation', single parents have been encouraged to participate in the formal labour market (the UK's New Deal for Lone Parents is a good example). Potentially, policy-makers have available a mixture of carrots (better and cheaper childcare, in-work benefits for the low-paid, education and training opportunities) and sticks (more intrusive case management, lower and more restricted benefits). Recent evidence (from reform proposals in the UK and Australia) suggests that there are attempts to broaden the range of opportunities but in a context of more compulsion (DWP, 2006; Dean, 1998).

A further species of 'new' risk is a by-product of the rising numbers of older people – especially those who are frail or who belong to the 'older elderly' (over seventy-five or eighty). As we have seen (above, pp. 213–14), absolute numbers and the proportion of older people in the population are growing and this represents not just a challenge in terms of the sufficiency of pensions but also in respect of healthcare systems and nursing or residential care. As needs rise (with increases in the proportion of older people), the supply of informal carers (mostly middle-aged women) is falling (as female labour force participation increases). Elder care is expensive and neither the state nor families are well placed to take up the strain.

Labour market changes

A second species of risk arises from changes in the typical labour markets in developed welfare states. We have seen that, whether under the impress of globalization or of technological change, patterns of employment in developed welfare states have shifted significantly over the past twenty or thirty years. These years have been characterized by a decline in traditional 'blue-collar' labour, a growth in employment in services (in both public and private sectors), an enhanced premium for skills, a greater association between educational achievement and employability, the (re-)emergence of large-scale unemployment (and especially, of long-term unemployment), difficulties in the transition from education to work (particularly for young people with the fewest skills), an increase in irregular forms of employment (either in the informal economy or with short-term contracts) and growing wage inequality. Levels of unionization have fallen and so (to a varying degree and from very different starting points) have forms of intermediation between the 'social partners' (organized labour and organized capital). In general, long-term rates of economic growth have fallen and this has been widely associated with the growth in the service sector and the reduced opportunities for raised productivity which are seen to be typical of this sector. (For a discussion, see P. Pierson, 2000.)

This has a number of consequences for the morphology of welfare risk. First, in so far as the typical postwar welfare state and its social insurance provision was built around a 'typical' blue-collar working career that was itself based on secure and reasonably well-paid continuous employment throughout a lengthy working life, the 'new' economy undermines the underpinnings of that older welfare state regime. Increasingly, employment is less secure and, for the less skilled (either those who have acquired no skills or whose job-specific skills have become obsolete), both less secure and less adequately rewarded. High levels of unionization and intermediation tended to keep wages relatively high and employment (for those already in post at least) relatively secure. These conditions have changed. Increasingly wage levels are too low to lift unskilled workers out of poverty and/or to enable them to build up the appropriate record of social insurance contributions which will enable them to rely on this as a source of income maintenance in times of illness, unemployment or in old age. 'New' economies seem to offer either too little work (for example, in continental welfare states, such as France and Germany) or wages too low to keep all of the employed out of poverty (as in the US and the UK).

These risks are particularly acute for those who face other forms of employment disadvantage – single parents, those with low skills, young people (or those without a previous record of employment) and immigrants. Over the past twenty years, growing numbers of older workers (especially men in traditional industries) have been forced out of the active workforce – either through early retirement or by a very liberal interpretation of the rules allowing for a transfer to disability benefits (for a long time, a favoured device to get ageing workers out of the workforce without raising official levels of unemployment). The overall consequence is a growing risk of unemployment or poverty or both for individuals and a growing pressure on states' welfare budgets as social policy struggles to secure income maintenance for a growing number of the economically inactive out of resources provided by a declining actively employed population under circumstances of sluggish economic growth.

Insufficiency of social insurance, insecurity of private alternatives

Two further and associated new risks have been widely identified. As we have already seen, the 'traditional' patterns of family formation and employment careers on which the 'old' welfare states were built have largely disappeared. This places a real squeeze on existing welfare budgets. Fewer individuals are able to build up appropriate levels of social insurance cover and, to this extent, they are increasingly dependent on means-tested forms of social assistance. This is especially a problem for those Continental/ Bismarckian welfare states which are large on both expenditure and entitlement. At the same time, such states have difficulties in raising revenues (either through taxation or social insurance contributions) without further depressing economic activity or further depressing levels of employment (by the addition of ever increasing non-wage labour costs) or both. They also face those challenges that arise from underlying demographic change – above all a substantial increase in the numbers of people beyond retirement. Changing employment patterns, growing numbers of older people and slowing economic growth lead to a severe challenge to existing pensions regimes (as we saw in the preceding section), which developed welfare states cannot yet be said adequately to have addressed (let alone solved).

Finally, there is an issue that arises in substantial part from the responses that governments have made to the 'new' challenges discussed above. One important response of government to the twin challenge of increasing demands and (at least potentially) declining revenues is to try to transfer some welfare activity into the market sector and to discharge some of these costs on private citizens (either through user charges or by simply transferring some activity, for example the provision of long-term residential care for the elderly or supplementary pensions, into the private sector) or simply declining to provide certain forms of welfare (for example, making childcare entirely a parental responsibility). There are at least three risks associated with such a strategy. The first is that the nature and level of provision are simply inadequate. Standards of childcare may be unacceptably low or pension provision may be so inadequate that the state is forced to subsidize pensioners. Secondly, individuals may be exposed to unacceptable levels of economic risk (after all, one of the purposes of social insurance is to ensure that individuals are not fully exposed to the risks of investing on the money markets). Thirdly, state regulation of private providers may fail (as it clearly did in the UK in relation to the mis-selling of private pensions) or it may prove to be wastefully expensive to maintain (again, whatever its other supposed weaknesses, the traditional NHS is notoriously *efficient* in its administration compared with other insurance-based healthcare alternatives).

New risks and a new welfare state?

As I have already indicated, the 'new' social risks do not replace the 'old'; they add to them. In responding to these challenges, governments and policy-makers have not, for the most part, abandoned the older (and generally most expensive) areas of welfare state expenditure. Rather, they have added to them new measures (often with an emphasis on regulation rather than new expenditure) or else (as in the case of compensation for the unemployed) they have set out to alter the terms and conditions (and incentives) under which expenditure is authorized or services delivered. In general terms, this has often been characterized as a transition from a 'passive' to an 'active' welfare state or, in relation to the working-age population, as 'making work pay'. We have already considered some of the most characteristic measures (workfare, in-work benefits, childcare tax credits) in earlier sections. Here I want to focus on some of the most typical policy responses of different governments to the challenges that the new social risks represent.

The first thing to note is that, although there are common features in these responses, differing governments in differing regimes have responded in different ways to the challenge of new risks. We can still trace the lines of regime diversity under these changing circumstances. It is widely remarked that the Scandinavian/social democratic welfare states, with their much longer-standing and perhaps more serious commitment to gender equity, have long since addressed questions of the life–work balance which enable women to participate fully in formal economic life. State-funded childcare provision is much better established in these states and they generally have a better record on women's participation in (full-time) work and a better (if still imperfect) record on equal pay (still within a strongly gender-segregated division of labour). They have also much longer experience of active labour markets, associated with their longstanding commitment to full employment. This is reflected in much higher levels of expenditure on the new social risks. Although quite low in absolute terms (compared to other areas of social spending), in the period between 1980 and 1999 the Scandinavian states spent three times as much as the EU average on care for the elderly and twice as much on family services (Taylor-Gooby, 2005, pp. 15–16). Still, the inclusive Scandinavian welfare states have come under increasing stress over the past decade. In Sweden, for example, there have been limited though significant changes to the main public pension programme and (long-term) unemployment has risen (from historically extremely low levels). There is a fear, articulated for example by Virpi Timonen (2004, pp. 100–1), that immigrants may be emerging as the 'new Swedish underclass'.

If the challenge of new social risks is still 'potential' or at least 'underdeveloped' in Scandinavian states, it is already a pressing reality elsewhere.

The challenge is perhaps most severe for Europe's major corporatist/ conservative regimes – above all, for France and Germany. Here, existing welfare regimes are large. Historically, they have had a quite limited role for markets and the status quo is defended by well-organized and entrenched interests outside the state. France benefits from an unusually well-developed and long-established system of childcare which has long enabled women to participate in (full-time) employment (Taylor-Gooby, 2005, p. 18). Other areas of the entrenched French system have proven difficult (though not quite impossible) to reform. Pensions provide a good example. (For an account of recent movement on pensions reform, see Mandin and Palier, 2005.) Generally, the last decade has been one of welfare activism in France, not just on pensions, but also in response to the problems of 'social exclusion' and the frail elderly. Commentators (see Palier and Mandin, 2004) have written of the construction of a 'second world of social protection', a system of tax-funded means-tested benefits designed to meet the needs of those excluded from the traditional 'con-tributions-based' French welfare state. Various work subsidy measures and benefits to the low-paid in work have been taken to increase levels of employment. Steps have also been taken to reverse the trend towards early exit from the labour force which had become characteristic of welfare regimes across continental Europe. A new means-tested benefit for the frail elderly was introduced by the Jospin government in 2001 and now covers more than half a million older French citizens (Palier and Mandin, 2004, pp. 124–5).

Until very recently at least, the same level of activism has not really been apparent in the other 'giant' of continental European welfare states: Germany. As we have already seen (above, pp. 191–3), Germany's welfare system came under severe strain following the process of reunification in the early 1990s. It has certainly faced a range of new social risks, including a decline in family stability, the destandardization of employment and a weakening of the labour market position of the low-skilled. It has also faced the problem of mass early withdrawal from the labour force by displaced older workers. Under these circumstances, it has become increasingly difficult to maintain even an amended version of the 'social market economy' under which Germany has operated since the early postwar period. German governments under Kohl and then Schröder have attempted a series of reforms designed to address new social risks. Historically, the employment role of mothers in the German economy has been strictly limited. Under the Kohl government, there were some moves to encourage women into (part-time) employment (through reform of parental leave), but very limited attempts to address the crucial question of childcare. The introduction in 1994 of a long-term care insurance scheme represented an attempt to address the issue of the growth in the frail elderly population outside the traditional framework of informal care (provided by women). After 2000, the Schröder government was more active in pursuing labour market reforms (especially under Hartz IV), introducing significant cuts and recalibration of pension entitlements and new charges in the public healthcare system (see above, pp. 192–3). The context for reform is difficult for national governments. There are strongly entrenched interests in the established German welfare order, and the federal structure of government and welfare provision makes reform difficult to achieve. Successes to date have been limited.

We have already discussed recent reforms in the UK in some detail. As we have seen, the 'Third Way' is substantially about the reform of the broad welfare state and the agenda for change is very much one that is written around the challenge of new social risks – changing family formation, a changing role for women, a new emphasis on skills, training and lifetime earning, 'making work pay'. The Blair governments have claimed (with some justification) to have achieved real changes in participation in employment (with active labour market measures, increasing provision of childcare and in-work benefits). The government can even claim to have had some impact on the rapidly accelerating rise in income inequality which has typified Britain over the last twenty-five years (Brewer et al., 2004). In some ways, this reform process has been made easier in Britain by the fact that it was already a pretty mean and market-oriented welfare system. The one area in which reform can be said to have made disappointingly little progress is in pension provision. In fact, Britain's pension *funding* crisis is quite modest compared with that of its continental neighbours but still it has substantially failed in terms of income adequacy for the elderly, in encouraging savings among current wage-earners and in the regulation of a private pensions market in which very few potential investors have any real confidence.

Conclusion

In this chapter we have assessed three (interrelated) sets of challenges to the contemporary welfare state arising from globalization, from societal ageing and from the emergence of 'new' social risks. As we have seen, none of these challenges represents a 'knock-out blow' to existing welfare regimes, though each of them presents very real and substantial difficulties. We have also seen that the direction of causation is not straightforward. To some extent, some of the processes captured by the idea of globalization do have an impact on welfare states but, at the same time, welfare state regimes themselves have shaped the processes of globalization (at the extreme, in Rieger and Leibfried's account, it was the emergence of postwar welfare states that made the subsequent internationalization of the economy possible). In relation to the new social risks, we see that the particular form that these risks take, indeed their historical emergence, is itself at least in part a product of existing welfare regimes. The ways in which these regimes have (variously) responded to the new social risks in turn changes the character and costs of these risks themselves. What we are left with is a complex interweaving of different pressures and counterpressures on the welfare state which proves to be both *explanandum* and *explanans*, both that which we have to explain and that which explains patterns of contemporary social change. Not only is it not a question of the welfare state disappearing (it will not), it is also not principally a question of whether the welfare state has 'grown to its limits' (maybe it has). The real issue is what future social policy regimes can look like faced with this elaborate cocktail of social changes and (for social democrats at least) whether it can still be a part of the answer to the question of how to marry economic efficiency with social justice. It is to these questions that I return briefly in the final chapter.

Conclusion: Defending the Welfare State

No one who reflects for a moment on the history of the twentieth century can write innocently of the benevolent power of the state. If the experience of Stalinism and fascism, to name but two of the most infamous tyrannies of the twentieth century, were not enough, there is also a tradition, perhaps best represented by Foucault, which charts the chronic and petty incursions of the state in the day-to-day life of the modern citizen. If we add to this the rather more mundane 'failures' of social democracy, there can be little surprise that the state in general, and the welfare state in particular, should have become so unfashionable. Yet, in these concluding pages I wish to mount a partial defence of the state's role in welfare, based on the comparative and historical evidence collated in this study.

Perhaps the most basic premise of this defence is the ubiquity of the welfare state. We have seen that welfare states come in a variety of forms and sizes, supported by disparate political and economic forces, seeking to realize differing social outcomes. Certainly, the state may not be needed in all those areas in which it presently intervenes and it may be that such interventions as it does make need not take their present form. Nonetheless, the prospects of any developed society moving towards a 'minimal state' are extremely remote and the idea of marginalizing the welfare state is likely to prove to be both utopian and socially regressive. As we saw in chapter 6, within the envisageable future, the 'real' issue is not going to be whether we have a welfare state (perhaps not even how much it will cost) but what sort of a welfare state regime it will be. The state's allocation of welfare may be changing but nowhere is it disappearing or yielding to a minimal state uninterested in the welfare status of its population. Indeed, the aspiration to move towards a more 'active' welfare state indicates a growing interest on the part of the state in the status and conduct of its welfare clients.

One response to this universality of the welfare state is to insist that, if it has to be maintained as a 'regrettable necessity', we should at least be seeking to minimize its size and the scale of its social interventions. This aspiration to move welfare allocation away from the state takes two especially influential forms. First, there is an initiative, popular in a range of new social movements, to bypass the state by returning welfare to more localized, non-hierarchical and non-bureaucratized forms of communal self-administration. Secondly, there is the neoconservative strategy of limiting the state's intervention by returning the allocation of welfare to markets (and families). Whatever the practical limitations of these initiatives (and I have attempted to show earlier in the book that these are considerable), they also suffer from a number of weaknesses in principle.

On the first initiative, critics are surely right to point to the difficulties of securing personalized and sensitive social provision through the massified institutions of a legal-administrative state apparatus. But while the development of new forms of welfare self-administration which they recommend is extremely healthy (and ought where appropriate to be supported by the state itself) this is not best understood as an *alternative* to the welfare state. For example, there are circumstances in which anonymity, non-discretionary provision and a professional relationship (which are often seen as characteristic *weaknesses* of the state sector) may be preferable to a less formal and more community-based response. On the ground, the voluntary and not-for-profit sectors are often developing not as an alternative to, but in partnership with, the local state. The state may still be needed to support those who lack the various resources to secure self-help, to benchmark acceptable levels of informal provision and to protect individuals where the interventions of their carers are inappropriate. It is difficult to see how the compulsory revenue-raising power of the state, or many of the services that it funds, could be replaced by some other agency. We may even feel, as Titmuss argued, that there is a special moral quality in meeting the 'needs of strangers' which is best effected through the anonymity of the state. Feminists are surely right to argue that welfare citizenship needs to be rethought and recast – but not abandoned. Strengthening social citizenship and guaranteeing the integrity of the sorts of alternative welfare institutions which new social movements commend may well require a selective strengthening of some of the powers of the interventionist state.

In turning to the neoconservative response, it is necessary to confront directly the claim that returning welfare functions from the state to the market can be properly considered a process of empowering ordinary citizens. It may certainly enhance the power of certain actors (and sometimes quite 'ordinary' ones) in certain contexts, but consumer sovereignty is not a surrogate for citizen sovereignty. Returning the allocation of (still more) welfare opportunities to the market is likely to make welfare outcomes still less equitable than under existing welfare state regimes. And, in the end, claims about the greater efficiency of markets are empirical. If markets or quasi-markets do not deliver greater efficiency (as at least some critics have insisted is the case with NHS reform) we have a good case for seeking an alternative. Furthermore, it is not clear that the intensified individuation of welfare choices is a viable long-term option. In many ways our current global position requires us to make more not fewer collective choices and, alongside a possible enhancement of the market in some areas, its stricter regulation in others. In the end, it is not at all clear that, in the welfare field, the state which governs least, governs best. To choose a state which intervenes as little as possible in the social allocation of welfare is to choose a very particular type of social regime – and not necessarily one we should all be disposed to call 'the best available option'.

Some of these points can be illustrated by returning to the green agenda for social and political reform. Green activists are among those who call for a decentralization of welfare provision and for more local, informal and discursive forms of decision-taking ('thinking globally while acting locally'). Yet the problems which the greens have helped to isolate – of unsustainable growth and maldistribution of global resources – clearly require enhanced decision-making and powers of enforcement at a national and especially a supranational level. Certain green welfare initiatives (for example, a guaranteed basic income or a guaranteed right to sabbatical leave in all forms of employment) actually imply a much larger role for the state (Dobson, 1995, pp. 112–5). If green politics is to be something more than an act of faith, the question of institutional and constitutional reform in large-scale contexts is unavoidable. The market, with its seeming decentralization of decision-making, is not in itself a solution. If we think of a position that is sympathetic to both the green agenda and to markets (as, for example, in the Pearce report *Blueprint for a Green Economy*) we see that markets are imagined to give environmentally 'efficient' allocations only within a previously given and *politically chosen* framework. Pearce argues that markets can maximize efficiency and effectiveness at a given level of resource exhaustion or environmental spoilation, but these framework-setting levels (and crucially decisions about intergenerational distribution) must be the outcome of political processes and can only be reached through the agency of the state (Pearce et al., 1989). Thus, if we accept even a very *weak* and market-sympathetic form of the green argument that unsustainable economic growth cannot be allowed to continue, then we have a very *strong* case for the increased politicization of economic decision-making.

Still the Social Democratic Challenge

All this still leaves us with a formidable challenge, one which is most severe
for social democracy and its sympathizers. Historically, social democrats
'abandoned' the political agenda of a more traditional socialism on the
grounds that the welfare state could deliver an expansive sense of citizenship and increasing social and economic equality within the framework of
a (largely) privately owned market economy. Now it seems that, for a whole
series of reasons outlined in this book, welfare states are less and less able
to guarantee these forms of citizenship and equality but that, often for
the very same reasons, alternative routes to 'progressive' outcomes are
blocked. For Giddens (1994), this leaves the rather sad spectre of social
democrats reduced to defending the ever diminishing terrain of a form of
welfare state which social change has rendered obsolete. Are there any
viable alternatives? In the closing pages of this chapter, I consider three
possible responses. Broadly described, these respond to the difficulties of
the social democratic welfare state by advocating (1) an enhancement of
the commitment to a *social investment state*; (2) an enhancement of the
role of *asset-based* welfare through *basic capital* grants; and 3) the introduction of a maximum *basic income* for all citizens.

The Social Investment State

The reform agenda of the 'new' social policy advocated by Labour in the
UK after 1997 has sometimes been described by its key advocates as the
promotion of a 'social investment state' under the rubric of a 'Third Way'
(see above, pp. 182–9; Giddens, 1998, p. 117). Here, I focus on an account
which seeks explicitly to distance itself from Labour's reforms, but which
uses the idea of a 'child-centred social investment strategy' to promote a
'new welfare architecture' for the reform of Europe's welfare states. This
is the perspective developed by Gøsta Esping-Andersen and his collaborators in *Why We Need a New Welfare State* (2002; for a critical evaluation see Lister, 2003).

The by now somewhat familiar premise from which Esping-Andersen
et al. proceed is that the social and economic circumstances under which
the welfare states that emerged after 1945 flourished have now changed in
ways which make the old welfare architecture ineffective or, still worse,
counterproductive in meeting the twin (social democratic) goals of social
justice and economic efficiency. On the one hand, the nature of family formation and family behaviour has changed profoundly. We now have a pro-
liferation of new and far less stable households and family arrangements
within which women are ever more active in the formal economy (and

correspondingly less available to provide unpaid informal care for dependants, although this work is still radically unequally distributed between men and women). At the same time, the character of the formal economy has itself been transformed. An economy built around the 'standard' (and male) production worker in relatively secure lifelong employment has given way to a much more flexible economy in which the service sector is dominant, in which employment is more precarious, the requirement for multivalent skills much higher and in which there is a growing tendency for employment to bifurcate into 'lovely' jobs (well paid and secure, with relatively high autonomy) and 'lousy' jobs (poorly paid, intermittent and insecure, with low levels of job satisfaction). This division is reflected in a tendency for wage inequalities to grow.

In general terms, the aspiration to respond to these changes with a more 'active' welfare regime is correct but, to date, this response has been too piecemeal and reactive. The focus on labour market activation of the discouraged or those with obsolete skills is generally 'too little, too late'. The key to social investment lies in childhood and, hence, with policies that support families both in terms of income but also of educational opportunities (including pre-school support): 'a recast family policy and, in particular, one which is powerfully child-oriented, must be regarded as a social investment' (Esping-Andersen et al., 2002, p. 9). This requires a commitment to eradicate child poverty (through strong income guarantees to families with children) plus substantial investment in high quality preschool daycare, good quality schooling (that will enable real social mobility) and additional support for single parent families. A complementary requirement is heavy investment in 'women-friendly' policies. Such womenfriendly policies – especially those that enable women to combine full participation in the formal economy with the choice to have children – are an important aspect of gender justice. But they are also crucial to the efficient operation of the contemporary political economy, and with it, the social investment state: 'improving the welfare of women means improving the collective welfare of society at large' (Esping-Andersen et al., 2002, p. 20). At the very least, the new gender contract requires affordable and highquality daycare, paid maternity *and* paternity leave (with the latter seen as a first step in adjusting the unequal division of domestic/caring labour between men and women) and provision for (paid) absence from work when children are ill. Facilitating the fuller participation of women in paid work is *not just* an issue of gender equality; it should also enhance economic growth, help to sustain household incomes and (so Esping-Andersen imagines) enable women to reconcile their roles as workers and mothers in ways which enable them to have the numbers of children they want (and thus potentially address the current 'crisis' of declining fertility).

In pursuing this agenda, the focus of our attention and our concern should not be on a 'snapshot' of inequality at one moment in time but rather on welfare outcomes across the (individual's) 'life course'. The 'new' economy and our increasingly unpredictable personal trajectories may mean that it is not possible (any longer) to secure for everyone and at all times well-paid and secure employment, but it should be the function of our social policy regimes to ensure that no one faces the prospect of 'life-long entrapment' in poverty or insecurity. A 'life course' focus also gives us the best prospects of resolving the challenge of demographic ageing. Our intention must be not to exacerbate intergenerational conflict (of the interests of the young versus the elderly) but rather to emphasize that investment in the very young will yield a long-term economic premium (both for the individual involved and for society more generally).

Asset-Based Welfare: Basic Capital

Like the 'social investment state', a variant of the idea of an 'asset-based welfare' can be found in many accounts of the Third Way. Stuart White (2001) describes 'asset-based egalitarianism' as one of those five 'pro-grammatic realignments' which help to define New Labour's Third Way. In the New Labour formulation, the idea of an 'asset-based egalitarian-ism' is frequently taken to suggest that issues of social inequality should be addressed through equipping citizens with social capital, skills and edu-cation rather than through the redistribution of resources. It is suggested that a transfer of assets generates positive values – an orientation towards the future, a capacity for self-management – which income transfers cannot (an argument often retraced to Sherraden, 1991). In many Third Way accounts this is tied to a preference for replacing a concern with poverty with a concern for social inclusion. Critics (see, for example, Levitas, 1998) see in this move a shift from a concern with equality towards a focus on the (much more conservative) notion of social cohesion. Some have adopted what we might call an intermediary position. Esping-Andersen (2000), for example, argues that while we should retain our concern with equality, this has in some sense to be reclassified as a concern with 'equality across the life-cycle' rather than at every point in time – and, in part, as we have seen, this is a response to the greater flexibility and diversity of the 'new economy'. At the same time, he warns against expect-ing that education and training can do all the work of securing equitable social outcomes, retaining a place for the old-fashioned mechanisms of redistribution.

There is a more radical reading of the asset-based welfare argument which characterizes it in terms not of social capital but of *real* capital, such as money. Stuart White (2003) describes such proposals as aiming to furnish all citizens with 'basic capital'. In fact, this is less an aspect of welfare endowment and more an element of citizenship *entitlement*. In its more radical form, it is a proposal which opens up questions about ownership which the traditional social democratic approach (Keynes-plus-modified-capitalism-plus-the-welfare-state) had very deliberately bracketed out. At its simplest, the essence of the basic capital approach to welfare is this. For a variety of reasons (and in the face of a number of commonplace assumptions about the inviolability of private property), all citizens are entitled to a part of a society's historically inherited assets. Reflecting this, it is appropriate for the state to give to every citizen (perhaps at the point at which they enter adulthood/full citizenship), a capital grant representing their share in the national patrimony. (There is a more pragmatic view which is unconcerned with the citizen's *right* to a share in the national wealth and holds simply that such provision is (1) sound policy, and (2) affordable.)

There are disagreements about how large such a grant should be and whether there should be restrictions on the ways in which citizens may use these assets. Recommendations in the literature range from a one-off grant of $80,000 (proposed by Bruce Ackerman and Anne Alstott in the US) to a much more modest £1,000 (to be granted at birth in the proposal made in Gavin Kelly and Rachel Lissauer's (2000) report for the Institute for Public Policy Research). Ackerman and Alstott (1999) propose almost no limitations on the uses to which a capital grant may be put. More typically, as for example in the scheme proposed by Julian LeGrand, funds are to be earmarked for particular and sanctioned welfare purposes – funding higher education or training, business start-up costs or paying the deposit on a home (LeGrand and Nissan, 2000). There is also a range of opinions about how the funds for these capital grants should be raised. They could come from general taxation but there is also an aspiration, which again reflects the more radical version of the argument, that the appropriate funds should (at least in part) derive from inheritance tax (reflecting the desire to redistribute the unearned income which inherited wealth represents). Almost nobody imagines that asset-based welfare could *replace* the existing welfare system. How much of the work of existing welfare states it could do depends, of course, on the size of the endowments. But it clearly represents an attempt both (1) to give greater welfare autonomy to individual citizens, while (2) directly addressing issues of the inequality of wealth (rather than just moderating inequalities of income).

Most of the discussion of basic capital has centred on initiatives which are modest in terms of expenditure and proscriptive in terms of approved uses. A great deal of attention has focused on the issue in the UK since the Labour government's introduction of the Child Trust Fund (CTF) in 2002. Under the terms of the CTF, the government pays an endowment to every child at birth and at age seven, generating a fund to which additional contributions can be made by family and friends and to which the government will itself make some additional means-related contributions. The account can be cashed in when a child reaches the age of eighteen.

The sums involved are extremely modest (up to £500 in the first instance) and it has been presented primarily as a reform that will encourage financial responsibility and 'strengthen the saving habit' rather than having a real impact on the distribution of the ownership of wealth (HM Treasury, 2003). Any more generously endowed system would almost certainly come with a list of acceptable uses.

The UK government's initiative has attracted plenty of attention abroad (not least in Australia, with its own proposals for a 'nest egg fund'; see IPPR, 2003). Potentially it represents a quite radical breach with traditional social democratic practice in so far as it opens up questions of asset ownership which it was one of the founding purposes of social democracy to shut down (see C. Pierson, 2001). Nonetheless, its real world impact to date has been strictly limited and it is, of course, completely dwarfed by welfare spending in its traditional, 'mainstream' forms.

Asset-Based Welfare: Basic Income

Perhaps the most radical of the alternatives on offer and, to date, the theoretically best developed is the case for a maximum basic income. For its advocates, securing the enduring core *values* which the best of social democratic welfare states embodied – perhaps, above all, the promotion of social justice – is only possible now through a radical institutional reform which abandons many of social democracy's traditional solutions. At the heart of this reform agenda is the proposal to introduce for all citizens an unconditional basic income (BI).

> A *basic income* . . . is an income paid by the government to each full member of society (1) even if she is not willing to work, (2) irrespective of being rich or poor, (3) whoever she lives with, and (4) no matter which part of the country she lives in. (Van Parijs, 1995, p. 35)

BI might be set at different levels for different categories of persons (with a higher rate for the elderly and disabled and a lower rate for children) but it is unconditional inasmuch as it is paid to all residents/citizens of a political community as individuals without any test of income or wealth and irrespective of employment status or indication of a 'willingness to work'. The level of BI is an open question. It is not defined in terms of some notional set of 'basic needs'. A BI might fall below subsistence level (and need to be 'topped up' by other sources of income) or it could, as in the account of BI's most sophisticated contemporary advocate, Philippe van Parijs (1995), be set at the maximum sustainable level (presumed to be much above subsistence). Certainly, most supporters aspire to see the BI reaching a level at which it would 'replace' all existing income maintenance benefits and allow for the abolition of all personal reliefs set against income tax (McKay, 1998).

The advocates of BI devote considerable intellectual energy to showing, perhaps at first sight counterintuitively, that their scheme has a powerful claim to be both just and efficient. Objections to the claim that BI is just have focused on the belief that an *unconditional* BI gives the idle 'something for nothing', enabling them to exploit the hard-working members of society whose efforts are taxed to pay for their idleness. This objection is resisted on the basis that a part of economic wealth in any period is the consequence of the accumulated assets and knowledge of earlier generations and the productive capacity of our natural environment, both of which constitute a common stock of resources for the use of which *all* of society's members are entitled to some compensation. In the account of van Parijs (1995), all of those who take up scarce resources (including in his account the scarce resource of jobs) owe a rent to the rest of society and this would be the source of BI. A second claim – that a maximal BI would be economically efficient – is also resisted with some well-worn arguments. Critics insist that a BI set at even a quite modest level would undermine incentives, discouraging the less skilled from entering the labour market and placing a fiscal burden on capital and more-skilled workers which would encourage them to lessen their effort or withdraw from the formal economy. Supporters of a BI are generally sanguine about these objections. At one level, they resist the idea that maximizing GDP and participation in paid employment is so desirable. Critics, like van Parijs, argue that what we should be seeking to maximize is not income but *real-freedom-for-all* (allowing individuals to choose as freely as possible what it is they want to do with their lives). They argue, too, that traditional accounts have privileged paid employment over other forms of work (especially the unpaid labour of women within the household) which have often not been seen to count as work at all. But even within a more traditional framework, BI is recommended as efficient – allowing individuals to take on work at very low wages (because of the income support that a BI would provide), allowing workers to retrain without excessive cost, and to start new enterprises without undue risk, encouraging greater flexibility in forms of work and easier movement between household and employment. In general, the greater economic flexibility which a BI underwrites is said to 'completely overshadow' concerns about the disincentive effects of the new tax regime on which it would be based (van Parijs, 1992, p. 233).

The proponents of an unconditional BI have some very powerful arguments on their side. A part of the promise of postwar social democracy was to check income inequality. Yet the last twenty years has seen a systematic trend towards greater income inequality which has now spread to virtually all the developed welfare states. The provision of a BI promises to reverse this trend. Set at a moderately high level, it would also replace the jungle of existing conditional benefits and entitlements (and various poverty traps) with a clear and unambiguous commitment to adequate baseline incomes. For its proponents, it offers a reform which is radical and egalitarian but without posing an implausible challenge to the institutional apparatus of existing private-ownership market economies. Its breach with traditional social democracy's unrelenting (if sometimes unstated) commitment to economic growth will seem timely to many. But problems remain. Some (quite sympathetic) critics challenge the plausibility of the ethical case for an *unconditional* BI. Stuart White (1997), for example, takes issue with van Parijs over the latter's insistence that an unconditional BI does not entail the exploitation of those who work by those who choose not to work. While a small unconditional BI might be justified on the basis of equal entitlement to the world's inanimate assets, most economic wealth is the product of cooperative social effort and those who will not contribute in any way to this collective effort are, so White concludes, not entitled to draw an income from the efforts of those who do. Similarly, many remain sceptical about what is in the end an empirical claim that the efficiency-enhancing side-effects of reform (enhanced flexibility) will outweigh the disincentive effects of the increased tax take required to fund a BI.

But perhaps the most profound problem for the BI case is political. BI's two great claims to feasibility are first, that dysfunctional societies of intensifying environmental degradation allied to growing inequality like ours are in the medium to long term unsustainable, and second, that the reform it promises is radical and egalitarian but consonant with capitalist market economies. Unfortunately, as a wealth of public choice literature shows, the existence of dysfunctionality is not in itself a guarantee that reform – even a reform that disadvantages no one – will be forthcoming. Certainly, the property regime of a fully implemented BI capitalism would be quite different from anything that operates under that label now – and would not necessarily recommend itself to everyone as an improvement on the present order. At the same time, it is hard to see where the large-scale political support for BI is to be found. In Britain, for example, the greens are the only party committed to BI. The Liberal Democrats, who were the only major party committed to (a very low level of) BI have reversed that commitment. The Labour Party is pursuing a 'welfare to work' alternative which *intensifies* the connection between employment and income. The context for reform, which the advocates of a BI do so much to illuminate, is, of course, one in which traditional social democratic solutions have been rendered obsolete at least in part because of a perceived tax reluctance on the part of democratic publics. It is not yet clear that democratic publics in developed welfare states are ready for the cultural revolution which the explicit disconnection of employment and income allied to a significantly increased tax burden (whatever the attendant benefits) would bring.

One further issue of feasibility concerns the community within which reform (however gradualist) might be introduced. Can there be BI capitalism in just one country or one economic community and, if not, through what sort of political mechanism (and what enforcement agency) might it be introduced? None of these objections could be said to weigh exhaustively against the idea of BI. It is about as clear as it can be that the old solutions (of various kinds) do not work. If the advocates of BI are right about the sorts of changes that our societies are undergoing, the time is coming when politicians and public will *have* to take these ideas seriously. But in a context where most people believe that politics is about the serving of powerful interests before it is about the promotion of an ethically optimal community, BI may still struggle to get a fair hearing.

One final and more general point is worth making here. Esping-Andersen (1985) was right to argue that the welfare state cannot carry all the burden of society's responsibility for social welfare and collective provision, while leaving the economy 'to look after itself'. If the sole focus on redistribution was a plausible social democratic strategy at some earlier historical stage, it is not so any longer. Paradoxically, the weakening of *indirect* control over investment decisions requires that the question of *direct* control be readdressed and social democrats need to consider policies and practices which might make for a more equitable distribution of primary (rather than redistributed) income. This may look fanciful in a world of sharpening income inequality and for some even a 'step back' to a set of traditional socialist concerns that have been even more comprehensively outmoded by the changes that have imperilled welfare states. But the situation need not be quite so hopeless. In addition to the proposals for basic capital or basic income, there are a number of policy instruments, some of them quite modest, which might afford the possibility of redistributing economic power. Perversely, some of these (including, for example, reform of pension funds) might be more 'respectable' or 'with the grain of public opinion' than attempts at more redistributive taxation or an increase in social expenditure.

Conclusion

The welfare state is certainly paradoxical. On the one hand, it is extraordinarily mundane, concerned with the minutiae of the pension and benefit rights of millions of citizens. On the other, the sheer scale of its growth is one of the most remarkable features of the postwar capitalist world and it remains one of the dominant, if sometimes unnoticed, institutions of the modern world. In recent years, it has become a major political concern of both the political left and, more especially, the political right. But this new or revived interest is, as we have seen, often based on a quite mistaken reading of its historical evolution and its political consequences. Recommendations from most political quarters are substantially weakened by these misunderstandings.

In particular, we have seen that the notorious spectre of a 'crisis of the welfare state' is itself a part of this wider misunderstanding. For many, the crisis was real enough, but is now passing. For others, the crisis looms in front of us, brought on by 'irresistible' changes to the global economy or the 'unmanageable' ageing of the population. It is certainly true that many of the most difficult and the most 'political' decisions about welfare lie in the future. Questions about the relationship between economic and social policy, between employment and income, between political decision-making and economic decision-making, between state and market, between this and subsequent generations, will have to be addressed anew. When they are, it is likely that the welfare state will prove to be not just part of the problem, but part of the solution too.

References

Aaron, H. J. 1966: The social insurance paradox. *Canadian Journal of Economics and Political Science*, 32 (Aug.), 371–4.

Ackerman, B. and Alstott, A. 1999: *The Stakeholder Society*. New Haven: Yale University Press.

Addison, P. 1977: *The Road to 1945*. London: Quartet.

Alber, J. 1982: *Von Armenhaus zum Wohlfahrtsstaat*. Frankfurt: Campus.

Alber, J. 1986: Germany. In P. Flora (ed.), *Growth to Limits*, vol. 2. Berlin: De Gruyter, pp. 1–154.

Alber, J. 1988a: Continuities and changes in the idea of the welfare state. *Politics and Society*, 16(4), 451–68.

Alber, J. 1988b: Is there a crisis of the welfare state? Cross-national evidence from Europe, North America, and Japan. *European Sociological Review*, 4(3), 181–207.

Albertsen, N. 1988: Postmodernism, post-Fordism and critical social theory. *Environment and Planning D: Society and Space*, 6, 339–65.

Alesina, A. and Glaeser, E. 2004: *Fighting Poverty in the US and Europe: A World of Difference*. Oxford: Oxford University Press.

Alestalo, M. and Uusitalo, M. 1986: Finland. In P. Flora (ed.), *Growth to Limits*, vol 1. Berlin: De Gruyter, pp. 197–292.

Allan, J. P. and Scruggs, L. 2004: Political partisanship and welfare state reform in advanced industrial societies. *American Journal of Political Science*, 48(3), 496–512.

Alston, L. J. and Ferrie, J. P. 1985: Labour costs, paternalism and loyalty in southern agriculture: a constraint on the growth of the welfare state. *Journal of Economic History*, 45 (Mar.), 95–117.

Alt, J. 1979: *The Politics of Economic Decline*. Cambridge: Cambridge University Press.

Alt, J. and Chrystal, K. A. 1983: Political business cycles. In J. Alt and K. A. Chrystal (eds), *Political Economics*. Brighton: Wheatsheaf, pp. 103–25.

Amenta, E. and Carruthers, B. G. 1988: The formative years of US social spending policies: theories of the welfare state and the American states during the Great Depression. *American Sociological Review*, 53, 661–78.

Amenta, E. and Skocpol, T. 1989: Taking exception: explaining the distinctiveness of American public policies in the last century. In F. Castles (ed.), *The Comparative History of Public Policy*. Cambridge: Polity.

Anderson, P. 1977: The antinomies of Antonio Gramsci. *New Left Review*, 100, 5–78.

Arts, W. and Gelissen, A. 2006: Three worlds of welfare capitalism or more? A state-of-the-art report. In C. Pierson and F. Castles (eds), *The Welfare State Reader* (2nd edn). Cambridge: Polity.

Ashford, D. E. 1982: *British Dogmatism and French Pragmatism: Central-Local Policymaking in the Welfare State*. London: Allen and Unwin.

Ashford, D. E. 1986a: The British and French social security systems: welfare states by intent and default. In D. E. Ashford and E. W. Kelley (eds), *Nationalizing Social Security in Europe and America*. London: JAI Press, pp. 245–71.

Ashford, D. E. 1986b: *The Emergence of the Welfare States*. Oxford: Blackwell.

Ashford, D. E. and Kelley, E. W. (eds) 1986: *Nationalizing Social Security in Europe and America*. London: JAI Press.

Axinn, J. and Levin, H. 1975: *Social Welfare: A History of the American Response to Need*. New York: Dodd, Mead.

Bacon, R. and Eltis, W. 1978: *Britain's Economic Problem: Too Few Producers*. London: Macmillan.

Balbo, L. 1987: Family, women and the state: notes towards a typology of family roles and public intervention. In C. S. Maier (ed.), *Changing Boundaries of the Political*. Cambridge: Cambridge University Press.

Baldwin, P. 1990: *The Politics of Social Solidarity: Class Bases of the European Welfare State 1875–1975*. Cambridge: Cambridge University Press.

Bane, M. J. 1988: Politics and policies of the feminization of poverty. In M. Weir, A. S. Orloff and T. Skocpol (eds), *The Politics of Social Policy in the United States*. Princeton: Princeton University Press, pp. 381–96.

Banting, K. G. 2005: The multicultural welfare state: international experience and North American narratives. *Social Policy and Administration*, 39(2), 98–115.

Barbalet, J. M. 1988: *Citizenship: Rights, Struggle and Class Inequality*. Milton Keynes: Open University Press.

Barnett, C. 1986: *The Audit of War*. London: Macmillan.

Barr, N. 1987: *The Economics of the Welfare State*. London: Weidenfeld and Nicolson.

Barrett, M. 1980: *Women's Oppression Today: Problems in Marxist Feminist Analysis*. London: Verso.

Barry, J. 1998: Social policy and social movements: ecology and social policy. In N. Ellison and C. Pierson (eds), *Developments in British Social Policy*. London: Macmillan.

Beattie, R. and McGillivray, W. 2000: On *Averting the Old Age Crisis*. In C. Pierson and F. G. Castles (eds), *The Welfare State Reader* (1st edn). Cambridge: Polity, pp. 281–92.

Beechey, V. and Perkins, T. 1987: *A Matter of Hours: Women, Part-time work and the Labour Movement*. Polity: Cambridge.

Bellamy, D. F. and Irving, A. 1989: Canada. In J. Dixon and R. P. Scheurell, *Social Welfare in Developed Market Countries*. London: Routledge, pp. 47–88.

Bendix, R. 1970: *Embattled Reason: Essays on Social Knowledge*. New York: Oxford University Press.

Benton, T. 1977: *Philosophical Foundation of the Three Sociologies*. London: Routledge and Kegan Paul.

Berkowitz, E. and McQuaid, K. 1980: *Creating the Welfare State: The Political Economy of Twentieth Century Reform*. New York: Praeger.

Bernstein, E. 1909: *Evolutionary Socialism*. London: Independent Labour Party.

Beveridge, W. H. 1942: *Report: Social Insurance and Allied Services*. London: HMSO.

Bhavnani, R. 1994: *Black Women in the Labour Market*. London: Equal Opportunities Commission.

Birch, A. 1984: Overload, ungovernability and delegitimation. *British Journal of Political Science*, 14(2), 135–60.

Blair, T. 1998: *The Third Way: New Politics for a New Century*. London: Fabian Society.

Blair, T. 2002: *The Courage of our Convictions*. London: Fabian Society.

Blair, T. 2004: Choice, excellence and equality. At www.labour.org.uk (accessed 1 July 2005).

Blair, T. and Schröder, G. 1999: Europe: the Third Way/Die Neue Mitte. At www.xs4all.nl/~adampost/Archive/arc000006.html (accessed 1 Oct. 2004).

Blake, D. and Ormerod, P. 1980: *The Economics of Prosperity: Social Priorities in the Eighties*. London: Grant Macintyre.

Blank, R. 2002: Evaluating welfare reform in the US. *Journal of Economic Literature*, 40(4), 1105–56.

Blitz, R. C. 1977: A benefit-cost analysis of foreign workers in West-Germany. *Kyklos*, 30, 479–502.

Block, F. 1987: Social policy and accumulation: a critique of the new consensus. In M. Rein, G. Esping-Andersen and M. Rainwater (eds), *Stagnation and Renewal in Social Policy: The Rise and Fall of Policy Regimes*. New York: Sharpe.

Block, F., Cloward, R. A., Ehrenreich, B. and Piven, F. F. 1987: *The Mean Season: The Attack on the Welfare State*. New York: Pantheon.

Bonoli, G. 2000: *The Politics of Pension Reform: Institutions and Policy Change in Western Europe*. Cambridge: Cambridge University Press.

Bonoli, G. 2005: New social risks and the politics of the new social policies. In P. Taylor-Gooby (ed.), *New Risks, New Welfare*. Oxford: Oxford University Press.

Bosanquet, N. 1983: *After the New Right*. London: Heinemann Education.

Bottomore, T. and Goode, P. (eds) 1978: *Austro-Marxism*. Oxford: Oxford University Press.

Bowles, S. and Gintis, H. 1982: The crisis of liberal democratic capitalism: the case of the US. *Politics and Society*, 11(1), 51–93.

Bowley, M. 1967: *Nassau Senior and Classical Economics*. New York: Octagon.

Brenner, J. and Ramas, M. 1984: Rethinking women's oppression. *New Left Review*, 144, 33–71.

Brewer, M., Goodman, A., Myck, M., Shaw, J. and Shephard, A. 2004: *Poverty and Inequality in Britain: 2004*. London: Institute for Fiscal Studies.

Brittan, S. 1975: The economic contradictions of democracy. *British Journal of Political Science*, 5(2), 129–59.

Brody, D. 1980: The rise and decline of welfare capitalism. In D. Brody (ed.), *Workers in Industrial America: Essays on the Twentieth Century Struggle*. New York: Oxford University Press, pp. 48–81.

Brown, C. 1984: *Black and White Britain: The Third PSI Survey*. London: Heinemann.

Brown, M. and Madge, N. 1982: *Despite the Welfare State: A Report on the SSRC/DHSS Programme of Research into Transmitted Deprivation*. London: Heinemann Educational.

Brownlie, I. (ed.) 1971: *Basic Documents on Human Rights*. London: Oxford University Press.

Brubaker, W. R. (ed.) 1989: *Immigration and the Politics of Citizenship in Europe and North America*. London: University Press of America.

Bruce, M. 1968: *The Coming of the Welfare State* (4th edn). London: Batsford.

Bruno, M. and Sachs, J. D. 1985: *Economics of Worldwide Stagflation*. Oxford: Blackwell.

Burrows, R. and Loader, B. 1994: *Towards a Post-Fordist Welfare State?* London: Routledge.

Cameron, D. R. 1978: The expansion of the public economy: a comparative analysis. *American Political Science Review*, 72(4), 1243–61.

Caraley, D. J. 2001–2: Ending welfare as we know it: a reform still in progress. *Political Science Quarterly*, 116(4), 525–60.

Carby, H. V. 1982: White woman listen! Black feminism and the boundaries of sisterhood. In Centre for Contemporary Cultural Studies, *The Empire Strikes Back*. London: Hutchinson, pp. 212–35.

Carens, J. H. 1988: Immigration and the welfare state. In A. Gutmann (ed.), *Democracy and the Welfare State*. Princeton: Princeton University Press, pp. 207–30.

Cashmore, E. E. and Troyna, B. 1983: *Introduction to Race Relations*. London: Routledge and Kegan Paul.

Castles, F. G. 1978: *The Social Democratic Image of Society: A Study in the Achievements and Origins of Scandinavian Social Democracy in Comparative Perspective*. London: Routledge and Kegan Paul.

Castles, F. G. 1982: The impact of parties on public expenditure. In F. G. Castles (ed.), *The Impact of Parties: Politics and Policies in Democratic Capitalist States*. London: Sage, pp. 21–96.

Castles, F. G. 1985: *The Working Class and Welfare*. Wellington: Allen and Unwin.

Castles, F. 1998: *Comparative Public Policy: Patterns of Post-war Transformation*. Cheltenham: Edward Elgar.

Castles, F. 2004: *The Future of the Welfare State: Crisis Myths and Crisis Realities*. Oxford: Oxford University Press.

Castles, F. and Mitchell, D. 1992: Identifying welfare state regimes. *Governance*, 5(1), 1–26.

Cawson, A. 1986: *Corporatism and Political Theory*. Oxford: Blackwell.

Cerny, P. 1990: *The Changing Architecture of Politics*. London: Sage.

Cerny, P. 1995: Globalization and the changing logic of collective action. *International Organization*, 49(4), 595–625.

Childs, M. 1961: *Sweden: The Middle Way*. New Haven: Yale University Press.

Christopher, K., England, P., Smeeding, T. M. and Ross Phillips, K. 2002: The gender gap in poverty in modern nations: single motherhood, the market, and the state. *Sociological Perspectives*, 45(3), 219–42.

Clarke, T. and Clements, L. (eds) 1977: *Trade Unions under Capitalism*. London: Fontana.

Cline, W. R. 1997: *Trade and Wage Inequality*. Washington: Institute for International Economics.

Collier, D. and Messick, R. E. 1975: Prerequisites versus diffusion: testing alternative explanations of social security adoption. *American Political Science Review*, 69(4), 1299–315.

Commission on Social Justice 1994: *Social Justice: Strategies for National Renewal*. London: Vintage.

Commonwealth Bureau of Census and Statistics (Australia) 1910– : *Official Year Book of the Commonwealth of Australia*. Canberra.

Cook, J. and Watt, S. 1987: Racism, women and poverty. In C. Glendinning and J. Millar, *Women and Poverty in Britain*. Brighton: Wheatsheaf, pp. 53–70.

Cook, J. and Watt, S. 1992: Racism, women and poverty. In C. Glendinning and J. Millar, *Women and Poverty in Britain: The 1990s*. London: Harvester-Wheatsheaf, pp. 11–23.

Corti, L. and Dex, S. 1995: Informal carers and employment. *Employment Gazette* (Mar.). London: Department of Employment/HMSO.

Coughlin, R. 1980: *Ideology, Public Opinion, and Welfare Policy*. Berkeley: University of California Press.

Cox, R. 1993: Gramsci, hegemony and international relations: an essay in method. In S. Gill (ed.), *Gramsci, Historical Materialism and International Relations*. Cambridge: Cambridge University Press.

CRE (Commission for Racial Equality) 2005a: Race equality impact statement: education. At www.cre.gov.uk/duty/reia/statistics_education.html (accessed 1 July 2005).

CRE (Commission for Racial Equality) 2005b: Race equality impact statement: housing. At www.cre.gov.uk/duty/reia/statistics_housing.html (accessed 1 July 2005).

CRE (Commission for Racial Equality) 2005c: Race equality impact statement: the labour market. At www.cre.gov.uk/duty/reia/statistics_labour.html (accessed 1 July 2005).

CRE (Commission for Racial Equality) 2005d: Refugees and asylum seekers: the facts. At www.cre.gov.uk/gdpract/refuge.html (accessed 1 July 2005).

Crosland, A. 1964: *The Future of Socialism*. London: Cape.

Crozier, M., Huntington, S. P. and Watanuki, J. (eds) 1975: *The Crisis of Democracy*. New York: New York University Press.

CSIS (Center for Strategic and International Studies) 2002: *The Global Retirement Crisis*. Washington, DC: CSIS.

Cutright, P. 1965: Political structure, economic development, and national social security programs. *American Journal of Sociology*, 70, 537–50.

Daly, M. and Lewis, J. 2000: 'The concept of social care and the analysis of contemporary welfare states. *British Journal of Sociology*, 51(2), 281–98.

Daly, M. and Rake, K. 2003: *Gender and the Welfare State*. Cambridge: Polity.

De Swaan, A. 1988: *In Care of the State: Health Care, Education and Welfare in Europe and the USA in the Modern Era*. Cambridge: Polity.

Deacon, Bob 1992: *The New Eastern Europe*. London: Sage.

Deacon, Bob 1997: *Global Social Policy*. London: Sage.

Deakin, N. 1987: *In Search of the Postwar Consensus*. London: Suntory International Centre for Economics and Related Disciplines, LSE.

Dean, M. 1998: Administering asceticism: reworking the ethical life of the unemployed citizen. In B. Hindess and M. Dean (eds), *Governing Australia*. Cambridge: Cambridge University Press.

Department of Health 1989: *Working for Patients*. London: HMSO.

Department of Health 1997: *The New NHS: Modern, Dependable*. London: HMSO.

DHSS (Department of Health and Social Security) 1985: *The Reform of Social Security*. Cmnd 9517, vol 1. London: HMSO.

Dixon, J. and Scheurell, R. P. (eds) 1989: *Social Welfare in Developed Market Countries*. London: Routledge and Kegan Paul.

Dobson, A. 1995: *Green Political Thought* (2nd edn). London: Routledge.

Donnison, D. 1979: Social policy since Titmuss. *Journal of Social Policy*, 8(2), 145–56.

Downs, A. 1957: *An Economic Theory of Democracy*. New York: Harper and Row.

Dryzek, J. and Goodin, R. E. 1986: Risk-sharing and social justice: the motivational foundations of the post-war welfare state. *British Journal of Political Science*, 16(1), 1–34.

DSS (Department of Social Security) 1998a: *New Ambitions for Our Country: A New Contract for Welfare*. London: HMSO.

DSS (Department of Social Security) 1998b: *A New Contract for Welfare: Partnership in Pensions*. London: HMSO.

DTI (Department of Trade and Industry) 2004: Individual incomes of men and women by ethnicity. At www.womenandequalityunit.gov.uk/publications/II_ethnicity_factsheets.pdf (accessed 1 July 2005).

Dunleavy, P. 1980: The political implications of sectoral cleavages and the growth of state employment. *Political Studies*, 28, 364–84 and 527–49.

DWP (Department for Work and Pensions, UK) 2006: *New Deal*. At www.newdeal.gov.uk.

Dyer, C. 1978: *Population and Society in Twentieth Century France*. New York: Holmes and Meier.

ECLAC (Economic Commission for Latin America and the Caribbean, UN) 2003: *Social Panorama of Latin America 2002–3*. At www.eclac.org.

Economist 1982a: Europe's socialists are losing their taste for power. *The Economist*, 284(7249).

Economist 1982b: The withering of Europe's welfare states. *The Economist*, 285(7259).

Economist 1997: Survey: The world economy. *The Economist*, 344(8035).

EIRO (European Industrial Relations Observatory) 2004: Working time developments, 2004. At www.eiro.eurofound.eu.int/2005/03/update/tn0503104u.html (accessed 6 Jan. 2006).

Electoral Studies 1989: *Electoral Studies*, 8(1), 102.

Ellison, N. 2005: *The Transformation of Welfare States.* London: Routledge.

Emmanuel, A. 1979: The state in the transitional period. *New Left Review*, 113–14, 111–31.

Ensor, R. C. K. 1936: *The Oxford History of England 1870–1914.* Oxford: Clarendon.

EOC (Equal Opportunities Commission) 1987: *Women and Men in Britain: A Statistical Profile.* London: HMSO.

EOC (Equal Opportunities Commission) 2003: *Women and Men in Britain: The Labour Market.* London: HMSO.

Esping-Andersen, G. 1985: *Politics against Markets.* Princeton: Princeton University Press.

Esping-Andersen, G. 1990: *The Three Worlds of Welfare Capitalism.* Cambridge: Polity.

Esping-Andersen, G. (ed.) 1996: *Welfare States in Transition.* London: Sage.

Esping-Andersen, G. 1997: Hybrid or unique? The Japanese welfare state between Europe and America. *Journal of European Social Policy*, 7(3), 179–89.

Esping-Andersen, G. 1999: *Social Foundations of Postindustrial Economies.* Oxford: Oxford University Press.

Esping-Andersen, G. 2000: The sustainability of welfare states into the twenty-first century. *International Journal of Health Services*, 30(1), 1–12.

Esping-Andersen, G. and Korpi, W. 1984: Social policy and class politics in post-war capitalism: Scandinavia, Austria and Germany. In J. Goldthorpe (ed.), *Order and Conflict in Contemporary Capitalism.* Oxford: Oxford University Press, pp. 179–208.

Esping-Andersen, G. and Korpi, W. 1987: From poor relief to institutional welfare states: the development of Scandinavian social policy. In R. Erikson et al., *The Scandinavian Model: Welfare States and Welfare Research.* Armonk, New York: Sharpe.

Esping-Andersen, G. with Gallie, D., Hemerjick, A. and Myles, J. 2002: *Why We Need a New Welfare State.* Oxford: Oxford University Press.

Eurostat 1996a: *Basic Statistics of the European Union* (33rd edn). Luxemburg: Office for Official Publications of the European Communities.

Eurostat 1996b: Principal demographic trends in the EU in 1995. *Key Figures*, 11, 96.

Eurostat 1996c: *Social Portrait of Europe.* Luxemburg: Office for Official Publications of the European Communities.

Eurostat 2002: *The Life of Women and Men in Europe, 1980–2000.* Luxemburg: Office for Official Publications of the European Communities.

Eurostat 2005a: Employment rate lower and part-time rates higher for women with children. Eurostat news release, 12 Apr.

Eurostat 2005b: *Gender Pay Gap.* At www.eurostat.cec.eu.int/ (accessed 1 July 2005).

Eurostat 2005c: *Poverty and Social Exclusion.* At www.europa.eu.int/eurostat/ newcronos/reference (accessed 1 July 2005).

Evans, E. J. 1978: *Social Policy 1830–1914: Individualism, Collectivism and the Origins of the Welfare State.* London: Routledge and Kegan Paul.

Feldstein, M. and Horoika, C. 1980: Domestic savings and international capital flows. *Economic Journal*, 90, 314–29.

Ferrera, M. 1986: Italy. In P. Flora (ed.), *Growth to Limits*, vol. 2. Berlin: De Gruyter, pp. 385–482.

Ferrera, M. 1989: Italy. In J. Dixon and R. P. Scheurell (eds), *Social Welfare in Developed Market Countries*. London: Routledge, pp. 122–46.

Ferrera, M. 1996: The 'southern model' of welfare in social Europe. *Journal of European Social Policy*, 6(1), 17–37.

Finch, J. and Groves, D. 1983: *A Labour of Love: Women, Work and Caring*. London: Routledge and Kegan Paul.

Finn, D. 2003: Employment policy. In N. Ellison and C. Pierson (eds), *Developments in British Social Policy* (2nd edn). London: Palgrave Macmillan, pp. 111–28.

Fligstein, N. 1998: *Is Globalization the Cause of the Crises of Welfare States*. EUI Working Paper SPS 98/5. Florence: European University Institute.

Flinders, M. 2005: The politics of public–private partnerships. *British Journal of Politics and International Relations*, 7(2), 215–39.

Flora, P. (ed.) 1986: *Growth to Limits*, vols 1 and 2. Berlin: De Gruyter.

Flora, P. (ed.) 1987a: *Growth to Limits*, vol. 4. Berlin: De Gruyter.

Flora, P. (ed.) 1987b: *State, Economy and Society*. 2 vols, London: Macmillan.

Flora, P. and Alber, J. 1981: Modernization, democratization and the development of welfare states in Western Europe. In P. Flora and A. J. Heidenheimer (eds), *The Development of Welfare States in Europe and America*. London: Transaction, pp. 37–80.

Flora, P. and Heidenheimer, A. J. (eds) 1981a: *The Development of Welfare States in Europe and America*. London: Transaction.

Flora, P. and Heidenheimer, A. J. 1981b: The historical core and changing boundaries of the welfare state. In P. Flora and A. Heidenheimer (eds), *The Development of the Welfare States*. London: Transaction, pp. 17–34.

Foot, M. 1975: *Aneurin Bevan*, vol. 2. London: Paladin.

Foucault, M. 1975: *Discipline and Punish*. Harmondsworth: Penguin.

Fougere, M. and Merette, M. 1999: Population ageing and economic growth in seven OECD countries. *Economic Modelling*, 16, 411–27.

Fowle, T. W. 1890: *The Poor Law*. London: Macmillan.

Fraser, D. 1973: *The Evolution of the Welfare State*. London: Macmillan.

Fraser, D. 1981: The English poor law and the origins of the British welfare state. In W. Mommsen (ed.), *The Emergence of the Welfare State in Britain and Germany 1850–1950*. London: Croom Helm, pp. 9–31.

Fraser, N. and Gordon, L. 1994: 'Dependency' demystified: inscriptions of power in a keyword of the welfare state. *Social Politics*, 1(1), 4–31.

Freeman, G. P. 1986: Migration and the political economy of the welfare state. *Annals of the American Academy of Political and Social Science*, 485, 51–63.

Friedman, M. 1962: *Capitalism and Freedom*. Chicago: University of Chicago Press.

Friedman, M. and Friedman, R. 1980: *Free to Choose*. London: Secker and Warburg.

Froebel, F., Heinrichs, J. and Kreile, O. 1980: *The New International Division of Labour*. Cambridge: Cambridge University Press.

Furniss, N. and Tilton, T. 1979: *The Case for the Welfare State*. London: University of Indiana Press.

Gale Research Co. 1985: *Encyclopaedia of Associations*. Detroit: Gale Research Company.

Gamble, A. 1981: *Britain in Decline*. London: Macmillan.

Gamble, A. 1988: *The Free Economy and the Strong State: The Politics of Thatcherism*. London: Macmillan.

Garrett, G. 1998: *Partisan Politics in the Global Economy*. Cambridge: Cambridge University Press.

Garrett, G. 1999: Globalization and government spending around the world. Working paper, Yale University, at http://pantheon.yale.edu/~gmg8 (accessed 1 July 2004).

Geist, C. 2005: The welfare state and the home: regime differences in the domestic division of labour. *European Sociological Review*, 21(1), 23–41.

Genschel, P. 2002: Globalization, tax competition, and the welfare state. *Politics and Society*, 30(2), 245–72.

Geyer, R. 2000: *Exploring European Social Policy*. Cambridge: Polity.

Geyer, R. 2003: The European Union and British social policy. In N. Ellison and C. Pierson (eds), *Developments in British Social Policy* (2nd edn). London: Palgrave Macmillan, pp. 286–300.

Giddens, A. 1981a: Class division, class conflict and citizenship rights. In A. Giddens, *Profiles and Critiques in Social Theory*. London: Macmillan.

Giddens, A. 1981b: *The Class Structure of the Advanced Societies*. London: Hutchinson.

Giddens, A. 1985: *The Nation-State and Violence*. Cambridge: Polity.

Giddens, A. 1994: *Beyond Left and Right*. Cambridge: Polity.

Giddens, A. 1998: *The Third Way: The Renewal of Social Democracy*. Cambridge: Polity.

Giddens, A. 2000: *The Third Way and Its Critics*. Cambridge: Polity.

Giddens, A. (ed.) 2001: *The Global Third Way Debate*. Cambridge: Polity.

Gilbert, B. B. 1966: *The Evolution of National Insurance in Great Britain*. London: Michael Joseph.

Gilbert, B. B. 1970: *British Social Policy 1914–1939*. London: Batsford.

Gilder, G. 1982: *Wealth and Poverty*. London: Buchan and Enright.

Gilens, M. 1999: *Why Americans Hate Welfare*. Chicago: University of Chicago Press.

Ginsburg, N. 1979: *Class, Capital and Social Policy*. London: Macmillan.

Glass, D. 1940: *Population: Policies and Movements in Europe*. Oxford: Clarendon Press.

Glendinning, C. and Millar, J. 1987: Invisible women, invisible poverty. In C. Glendinning and J. Millar (eds), *Women and Poverty in Britain*. Brighton: Wheatsheaf, pp. 3–27.

Glennerster, H., Power, A. and Travers, T. 1991: A new era for social policy. *Journal of Social Policy*, 20, 389–414.

Godfrey, M. 1986: *Global Unemployment: The New Challenge of Economic Theory*. Brighton: Wheatsheaf.

Goldberg, G. S. and Kremen, E. (eds) 1990: *The Feminization of Poverty: Only in America?* London: Praeger.

Golding, P. and Middleton, S. 1982: *Images of Welfare*. Oxford: Blackwell.

Goldthorpe, J. H. 1984: *Order and Conflict in Contemporary Capitalism*. Oxford: Oxford University Press.

Goodhart, D. 2004: Too diverse? *Prospect* (Feb.), 30–7.

Goodin, R. 1988: *Reasons for Welfare*. Princeton: University of Princeton Press.

Goodin, R. E. and Le Grand, J. 1987: *Not Only the Poor: The Middle Classes and the Welfare State*. London: Allen and Unwin.

Goodman, R. and Peng, I. 1996: The East Asian welfare state. In G. Esping-Andersen (ed.), *Welfare States in Transition*. London: Sage/UNRISD.

Gordon, L. 1994: *Pitied but not Entitled: Single Mothers and the History of Welfare*. Cambridge, Mass.: Harvard University Press.

Gorz, A. 1985: *Paths to Paradise*. London: Pluto.

Gough, I. 1979: *The Political Economy of the Welfare State*. London: Macmillan.

Gough, I. 1983: Thatcherism and the welfare state. In S. Hall and M. Jacques (eds), *The Politics of Thatcherism*. London: Lawrence and Wishart, pp. 148–68.

Gough, I. 2001: 'Globalization and Regional Welfare Regimes. *Global Social Policy*, 1(2), 163–89.

Gould, A. 1999: The erosion of the welfare state: Swedish social policy and the EU. *Journal of European Social Policy*, 9, 165–74.

Graham, H. 1987: Women's poverty and caring. In C. Glendinning and J. Millar (eds), *Women and Poverty in Britain*. Brighton: Wheatsheaf, pp. 221–40.

Grammenos, S. 1982: *Migrant Labour in Western Europe*. Maastricht: European Centre for Work and Society.

Gramsci, A. 1971: *The Prison Notebooks*. London: Lawrence and Wishart.

Green Party (UK): *General Election Manifesto 2005*. At manifesto.greenparty.org.uk.

Gunnarsson, E. 2002: The vulnerable life course: poverty and social assistance among middle-aged and older women. *Ageing and Society*, 22, 709–28.

Habermas, J. 1976: *Legitimation Crisis*. London: Heinemann Educational.

Habermas, J. 1989a: The new obscurity: the crisis of the welfare state and the exhaustion of utopian energies. In J. Habermas, *The New Conservatism*. Cambridge, Mass.: MIT Press, pp. 48–70.

Habermas, J. 1989b: *The Structural Transformation of the Public Sphere: An Inquiry into a Category of Bourgeois Society*. Cambridge: Polity.

Hage, J., Hanneman, R. and Gargan, E. T. 1989: *State Responsiveness and State Activism*. London: Unwin Hyman.

Hall, P. 1952: *The Social Services of Modern England*. London: Routledge and Kegan Paul.

Hall, P. A. and Soskice, D. (eds) 2001: *Varieties of Capitalism*. Oxford: Oxford University Press.

Halligan, J. 2004: The quasi-autonomous agency in an ambiguous environment: the Centrelink case. *Public Administration and Development*, 24, 147–56.

Hammar, T. 1990: *Democracy and the Nation State: Aliens, Denizens and Citizens in a World of International Migration*. Aldershot: Avebury.

Hammar, T. and Lithman, Y. G. 1987: The integration of migrants: experiences, concepts and policies. In OECD, *The Future of Migration*. Paris: Organization for Economic Cooperation and Development, pp. 234–256.

Harris, J. 1977: *William Beveridge: A Biography*. Oxford: Clarendon Press.

Harris, R. and Seldon, A. 1979: *Over-ruled on Welfare*. London: Institute of Economic Affairs.

Harris, R. and Seldon, A. 1987: *Welfare without the State: A Quarter-Century of Suppressed Public Choice*. London: Institute of Economic Affairs.

Hartmann, H. 1981: The family as the locus of gender, class, and political struggle: the example of housework. *Signs*, 6(3), 366–94.

Hay, C. 1997: Anticipating accommodations, accommodating anticipations: the appeasement of capital in the modernisation of the British Labour Party, 1987–92. *Politics and Society*, 25(2), 234–56.

Hay, C. 1999: *The Political Economy of New Labour*. Manchester: Manchester University Press.

Hay, J. 1975: *Origins of the Liberal Welfare Reforms of 1908–14*. London: Macmillan.

Hay, J. 1978a: *The Development of the British Welfare State, 1880–1975*. London: Edward Arnold.

Hay, J. 1978b: Employers' attitudes to social policy and the concept of social control 1890–1920. In P. Thane (ed.), *The Origins of British Social Policy*. London: Croom Helm, pp. 107–25.

Hay, R. 1977: Employers and social policy: the evolution of welfare legislation 1905–14. *Social History*, 4, 435–55.

Hayek, F. 1960: *The Constitution of Liberty*. London: Routledge and Kegan Paul.

Hayek, F. 1982: *Law, Legislation and Liberty*. 3 vols, London: Routledge and Kegan Paul.

Heclo, H. 1974: *Modern Social Politics in Britain and Sweden: From Relief to Income Maintenance*. London: Yale University Press.

Heclo, H. 1981: Towards a new welfare state? In P. Flora and A. Heidenheimer (eds), *The Development of the Welfare States in Europe and North America*. London: Transaction, pp. 383–406.

Heikkinen, E. 1984: Implications of demographic change for the elderly population. In A. D. Lopez and R. L. Cliquet (eds), *Demographic Trends in the European Region*. Copenhagen: World Health Organization, pp. 161–75.

Held, D. 1987: *Models of Democracy*. Cambridge: Polity.

Held, D. 1989: Citizenship and autonomy. In D. Held (ed.), *Political Theory and the Modern State*. Cambridge: Polity.

Held, D., McGrew, A., Goldblatt, D. and Perraton, J. 1999: *Global Transformations: Politics, Economics and Culture*. Cambridge: Polity.

Hemerijck, A. and Visser, J. 2001: The Dutch model: an obvious candidate for the 'Third Way'? *Archives Européennes de Sociologie*, 42(1), 221–39.

Hennock, E. P. 1987: *British Social Reform and German Precedents: The Case of Social Insurance 1880–1914*. Oxford: Clarendon Press.

Henriques, U. R. O. 1979: *Before the Welfare State*. London: Longman.

Hernes, H. 1987: *Welfare State and Woman Power: Essays in State Feminism*. Oslo: Norwegian University Press.

Hewitt, C. 1977: The effect of political democracy and social democracy on equality in industrial societies: a cross-national comparison. *American Sociological Review*, 42, 450–64.

Hicks, A. 1988: Social democratic corporatism and economic growth. *Journal of Politics*, 50, 677–704.

Hicks, A. and Swank, D. 1984: On the political economy of welfare expansion: a comparative analysis of eighteen advanced capitalist democracies, 1960–1971. *Comparative Political Studies*, 17(1), 81–119.

Hill, D. C. D. and Tigges, L. M. 1995: Gendering welfare state theory: a cross-national study of women's public pension quality. *Gender and Society*, 9(1), 99–119.

Hills, J. 1997: *The Future of Welfare*, 2nd edn. York: LSE/Rowntree.

Himmelstrand, U. et al. 1981: *Beyond Welfare Capitalism*. London: Heinemann.

Hirst, P. and Thompson, G. 1996: *Globalization in Question: The International Economy and the Possibilities of Governance*. Cambridge: Polity.

HM Treasury 1979: *The Government's Expenditure Plans 1980–1*. Cmnd. 7746. London: HMSO.

HM Treasury 2003: *Detailed Proposals for the Child Trust Fund*. London: HMSO.

HM Treasury 2005: *2004 Spending Review*. London: HMSO.

Huber, E. and Stephens, J. D. 2001: *Development and Crisis of the Welfare State: Parties and Policies in Global Markets*. Chicago: University of Chicago Press.

Huber, E. and Stephens, J. 2006: Combatting old and new social risks. In K. Armingeon and G. Bonoli (eds), *The Politics of Postindustrial Welfare States*. London: Routledge.

Hutton, W. 1995: *The State We're In*. London: Cape.

Hyman, R. 1989a: Class struggle and the trade union movement. In R. Hyman (ed.), *The Political Economy of Industrial Relations*. London: Macmillan.

Hyman, R. 1989b: *Strikes*. London: Macmillan.

Illich, I. 1973: *Deschooling Society*. Harmondsworth: Penguin.

Illich, I. 1977: *Disabling Professions*. London: Boyars.

Illich, I. 1978: *The Right to Useful Employment*. London: Boyars.

IOM (International Organization for Migration) 2004: *Migration Trends in Selected EU Applicant Countries*. Geneva: IOM.

IPPR (Institute for Public Policy Research) 2003: *Nest-Egg Accounts*. London: IPPR. At www.chifley.org.au/publications/nest_egg_accounts.pdf (accessed 1 Sept. 2005).

ISSP 1985/1996: International Social Survey Programme. At www.gesis.org/en/data_service/issp/data/1985_Role_of_Government_I.htm and www.gesis.org/en/data_service/issp/data/1996_Role_of_Government_III.htm (accessed 1 July 2005).

Iversen, T. 2000: The dynamics of welfare state expansion: trade openness, de-industrialization, and partisan politics. In P. Pierson (ed.), *The New Politics of the Welfare State*. Oxford: Oxford University Press, pp. 45–79.

Jackson, B. and Jackson, S. 1979: *Childminder: A Study in Action Research*. London: Routledge and Kegan Paul.

Jackson, M. P. 1987: *Strikes*. Brighton: Wheatsheaf.

Jacobs, M. 1996: *The Politics of the Real World*. London: Earthscan.

James, E. 2000: Social security around the world. In C. Pierson and F. G. Castles (eds), *The Welfare State Reader* (1st edn). Cambridge: Polity, pp. 271–80.

Jay, P. 1977: Englanditis. In R. E. Tyrrell (ed.), *The Future That Doesn't Work*. New York: Doubleday, pp. 167–85.

Jennings, E. T. 1979: Competition, constituencies, and welfare policies in American states. *American Political Science Review*, 73(2), 414–29.

Jessop, B. 1988: *Conservative Regimes and the Transition to Post-Fordism*. Colchester: University of Essex Papers.

Jessop, B. 1991: Thatcherism and flexibility. In B. Jessop et al., *The Politics of Flexibility*. London: Edward Elgar.

Jessop, B. 1994: The Schumpeterian workfare state. In R. Burrows and B. Loader (eds), *Towards a Post-Fordist Welfare State*. London: Routledge.

Johansen, L. N. 1986: Denmark. In P. Flora (ed.), *Growth to Limits*, vol. 1. Berlin: De Gruyter, pp. 293–381.

Jones, C. 1985: *Patterns of Social Policy*. London: Tavistock.

Jones, C. 1993: The Pacific challenge: Confucian welfare states. In C. Jones (ed.), *New Perspectives on the Welfare State in Europe*. London: Routledge.

Jones, Martin 1996: Full steam ahead to a workfare state? *Policy and Politics*, 24(2), 137–57.

Jones, Michael A. 1980: *The Australian Welfare State*. London: Allen and Unwin.

Jones, T. 1993: *Britain's Ethnic Minorities*. London: Policy Studies Institute.

Joshi, S. and Carter, B. 1984: The role of Labour in the creation of a racist Britain. *Race and Class*, 25(3), 53–70.

Jowell, R. 1991: *British Social Attitudes: Eighth Report*. Aldershot: Dartmouth.

Kaim-Caudle, P. 1973: *Comparative Social Policy and Social Security*. Oxford: Martin Robertson.

Katz, M. 1986: *In the Shadow of the Poorhouse*. New York: Basic Books.

Katzenstein, P. 1985: *Small States in World Markets*. Ithaca: Cornell University Press.

Kautsky, K. 1909: *The Road to Power*. Chicago: Bloch.

Kautsky, K. 1910: *The Class Struggle*. New York: Kerr.

Kautsky, K. 1983: *Selected Political Writings*. London: Macmillan.

Kavanagh, D. 1987: *Thatcherism and British Politics: The End of Consensus?* Oxford: Oxford University Press.

Kavanagh, D. and Morris, P. 1989: *Consensus Politics from Attlee to Thatcher*. Oxford: Blackwell.

Kelly, G. and Lissauer, R. 2000: *Ownership for All*. London: Institute for Public Policy Research.

Kelsey, J. 1995: *The New Zealand Experiment: A World Model or Structural Adjustment?* Auckland: Auckland University Press/Bridget Williams Books.

Keman, H. 2003: Explaining miracles: third ways and work and welfare. *West European Politics*, 26(2), 115–35.

Kennedy, F. 1975: *Public Social Expenditure in Ireland*. Dublin: Economic and Social Research Institute.

Keohane, R. O. 1984: The world political economy and the crisis of embedded liberalism. In J. Goldthorpe, *Order and Conflict in Contemporary Capitalism*. Oxford: Oxford University Press, pp. 15–38.

Keynes, M. 1973: *The General Theory of Employment, Interest and Money*. London: Macmillan.

Kilkey, M. and Bradshaw, J. 1999: Lone mothers, economic well-being, and policies. In D. Sainsbury (ed.), *Gender and Welfare State Regimes*. Oxford: Oxford University Press, pp. 147–84.

King, D. S. 1987: *The New Right: Politics, Markets and Citizenship*. London: Macmillan.

Klein, R. 1983: *The Politics of the NHS*. London: Longman.

Korpi, W. 1979: *The Working Class in Welfare Capitalism*. London: Routledge and Kegan Paul.

Korpi, W. 1983: *The Democratic Class Struggle*. London: Routledge and Kegan Paul.

Korpi, W. 1989: Power, politics, and state autonomy in the development of social citizenship: social rights during sickness in eighteen OECD countries since 1930. *American Sociological Review*, 54(3), 309–28.

Korpi, W. and Palme, J. 2003: New politics and class politics in the context of austerity and globalization: welfare state regress in eighteen countries, 1975–95. *American Political Science Review*, 97(3), 425–46.

Kristol, I. 1978: *Two Cheers for Capitalism*. New York: Basic Books.

Kudrle, R. T. and Marmor, T. R. 1981: The development of welfare states in North America. In P. Flora and A. J. Heidenheimer (eds), *The Development of Welfare States in Europe and America*. London: Transaction, pp. 81–121.

Kuhnle, S. 1981: The growth of social insurance programs in Scandinavia: outside influences and internal forces. In P. Flora and A. J. Heidenheimer (eds), *The Development of Welfare States*. London: Transaction, pp. 125–50.

Lane, J. E. 1995: The decline of the Swedish model. *Governance*, 8(4), 179–90.

Lane, J.-E. and Ersson, S. O. 1987: *Politics and Society in Western Europe*. London: Sage.

Lane, J.-E., McKay, D. and Newton, K. 1997: *Political Data Handbook*. Oxford: Oxford University Press.

Langan, M. and Lee, P. (eds) 1989: *Radical Social Work Today*. London: Unwin Hyman.

Lasch, C. 1978: *The Culture of Narcissism*. New York: Norton.

Lash, S. and Urry, J. 1987: *The End of Organized Capitalism*. Cambridge: Polity.

Le Grand, J. and Nissan, D. 2000: *A Capital Idea: Start-up Grants for Young People*. London: Fabian Society.

Leibfried, S. 1993: Towards a European welfare state? In C. Jones (ed.), *New Perspectives on the Welfare State in Europe*. London: Routledge, pp. 133–56.

Leibfried, S. and Obinger, H. 2003: The state of the welfare state: German social policy between macroeconomic retrenchment and microeconomic recalibration. *West European Politics*, 26(4), 199–215.

Leman, C. 1977: Patterns of policy development: social security in the US and Canada. *Public Policy*, 25(2), 261–91.

Levine, D. 1983: Social democrats, socialism and social insurance in Germany and Denmark, 1918–1933. In R. F. Tomasson (ed.), *Comparative Social Research*, vol. 6: *The Welfare State, 1883–1983*. Connecticut: JAI Press, pp. 67–86.

Levinson, A. 2005: *Regularisation Programmes in the UK*. Oxford: Centre on Migration, Policy and Society, University of Oxford.

Levitas, R. 1998: *The Inclusive Society?* London: Macmillan.

Lewis, J. 1992: Gender and the development of welfare regimes. *Journal of European Social Policy*, 2(3), 159–73.

Lipset, S. M. 1969: *Political Man*. London, Heinemann.

Lister, R. 1993: Tracing the contours of women's citizenship. *Policy and Politics*, 21(1), 3–16.

Lister, R. 2001: Towards a citizens' welfare state: the 3 + 2 'R's of welfare reform. *Theory, Culture and Society*, 18(2–3), 91–111.

Lister, R. 2003: Investing in citizen-workers of the future: transformations in citizenship and the state under New Labour. *Social Policy and Administration*, 57(5), 427–43.

Luhmann, N. 1990: *Political Theory in the Welfare State*. Berlin: De Gruyter.

McEvedy, C. and Jones, R. 1978: *Atlas of World Population History*. Harmondsworth: Penguin.

McIntosh, C. A. 1983: *Population Policy in Western Europe*. Armonk, New York: M. E. Sharpe.

McIntosh, M. 1978: The state and the oppression of women. In A. Kuhn and A. Wolpe (eds), *Feminism and Materialism: Women and Modes of Production*. London: Routledge and Kegan Paul.

McKay, A. 1998: Basic income maintenance or basic income? In N. Ellison and C. Pierson (eds), *Developments in British Social Policy*. London: Macmillan.

Mackie, T. T. and Rose, R. 1991: *The International Almanac of Electoral History* (3rd edn). London, Macmillan.

Maclean, M. and Groves, D. (eds) 1991: *Women's Issues in Social Policy*. London: Routledge.

Maddison, A. 1984: Origins and impact of the welfare state. *Banca Nazionale del Lavoro Quarterly Review*, 148, 55–87.

Madison, B. Q. 1980: *The Meaning of Social Policy*. London: Croom Helm.

Maguire, M. 1986: Ireland. In P. Flora (ed.), *Growth to Limits*, vol. 2. Berlin: De Gruyter, pp. 241–384.

Maillat, D. 1987: Long-term aspects of international migration flows: the experience of European receiving countries. In OECD, *The Future of Migration*. Paris: Organization for Economic Cooperation and Development, pp. 38–63.

Malthus, T. R. 1890: *An Essay on the Principle of Population*. London: Ward, Lock.

Mandin, C. and Palier, B. 2005: The politics of pension reform in France: the end of exceptionalism? In G. Bonoli and T. Shinkawa (eds), *Ageing and Pension Reform around the World*. London: Edward Elgar, pp. 74–93.

Mann, M. 1970: The social cohesion of liberal democracy. *American Sociological Review*, 35(3), 423–39.

Manning, N. 2004: Diversity and change in pre-accession Central and Eastern European Europe since 1989. *Journal of European Social Policy*, 14(3), 211–32.

Manow, P. and Seils, E. 2000: The employment crisis of the German welfare state. *West European Politics*, 23(2), 137–60.

Marcuse, H. 1972: *One Dimensional Man*. London: Sphere.

Mares, I. 2003: *The Politics of Social Risk: Business and Welfare State Development*. Cambridge: Cambridge University Press.

Marshall, T. H. 1963: *Sociology at the Crossroads*. London: Heinemann.

Marshall, T. H. 1975: *Social Policy in the Twentieth Century*. London: Hutchinson Education.

Martin, A. 1997: *What Does Globalization Have to Do with the Erosion of Welfare States? Sorting out the Issues*. Bremen: Zentrum für Sozialpolitik.

Marwick, A. 1967: The Labour Party and the welfare state in Britain 1900–1948. *American Historical Review*, 73(2), 380–403.

Marx, K. 1973a: *Capital*. Harmondsworth: Penguin.

Marx, K. 1973b: *Surveys from Exile*. Harmondsworth: Penguin.

Middlemas, K. 1979: *Politics in Industrial Society: The Experience of the British System since 1911*. London: Andre Deutsch.

Miliband, R. 1969: *The State in Capitalist Society*. London: Weidenfeld and Nicolson.

Miller, D. 1995: *On Nationality*. Oxford: Oxford University Press.

Minami, R. 1986: *The Economic Development of Japan: A Quantitative Study*. London: Macmillan.

Minford, P. 1987: The role of the social services: a view from the New Right. In M. Loney (ed.), *The State or the Market: Politics and Welfare in Contemporary Britain*. London: Sage, pp. 70–82.

Mishra, R. 1984: *The Welfare State in Crisis*. Brighton: Wheatsheaf.

Mitchell, B. R. 1975: *European Historical Statistics 1750–1970*. New York: Columbia University Press.

Modood, T. and Berthoud, R. 1997: *Ethnic Minorities in Britain: Diversity and Disadvantage*. London: Policy Studies Institute.

Mommsen, W. J. (ed.) 1981: *The Emergence of the Welfare State in Britain and Germany*. London: Croom Helm.

Moran, M. 1988: Crises of the welfare state. *British Journal of Political Science*, 18, 397–414.

Moynihan, D. P. 1965: *The Negro Family: The Case for National Action*. Washington DC: Office of Planning and Research, US Department of Labor.

Murray, C. 1984: *Losing Ground: American Social Policy 1950–1980*. New York: Basic Books.

Navarro, V. 1978: *The Rise and Fall of Economic Justice*. Oxford: Oxford University Press.

New Zealand Census and Statistics Office 1882– : *New Zealand Official Year-Book*. Wellington: Census and Statistics Office.

Niskanen, W. A. 1971: *Bureaucracy and Representative Government*. New York: Aldine-Atherton.

Niskanen, W. A. 1973: *Bureaucracy: Servant or Master?* London: Institute for Economic Affairs.

Nordlinger, E. A. 1981: *On the Autonomy of the Democratic State*. Cambridge, Mass.: Harvard University Press.

Nozick, R. 1974: *Anarchy, State and Utopia*. New York: Basic Books.

Oakley, A. 1974: *Housewife*. Harmondsworth: Allen Lane.

O'Connor, J. 1973: *The Fiscal Crisis of the State*. New York: St Martin's Press.

O'Connor, J. 1987: *The Meaning of Crisis*. Oxford: Blackwell.

O'Connor, J. S. 1988: Convergence or divergence? Change in welfare effort in OECD countries, 1960–1980. *European Journal of Political Research*, 16, 277–99.

O'Connor, J. S. 1996: *From Women in the Welfare State to Gendering Welfare State Regimes*. Special issue of *Current Sociology*, 44(2).

O'Connor, J. S. and Brym, R. J. 1988: Public welfare expenditure in OECD countries: towards a reconciliation of inconsistent findings. *British Journal of Sociology*, 39(1), 47–68.

OECD 1966: *Economic Growth, 1960–1970*. Paris: Organization for Economic Cooperation and Development.

OECD 1977: *Towards Full Employment and Price Stability*. Paris: Organization for Economic Cooperation and Development.

OECD 1984: *OECD Observer*, 126.

OECD 1985a: *The Integration of Women into the Economy*. Paris: Organization for Economic Cooperation and Development.

OECD 1985b: *Social Expenditure 1960–1990: Problems of Growth and Control*. Paris: Organization for Economic Cooperation and Development.

OECD 1986a: *Employment Outlook*. Paris: Organization for Economic Cooperation and Development.

OECD 1986b: *OECD Observer*, 138.

OECD 1987a: *The Future of Migration*. Paris: Organization for Economic Cooperation and Development.

OECD 1987b: *Structural Adjustment and Economic Performance*. Paris: Organization for Economic Cooperation and Development.

OECD 1988a: *The Future of Social Protection*. Paris: Organization for Economic Cooperation and Development.

OECD 1988b: *Reforming Public Pensions*. Paris: Organization for Economic Cooperation and Development.

OECD 1989: *Economies in Transition*. Paris: Organization for Economic Cooperation and Development.

OECD 1992: *Private Pensions and Public Policy*. Paris: Organization for Economic Cooperation and Development.

OECD 1994: *New Orientations for Social Policy*. Paris: Organization for Economic Cooperation and Development.

OECD 1996: *Ageing in OECD Countries*. Paris: Organization for Economic Cooperation and Development.

OECD 1997: *Family, Market and Community: Equity and Efficiency in Social Policy*. Paris: Organization for Economic Cooperation and Development.

OECD 1998: *OECD Economic Outlook*, 63. Paris: Organization for Economic Cooperation and Development.

OECD 1999: *A Caring World: The New Social Policy Agenda*. Paris: Organization for Economic Cooperation and Development.

OECD 2001: *Labour Force Statistics 1980–2000*. Paris: Organization for Economic Cooperation and Development.

OECD 2002: *Employment Outlook*, 71 (June). Paris: Organization for Economic Cooperation and Development.

OECD 2004: *Employment Outlook*. Paris: Organization for Economic Cooperation and Development.

OECD 2005: *OECD Factbook 2005*. At http://thesius.sourceoecd.org/vl=16438087/cl=42/nw=1/rpsv/factbook/ (accessed 1 July 2005).

Offe, C. 1984: *Contradictions of the Welfare State*. London: Hutchinson Education.

Offe, C. 1985: *Disorganized Capitalism*. Cambridge: Polity.

Offe, C. 1985–6: New social movements: challenging the boundaries of institutional politics. *Social Research* (Winter). (A version is reprinted as 'Challenging the boundaries of institutional politics: social movements since the 1960s' in C. S. Maier (ed.), *Changing Boundaries of the Political: Essays on the Evolving Balance between the State and Society, Public and Private in Europe*. Cambridge: Cambridge University Press, 1987, pp. 63–105.)

Offe, C. 1987: Democracy against the welfare state? *Political Theory*, 15(4), 501–37.

Offe, C. and Wiesenthal, H. 1985: Two logics of collective action. In C. Offe, *Disorganized Capitalism*. Cambridge: Polity, pp. 170–220.

Official Year Book of the Commonwealth of Australia 1923: Melbourne: Australian Government.

Official Year Book of the Commonwealth of Australia 1932: Canberra: Australian Government.

Ohlin, B. 1938: Economic progress in Sweden. *Annals of the American Academy of Political and Social Science*, 197, 1–6.

Ohmae, K. 1990: *The Borderless World*. London: Collins.

Olson, M. 1965: *The Logic of Collective Action: Public Goods and the Theory of Groups*. Oxford: Oxford University Press.

Olson, M. 1982: *The Rise and Decline of Nations: Economic Growth, Stagflation, and Social Rigidities*. New Haven: Yale University Press.

Olsson, S. 1986: Sweden. In P. Flora (ed.), *Growth to Limits*, vol. 1. Berlin: De Gruyter, pp. 1–116.

Oppenheim, C. and Harker, L. 1996: *Poverty: The Facts* (3rd edn). London: Child Poverty Action Group.

Orban, O. 1908: *Le Droit constitutionnel de la Belgique. II: Les Pouvoirs de l'État*. Liège: Dessain.

Orloff, A. S. 1988: The origins of America's belated welfare state. In M. Weir, A. S. Orloff and T. Skocpol (eds), *The Politics of Social Policy in the United States*. Princeton: Princeton University Press.

Orloff, A. S. 1993: Gender and the social rights of citizenship: the comparative analysis of gender relations and welfare states. *American Sociological Review*, 38, 303–28.

Orloff, A. S. 1996: Gender in the welfare state. *Annual Review of Sociology*, 22, 51–78.

Orloff, A. S. and Skocpol, T. 1984: Why not equal protection? Explaining the politics of public social spending in Britain, 1900–1911, and the United States, 1880s–1920. *American Sociological Review*, 49(6), 726–50.

Osborne, D. and Gaebler, T. 1992: *Reinventing Government*. Boston: Addison-Wesley.

Oshima, H. T. 1965: Meiji fiscal policy and agricultural progress. In W. W. Lockwood (ed.), *The State and Economic Enterprise in Japan*. Princeton: Princeton University Press, pp. 353–89.

Owen, R. 1927: *A New View of Society and Other Writings*. London: Dent.

Paine, S. 1974: *Exporting Workers: The Turkish Case*. Cambridge: Cambridge University Press.

Paine, T. 1958: *The Rights of Man*. London: Dent.

Palier, B. 2000: 'Defrosting' the French welfare state. *West European Politics*, 23(2), 113–36.

Palier, B. and Mandin, C. 2004: France: a new world of welfare for new social risks? In P. Taylor-Gooby (ed.), *New Risks, New Welfare*. Oxford: Oxford University Press, pp. 111–29.

Pampel, F. and Stryker, R. 1990: Age structure, the state, and social welfare spending: a reanalysis. *British Journal of Sociology*, 41(1), 16–24.

Pampel, F. C. and Williamson, J. B. 1988: Welfare spending in advanced industrial democracies, 1950–1980. *American Journal of Sociology*, 93(6), 1424–56.

Pampel, F. C. and Williamson, J. B. 1989: *Age, Class, Politics and the Welfare State*. Cambridge: Cambridge University Press.

Parry, R. 1986: United Kingdom. In P. Flora (ed.), *Growth to Limits*, vol. 2. Berlin: De Gruyter, pp. 155–240.

Pascall, G. and Lewis, J. 2004: Emerging gender regimes and policies for gender equality in a wider Europe. *Journal of Social Policy*, 33(3), 373–94.

Pateman, C. 1988: The patriarchal welfare state. In A. Gutmann (ed.), *Democracy and the Welfare State*. Princeton: Princeton University Press, pp. 231–60.

Peacock, A. and Wiseman, J. 1961: *The Growth of Public Expenditure in the UK*. Oxford: Oxford University Press.

Pearce, D. 1978: The feminization of poverty: women, work and welfare. *Urban and Social Change Review*, 11(1–2), 28–36.

Pearce, D., Markandya, A. and Barbier, E. B. 1989: *Blueprint for a Green Economy: A Report*. London: Earthscan.

Pedersen, S. 1993: *Family, Dependence and the Origins of the Welfare State*. Cambridge: Cambridge University Press.

Pelling, H. 1968: The working class and the origins of the welfare state. In H. Pelling (ed.), *Popular Politics and Society in Late Victorian Britain*. London: Macmillan.

Pemberton, A. 1983: Marxism and social policy: a critique of the 'contradictions of welfare'. *Journal of Social Policy*, 12(3), 289–308.

Pen, J. 1987: Expanding budgets in a stagnating economy: the experience of the 1970s. In C. S. Maier (ed.), *Changing Boundaries of the Political*. Cambridge: Cambridge University Press.

Perraton, J., Goldblatt, D., Held, D. and McGrew, A. 1997: The globalisation of economic activity. *New Political Economy*, 2(2).

Pfaller, A., Gough, I. and Therborn, G. (eds) 1991: *Can the Welfare State Compete?* London: Macmillan.

Piachaud, D. 1984: *Round about Fifty Hours a Week*. London: Child Poverty Action Group.

Pierson, C. 1986: *Marxist Theory and Democratic Politics*. Cambridge: Polity.

Pierson, C. 1991: Welfare states and social democracies: Sweden's 'Austro-Marxism' and the 'Social Democratic Road to Power'. *Research in Political Sociology*, 5.

Pierson, C. 1998: Globalisation and the changing governance of welfare states: superannuation reform in Australia, *Global Society*, 12(1), 31–47.

Pierson, C. 2001: *Hard Choices*. Cambridge: Polity.

Pierson, C. 2002: 'Social democracy on the back foot': the ALP and the 'new' Australian model. *New Political Economy*, 7(2), 179–97.

Pierson, C. 2005a: 'Late industrialisers' and the development of the welfare state. *Acta Politica*, 40(4), 395–418.

Pierson, C. 2005b: Lost property: what the Third Way lacks. *Journal of Political Ideologies*, 10(2), 145–63.

Pierson, P. 1994: *Dismantling the Welfare State? Reagan, Thatcher, and the Politics of Retrenchment*. Cambridge: Cambridge University Press.

Pierson, P. 1996: The new politics of the welfare state. *World Politics*, 48, 143–79.

Pierson, P. 1998: Irresistible forces, immovable objects: post-industrial welfare states confront permanent austerity. *Journal of European Public Policy*, 5(4), 539–60.

References 263

Pierson, P. (ed.) 2000: *The New Politics of the Welfare State*. Oxford: Oxford University Press.

Pigou, A. C. 1912: *Wealth and Welfare*. London: Macmillan.

Pigou, A. C. 1929: *The Economics of Welfare*. London: Macmillan.

Pimlott, B. 1988: The myth of consensus. In L. M. Smith (ed.), *The Making of Britain: Echoes of Greatness*. London: Macmillan, pp. 129–41.

Piore, S. 1979: *Birds of Passage: Migrant Labour and Industrial Societies*. Cambridge: Cambridge University Press.

Pitruzzello, S. 1997: Social policy and the implementation of the Maastricht fiscal convergence criteria: the Italian and French attempts at welfare and pension reforms. *Social Research*, 64(4).

Piven, F. F. and Cloward, R. 1971: *Regulating the Poor: The Functions of Public Welfare*. New York: Pantheon.

Piven, F. F. and Cloward, R. 1977: *Poor People's Movements: Why They Succeed, How They Fail*. New York: Pantheon.

Piven, F. F. and Cloward, R. 1985: *The New Class War: Reagan's Attack on the Welfare State and its Consequences*. New York: Pantheon.

Piven, F. F. and Cloward, R. A. 1986: The new class war in the US. In E. Oyen (ed.), *Comparing Welfare States and their Futures*. London: Gower, pp. 47–63.

Ploug, N. 1995: The welfare state in liquidation? *International Social Security Review*, 2, 61–7.

Poguntke, T. 1987: New politics and party systems: the emergence of a new type of party? *West European Politics*, 10(1), 76–88.

Polanyi, K. 1944: *The Great Transformation*. New York: Rinehart.

Poulantzas, N. 1973: *Political Power and Social Classes*. London: Verso.

Poulantzas, N. 1978: *State, Power, Socialism*. London: Verso.

Przeworski, A. 1985: *Capitalism and Social Democracy*. Cambridge: Cambridge University Press.

Przeworski, A. and Sprague, J. 1986: *Paper Stones: A History of Electoral Socialism*. London: University of Chicago Press.

Quadagno, J. 1984: Welfare capitalism and the Social Security Act of 1935. *American Sociological Review*, 49, 632–47.

Quadagno, J. 1987: Women's welfare benefits and American exceptionalism. *Comparative Historical Sociology Newsletter*, 4(2), 1–2.

Quadagno, J. 1988a: From old-age assistance to supplemental security income: the political economy of relief in the south, 1935–1972. In M. Weir, A. S. Orloff and T. Skocpol (eds), *The Politics of Social Policy in the United States*. Princeton: Princeton University Press, pp. 235–63.

Quadagno, J. 1988b: *The Transformation of Old Age Security, Class and Politics in the American Welfare State*. Chicago: University of Chicago Press.

Quadagno, J. 1990: Race, class, and gender in the US welfare state: Nixon's failed family assistance plan. *American Sociological Review*, 55(1), 11–28.

Quadagno, J. 1994: *The Color of Welfare*. Oxford: Oxford University Press.

Rader, M. 1979: *Marx's Interpretation of History*. New York: Oxford University Press.

Rathbone, E. 1986: *The Disinherited Family*. Bristol: Falling Wall Press.

Rawlings, H. F. 1988: *Law and the Electoral Process*. London: Sweet and Maxwell.

Razin, A. and Sadka, E. 1999: Migration and pension with international capital mobility. *Journal of Public Economics*, 74, 141–50.

Reede, A. H. 1947: *Adequacy of Workmen's Compensation*. Cambridge, Mass.: Harvard University Press.

Regan, S. 2003: Paying for welfare in the twenty-first century. In N. Ellison and C. Pierson (eds), *Developments in British Social Policy* (2nd edn). London: Palgrave Macmillan, pp. 271–85.

Rein, M. 1985: Women, employment and social welfare. In R. Klein and M. O'Higgins (eds), *The Future of Welfare*. Oxford: Blackwell, pp. 37–58.

Rein, M., Esping-Andersen, G. and Rainwater, M. (eds) 1987: *Stagnation and Renewal in Social Policy: The Rise and Fall of Policy Regimes*. New York: Sharpe.

Rieger, E. and Leibfried, S. 2003: *Limits to Globalization*. Cambridge: Polity.

Rimlinger, G. V. 1974: *Welfare Policy and Industrialization in Europe, America and Russia*. New York: John Wiley.

Ritter, G. A. 1985: *Social Welfare in Germany and Britain*. Leamington Spa: Berg.

Roberts, D. 1960: *Victorian Origins of the Welfare State*. New Haven: Yale University Press.

Rodrik, D. 1997: *Has Globalization Gone Too Far?* Washington, DC: Institute for International Economics.

Rose, H. 1981: Rereading Titmuss: the sexual division of welfare. *Journal of Social Policy*, 10, 477–501.

Rose, R. and Peters, G. 1978: *Can Governments Go Bankrupt?* New York: Basic Books.

Rosenblum, G. 1973: *Immigrant Workers: Their Impact on American Labor Radicalism*. New York: Basic Books.

Sainsbury, D. (ed.) 1994: *Gendering Welfare States*. London: Sage.

Samuelsson, K. 1968: *From Great Power to Welfare State: Three Hundred Years of Swedish Social Development*. London: Allen and Unwin.

Saraceno, C. 1997: Family change, family policies and the restructuring of welfare. In P. Hennessy and M. Pearson (eds), *Family, Market and Community*. Paris: Organization for Economic Cooperation and Development.

Scase, R. (ed.) 1977a: *Readings in the Swedish Class Structure*. London: Pergamon.

Scase, R. 1977b: *Social Democracy in Capitalist Society: Working Class Politics in Britain and Sweden*. London: Croom Helm.

Schmidt, M. G. 1983: The welfare state and the economy in periods of economic crisis: a comparative study of twenty-three OECD nations. *European Journal of Political Research*, 11, 1–26.

Schmidt, M. G. 1989: Social policy in rich and poor countries: socio-economic trends and political-institutional determinants. *European Journal of Political Research*, 17(6), 641–59.

Schneider, S. K. 1982: The sequential development of social programs in eighteen welfare states. *Comparative Social Research*, 5, 195–219.

Schottland, C. 1969: *The Welfare State*. New York: Harper and Row.

Schumpeter, J. 1954: The crisis of the tax state. *International Economic Papers*, 4, 5–38.

Schumpeter, J. 1976: *Capitalism, Socialism, Democracy*. London: Allen and Unwin.

Schwartz, H. 2000: Round up the usual suspects! Globalization, domestic politics, and welfare state change. In P. Pierson (ed.), *The New Politics of the Welfare State*. Oxford: Oxford University Press, pp. 17–44.

Scruggs, L. and Allan, J. 2006: Welfare state decommodification in eighteen OECD countries: a replication and revision. *Journal of European Social Policy*, 16, 55–72.

Seeleib-Kaiser, M. 2002: A dual transformation of the German welfare state? *West European Politics*, 25(4), 25–48.

Selbourne, D. 1985: *Against Socialist Illusion*. London: Macmillan.

Senior, N. A. 1865: *Historical and Political Essays*. London.

Shalev, M. 1983: The social democratic model and beyond: 'two generations' of comparative research on the welfare state. In R. F. Tomasson (ed.), *The Welfare State, 1883–1983*, vol. 6 of *Comparative Social Research*. London: JAI Press, pp. 315–51.

Shaver, S. 1989: Gender, class and the welfare state: the case of income security in Australia. *Feminist Review*, 32, 91–108.

Sherraden, M. 1991: *Assets and the Poor: A New American Welfare Policy*. New York: Sharpe.

Sked, A. and Cook, C. 1984: *Post-war Britain*. Harmondsworth: Penguin.

Skellington, R. 1996: *'Race' in Britain Today* (2nd edn). London: Sage.

Skidelsky, R. 1979: The decline of Keynesian politics. In C. Crouch (ed.), *State and Economy in Contemporary Capitalism*. London: Croom Helm, pp. 55–87.

Skocpol, T. 1980: Political response to capitalist crisis: neo-Marxist theories of the state and the case of the New Deal. *Politics and Society*, 10, 155–201.

Skocpol, T. 1985: Bringing the state back in: strategies of analysis in current research. In P. B. Evans, D. Rueschemeyer and T. Skocpol (eds), *Bringing the State Back In*. Cambridge: Cambridge University Press, pp. 3–37.

Skocpol, T. 1987: America's incomplete welfare state. In M. Rein, G. Esping-Andersen and M. Rainwater (eds), *Stagnation and Renewal in Social Policy*. New York: Sharpe.

Skocpol, T. 1992: *Protecting Soldiers and Mothers: The Political Origins of Social Policy in the US*. Cambridge, Mass.: Harvard University Press.

Skocpol, T. and Amenta, E. 1986: States and social policies. *Annual Review of Sociology*, 12, 131–57.

Skocpol, T. and Ikenberry, J. 1983: The political formation of the American welfare state in historical and comparative perspective. In R. F. Tomasson (ed.), *Comparative Social Research*, vol. 6. London: JAI Press, pp. 87–148.

Smith, A. 1976a: *Theory of Moral Sentiments*. Oxford: Clarendon Press.

Smith, A. 1976b: *The Wealth of Nations*. Oxford: Clarendon Press.

Smith, H. L. 1986: *War and Social Change: British Society in the Second World War*. Manchester: Manchester University Press.

Soroka, S., Banting, K. and Johnston, R. (forthcoming): Immigration and redistribution in the global era. In P. Bardham, S. Bowles and M. Wallerstein (eds), *Globalization and Social Redistribution*. Princeton: Princeton University Press and Twentieth Century Fund.

Stephens, J. 1979: *The Transition from Capitalism to Socialism*. London: Macmillan.

Stockman, D. A. 1986: *The Triumph of Politics*. London: Bodley Head.

Swank, D. 1998a: Funding the welfare state: globalization and the taxation of business in advanced market economies. *Political Studies*, 46(4), 671–92.

Swank, D. 1998b: Global capital, democracy, and the welfare state: why political institutions are so important in shaping the domestic response to international-ization. Political Economy of European Integration Working Paper 1.66. Berkeley: University of California Center for German and European Studies.

Swann, M. (chair) 1985: *Education for All: The Report of the Committee of Inquiry into the Education of Children from Ethnic Minority Groups*. London: HMSO.

Swenson, P. A. 2002: *Capitalism against Markets: The Making of Labor Markets and Welfare States in the United States and Sweden*. Oxford: Oxford University Press.

Tampke, J. 1981: Bismarck's social legislation: a genuine breakthrough? In W. J. Mommsen (ed.), *The Emergence of the Welfare State in Britain and Germany 1850–1950*. London: Croom Helm, pp. 71–83.

Taylor, A. J. P. 1965: *English History 1914–1945*. Oxford: Clarendon Press.

Taylor, C. L. and Hudson, M. C. 1983: *World Handbook of Political and Social Indicators*. New Haven: Yale University Press.

Taylor-Gooby, P. 1985: *Public Opinion, Ideology and State Welfare*. London: Routledge and Kegan Paul.

Taylor-Gooby, P. 1989: The role of the state. In R. Jowell, S. Witherspoon and L. Brook (eds), *British Social Attitudes: Special International Report* (6th edn). Aldershot: Gower, pp. 35–58.

Taylor-Gooby, P. (ed.) 2005: *New Risks, New Welfare*. Oxford: Oxford University Press.

Taylor-Gooby, P. and Dale, J. 1981: *Social Theory and Social Welfare*. London: Arnold.

Temple, W. 1941: The state. In *Citizen and Churchman*. London: Eyre and Spottiswoode. Repr. in C. Schottland (ed.), *The Welfare State*. London: Harper and Row, 1967, pp. 20–4.

Temple, W. 1942: *Christianity and the Social Order*. London: Penguin.

Thane, P. 1982: *Foundations of the Welfare State*. London: Longman.

Thane, P. 1984: The working class and state 'welfare' in Britain, 1880–1914. *Historical Journal*, 27(4), 877–900.

Therborn, G. 1986: Karl Marx returning. *International Political Science Review*, 7(2), 131–64.

Therborn, G. 1987: Welfare state and capitalist markets. *Acta Sociologica*, 30(3–4), 237–54.

Timonen, V. 2004: New risks: are they still new for the Nordic welfare states? In P. Taylor-Gooby (ed.), *New Risks, New Welfare*. Oxford: Oxford University Press, pp. 83–109.

Tingsten, H. 1973: *The Swedish Social Democrats: Their Ideological Development*. Totowa: Bedminster.

Titmuss, R. M. 1963: *Essays on the Welfare State*. London: Allen and Unwin.

Tomasson, R. F. 1969: The extraordinary success of the Swedish Social Demo-crats. *Journal of Politics*, 31(3), 772–98.

Tomasson, R. F. 1970: *Sweden: Prototype of a Modern Society*. New York: Random House.

Tomasson, R. F. (ed.) 1983: *The Welfare State, 1883–1983*, vol. 6 of *Comparative Social Research*. London: JAI Press.

Trattner, W. 1988: The federal government and needy citizens in nineteenth century America. *Political Science Quarterly*, 103(2), 347–56.

Tullock, G. 1976: *The Vote Motive: An Essay in the Economics of Politics, with Applications to the British Economy*. Princeton: Princeton University Press.

Turner, B. S. 1986: *Citizenship and Capitalism: The Debate over Reformism*. London: Allen and Unwin.

Turner, B. S. 1990: Outline of a theory of citizenship. *Sociology*, 24(2), 189–217.

Ullman, H. P. 1981: German industry and Bismarck's social security system. In W. J. Mommsen (ed.), *The Emergence of the Welfare State in Britain and Germany*. London: Croom Helm, pp. 133–49.

United Nations 1948: *Universal Declaration of Human Rights*. New York: United Nations.

Urquhart, M. C. 1965: *Historical Statistics of Canada*. Cambridge: Cambridge University Press.

US Bureau of the Census 1996: *Poverty Statistics: 1995* (online). Washington, DC: US Bureau of the Census.

US Bureau of the Census 2003: *Income, Poverty and Health Insurance Coverage in the US*. Washington, DC: US Bureau of the Census.

US Bureau of the Census 2005: *Income, Poverty and Health Insurance Coverage in the US*. Washington DC: US Bureau of the Census.

US Bureau of Labor Statistics 2005: Employment situation summary. At www.bls.gov/ces (accessed 1 July 2005).

US Bureau of Statistics 1975: *Historical Statistics of the United States: From Colonial Times to 1970*. Washington, DC: US Government Printing Office.

US Department of Commerce 1975: *Historical Statistics of the US*, Washington, DC: Department of Commerce.

Uusitalo, H. 1984: Comparative research on the determinants of the welfare state: the state of the art. *European Journal of Political Research*, 12, 403–22.

Vail, M. 2004: The myth of the frozen welfare state and the dynamics of contemporary French and German social-Protection reform. *French Politics*, 2(2), 151–83.

Van Parijs, P. (ed.) 1992: *Arguing for Basic Income*. London: Verso.

Van Parijs, P. 1995: *Real Freedom for All*. Oxford: Oxford University Press.

Waine, B. 1995: A disaster foretold? The case of the personal pension. *Social Policy and Administration*, 29(4), 317–44.

Weale, A. 1983: *Political Theory and Social Policy*. London: Macmillan.

Webb, S. and Webb, B. 1910– : *English Local Government: English Poor Law History*, vols 7–10. London: Longmans, Green.

Webb, S. and Webb, B. 1927: *English Local Government: English Poor Law History: Part 1: The Old Poor Law*. London: Longmans, Green.

Weber, M. 1968: *Economy and Society*. 3 vols, New York: Bedminster.

Weir, A. 1974: The family, social work and the welfare state. In S. Allen, L. Sanders and J. Wallis, *Conditions of Illusion*. Leeds: Feminist Books, pp. 217–28.

Weir, M. and Skocpol, T. 1985: State structures and the possibilities for 'Keynesian' responses to the Great Depression in Sweden, Britain and the United States. In P. B. Evans, D. Rueschemeyer and T. Skocpol (eds), *Bringing the State Back In*. Cambridge: Cambridge University Press, pp. 107–63.

Weir, M., Orloff, A. S. and Skocpol, T. (eds) 1988a: *The Politics of Social Policy in the United States*. Princeton: Princeton University Press.

Weir, M., Orloff, A. S. and Skocpol, T. 1988b: Understanding American social politics. In M. Weir, A. S. Orloff, and T. Skocpol (eds), *The Politics of Social Policy in the United States*. Princeton: Princeton University Press, pp. 3–27.

White, S. 1997: Liberal equality, exploitation, and the case for an unconditional basic income. *Political Studies*, 45, 312–26.

White, S. 2001: The ambiguities of the Third Way. In S. White (ed.), *New Labour: The Progressive Future?* London: Palgrave, pp. 3–17.

White, S. 2003: *The Civic Minimum*. Oxford: Oxford University Press.

Wilensky, H. 1975: *The Welfare State and Equality: Structural and Ideological Roots of Public Expenditure*. Berkeley: University of California Press.

Wilensky, H. 1976: *The 'New Corporatism', Centralization and the Welfare State*. London: Sage.

Wilensky, H. L. 1981: Leftism, Catholicism, and democratic corporatism: the role of political parties in recent welfare state development. In P. Flora and A. J. Heidenheimer (eds), *The Development of Welfare States in Europe and America*. London: Transaction, pp. 345–82.

Williams, F. 1989: *Social Policy: A Critical Introduction: Issues of Race, Gender and Class*. Cambridge: Polity.

Williamson, J. (ed.) 1994: *The Political Economy of Policy Reform*. Washington, DC: Institute for International Economics.

Wilson, E. 1977: *Women and the Welfare State*. London: Tavistock.

Wilson, W. J. 1987: *The Truly Disadvantaged: The Inner City, the Underclass, and Public Policy*. London: University of Chicago Press.

Winter, J. M. 1982: The decline of mortality in Britain 1870–1950. In T. Barker and M. Drake (eds), *Population and Society in Britain 1850–1950*. London: Batsford, pp. 100–20.

Wolfe, A. 1979: *The Limits of Legitimacy*. London: Macmillan.

World Bank 1994: *Averting the Old Age Crisis*. New York: Oxford University Press.

Zimmern, A. 1934: *Quo Vadimus*. Oxford: Oxford University Press.

Index